Teaching World History as Mystery

Offering a philosophy, methodology, and examples for history instruction that are active, imaginative, and provocative, this text engages teachers and students in teaching and learning world history through a fully developed pedagogy based on problem-solving methods that promote reasoning and judgment and restore a sense of imagination and participation to classroom learning. It is designed to draw readers into the detective process that characterizes the work of professional historians and social scientists—sharing raw data, defining terms, building interpretations, and testing competing theories. An inquiry framework drives both the pedagogy and the choice of historical materials, with selections favoring the unsolved, problematical, controversial, and fragmented rather than the neatly wrapped-up analysis of past events.

Teaching World History as Mystery:

- Provides a balanced combination of interestingly arranged historical content and clearly explained instructional strategies
- Features "Mystery Packet" case studies of commonly and not so commonly taught topics within a typical world/global history curriculum using combinations of primary and secondary documents
- Discusses ways of dealing with ethical and moral issues in the world history classroom, drawing students into persisting questions of historical truth, bias, and judgment

Jack Zevin is Professor of Social Studies Education at Queens College, City University of New York.

David Gerwin is Associate Professor of Social Studies Education at Queens College, City University of New York.

Teaching World History as Mystery

JACK ZEVIN

QUEENS COLLEGE, CITY UNIVERSITY OF NEW YORK

DAVID GERWIN

QUEENS COLLEGE, CITY UNIVERSITY OF NEW YORK

Routledge
Taylor & Francis Group

NEW YORK AND LONDON

First published 2011
by Routledge
711 Third Avenue, New York, NY 10017

Simultaneously published in the UK
by Routledge
2 Park Square, Milton Park, Abingdon, Oxon OX14 4RN

Routledge is an imprint of the Taylor & Francis Group, an informa business
© 2011 Taylor & Francis

Typeset in Minion Pro and Helvetica Neue LT Pro by Prepress Projects Ltd, Perth, UK

Library of Congress Cataloging in Publication Data
Zevin, Jack.
Teaching world history as mystery / Jack Zevin, David Gerwin.
p. cm.
1. History–Study and teaching–United States. I. Gerwin, David. II. Title.
D16.3.Z48 2010
907.1′073–dc22
2010015408

ISBN 13: 978–0–415–99224–4 (hbk)
ISBN 13: 978–0–415–99225–1 (pbk)
ISBN 13: 978–0–203–85605–5 (ebk)

Contents

Preface

We welcome teachers and students to learn history all over again by contact with original sources, and secondary interpreters. This book, and its companion, *Teaching U.S. History as Mystery*, are open invitations to engage you, our readers, and your students, and peers, with history more like it really is than as it is presented in large, heavy textbook accounts in which everything is explained and outlined precisely and efficiently, but perhaps without much pizzazz or mystery.

Our view is that history, the recapturing of our past, and our comprehension of the present, is a far messier and more complex affair than most texts or historians make it out to be, and we push this point as advantageous to all teachers of history.

Why?

Because recapturing the content and context of history is engaging and exciting, encouraging us to play detectives and solve problems on our way to drawing our own conclusions about any given historical topic.

You and your students get to examine the same original sources (at least a selected sample) that historians work on when they write books or carry out research. You and your students get to make judgments and apply values to people, places, and events that provoke discussions and perhaps are so pointed that they rouse those napping in class to an opinion here and there, despite boredom. You and your students have the opportunity to test conclusions that they have developed against a body of evidence, and against the work of professionals as well, learning how to do history rather than simply absorb ready-made conclusions.

In this particular book, *Teaching World History as Mystery*, we offer a delectable menu of case studies spread across time and place, each of which we hope motivates and sustains interest in the long ago and far away as well as the here and now. We begin with two orienting chapters, one discussing why we think history should be taught as mystery, and a second providing an overview of world historians' ideas about how to integrate global change and development through the ages. Then we move on to examples and case studies arranged roughly in chronological order and complexity, each case presenting a somewhat different set of problems for students to solve.

We begin with a favorite, Stonehenge, and then jump to Rome—but we ask why it lasted so long rather than why it fell. Then we provide a medieval example using the crusades as an opening to discuss how history and historians define events, moving on to a global contact case from the Columbian Exchange that asks students to trace the origins of pizza from Old- and New-World beginnings. (If you are really happy with this chapter, why not prepare a pizza from scratch in your classroom and eat the results!) The chapter on Incas and Spaniards should stimulate questions of contact and conflict, adaptation and cultural diffusion between the so-called Old and New World.

Then we offer two chapters that cross times and cultures, focusing on key ideas that relate to the present day. Here, we provide a cross-cultural mystery about the origins and purposes of secret societies in history, ranging from the Tai Pings in China to the Serbian Black Hand in WWI, to the present Al-Qaeda movement. A concluding case takes up the role of women in world history, using biographies of famous and not-so-famous women. We conclude with a final chapter designed to help you define your own goals in teaching history as mystery using primary and secondary sources that have the potential to be engaging and provocative.

To sum up, we invite you and your students to engage with history in all its glory, through sometimes confusing and difficult evidence, playing detective, reading cues, and looking for clues on the way to constructing and testing your own conclusions about events and historical methods. We invite you, our colleagues, to apply social science and historical methods, as well as the humanities and literacy techniques of careful reading, viewing, and listening to the wide variety of data we offer packaged into chapters that roughly parallel chronological changes in human history. Although we have taken the liberty of providing mystery packages for you and your students to work on, we also encourage you to develop suggestions, modifications, and inventions of your own. You are encouraged to investigate real mysteries where these exist and to create "manufactured" mysteries where your students have grown bored or overly familiar with a subject.

Most of all, we invite you to look at history as "it was left to us" and enjoy both the conclusions you can draw after struggling through evidence, and the admission of uncertainty and ambiguity that makes life interesting and history debatable.

Enjoy!

—Jack and David

Acknowledgments

We gratefully acknowledge the support of our wives, Iris Zevin and Lisa Gersten, in helping us create this expanded volume on teaching history as mystery, rather than as misery! We also want to express our special appreciation to our capable research assistants: Tom Hatsis, who did much of the legwork on sources; Tina Wexler, who did much of the organizing work; and Maria Malzone, whose contributions were invaluable to making this book whole and getting it to our publisher. And we thank our office support at Queens College: Evelyn Sanchez, for permission assistance, as well as our two loyal and tolerant department secretaries, Bonnie Wilichinsky and Kathy Nava.

Figures, Text Excerpts, and Sources

We would also like to thank the following people and organizations for allowing us to use their work in this book:

"History of the World" (poem): Courtesy of Micah Zevin, author.
Figure 1.1 (hand axe): Courtesy of José-Manuel Benito Álvarez, creator. This image has been released into the public domain and is available at Wikimedia Commons.*
Figures 1.2 and 1.3 (arrowheads/hand axes): Courtesy of Donutey.com. This image has been released into the public domain and is available online at http://donutey.com/arrowheads.php.
Figure 2.2 (Dymaxion map): Courtesy of Christopher Rywalt. This image is in the public domain.
Figure 3.2 (drawing of Stonehenge): Hand-colored wood engraving, 1849, purchased in England by Jack Zevin, co-author.
Figure 3.3 (druids at Stonehenge), Stock Photo, UK (May 1, 2004), Corbis.com
Figure 3.6 (map of megalithic architecture): Image adapted from original color map by Tharkun Coll. Used under Creative Commons Attribution Share-Alike** 3.0 license. Available at Wikimedia Commons.*

Figure 4.1 (Roman aqueduct, Pont du Gard): Photo by Armin Kübelbeck, original in color. Used under Creative Commons Attribution Share-Alike** 3.0 license.

Figure 4.3 (ancient Roman abacus): Photo by Mike Cowlishaw, original in color. Used under Creative Commons Attribution Share-Alike** 3.0 license. Available at Wikimedia Commons.*

Figure 4.6 (Appian Way): Photo by Wikimedia Commons user Longbow4U, original in color. Used under Creative Commons Attribution Share-Alike** 3.0 license. Available at Wikimedia Commons.*

Figure 4.7 (map of Roman Empire in 116 C.E.): Based on original map by Jani Niemenmaa. Used under Creative Commons Attribution Share-Alike** 3.0 license. Available at Wikimedia Commons.*

Figure 6.2 (homemade focaccia): Photo by J. P. Lon, original in color. Used under GNU Free Documentation License, Version 1.2 or later. Available at Wikimedia Commons.*

Figure 6.3 (Indian na'an bread): Photo by Leoboudv, original in color. Used under Creative Commons Attribution 2.0 Generic license. Available at Wikimedia Commons.*

Figure 6.4 (Turkish pizza): Photo by Kenneth Jorgensen, original in color. Used under GNU Free Documentation License, Version 1.2 or later. Available at Wikimedia Commons.*

Figure 6.6 (handmade shmura matza): Photo by Yoninah, original in color. Used under GNU Free Documentation License, Version 1.2 or later. Available at Wikimedia Commons.*

Figure 6.7 (bread from Pompeii): Photo by Beatrice. Used under Creative Commons Attribution ShareAlike 2.0 License, Italy. Available at Wikimedia Commons.*

The Tomato had to Go Abroad to Make Good, from the PLANTanswers gardening information archive provided by the Texas Cooperative Extension of Texas A&M University, available online at http://aggie-horticulture.tamu.edu/plantanswers.

Excerpt from "American Pie," originally published in *American Heritage Magazine*, volume 57, issue 2. Excerpted by permission of American Heritage Publishing.

Chen, P. (February 23, 2006) "*Tujia* Pizza Proves that Chinese Invented Pizza," originally published on the web by *The Shanghaiist*, available online at http://shanghaiist.com/2006/02/23/tujia_pizza_pro_1.php. Permission sought.

We Know Not Where, originally published on the web by *The Straight Dope*. Copyright 2001 Creative Loafing Media. Reprinted with permission of Straightdope.com.

Excerpt from *The Incas* by Garcilaso de la Vega, translated by Maria Jolas from the French translation by Alain Gheerbrant. Published by Cassell Plc., division of the Orion Publishing Group, London. All attempts to locate the copyright holder were unsuccessful.

Figure 9.2 (the goddess Athena): Original color photo by Photo: Yair Haklai. Used under Creative Commons Attribution Share-Alike** 3.0 license. Available at Wikimedia Commons.*

Figure 9.7 (Rigoberta Menchú): Modified from original color photo by Freddy Ballo.

Used under Creative Commons Attribution Share-Alike** 3.0 license. Available at Wikimedia Commons.*

Figure 9.8 (Zenobia coin): From modifications to a public domain image by Jone Johnson Lewis, © 2006. Available at http://womenshistory.about.com. Used with permission.

Excerpt from Gerda Lerner's 1982 Presidential Address to the Organization of American Historians, titled "The Necessity of History and the Professional Historian" and published in *Why History Matters,* pp. 119–120. Reprinted with permission of the Organization of American Historians.

"The Ballad of Hua Mulan," translated by Hans Frankel and originally published in *Flowering Plum and the Palace Lady: Interpretation of Chinese Poetry.* Copyright 1976, Yale University Press. Reprinted with permission from Yale University Press.

*Wikimedia Commons website is found at http://commons.wikimedia.org/wiki/Main_Page.

**You are free to share and make derivative works of the file under the condition that you appropriately attribute it, and that you distribute it only under a license identical to this one.

Note: All Creative Commons and GNU Free Documentation images are used under the corresponding licenses, and may be reproduced under the same license. Routledge, Taylor & Francis, and the authors of this book, make no copyright claims to these images. The full text of Creative Commons licenses is available at http://creativecommons.org/about/licenses.

World History in Poetry

The History of the World

Between 150,000 and
250, 000 years ago
The massive craniums of
Our forebears plodded
On this earth and didn't
Even know what fire was
Or invention until persistence
Burned into their eyes and with
Sticks and stones rubbed together
It was born. In Mesopotamia, Egypt
And then with the Sumerians
Civilization came to furious life
And then India, all its languages
Gods and temples showering the
Landscape with their devout splendor
Until the Chinese had one dynasty
One war after the other, a Great Wall dotting
The landscape, and the Greeks
Spread their intelligence around the world,
But especially to the Romans, conquerors
Of all nations, who adopted the Greek's
Bodies and minds as their own—
Throughout human beings' brief stay
On this planet, family, the tribe, emerged,
The all-powerful unit, the great support system
That commenced in the Paleolithic Age

Men and women hunted and gathered
Food together, and women bore children,
Then society rose up and marriage, property
And other possessions followed.
Today, despite electronic gadgets, the internet and
Electricity, and the semi-civilization
Of human kind, not much has changed,
Except the means, fire is our friend,
Lighting our bellies with its warmth
And when a light bulb is not available,
Guides us through the darkness
Back to where we started . . .

—By Micah Zevin

one
Teaching World History as Mystery

What I want is a movement toward a set of questions that all human data are theoretically needed to answer. I think we need to stop arguing over which books to read or which cultures to study and start talking about which questions to ask.

(Waldman, 2000, p. 95)

And the end of all our exploring
Will be to arrive where we started
And know the place for the first time.

(T. S. Eliot, "Little Gidding," 1942)

Teaching the world is a big job. There is just too much to do, too much to cover, too little time. World or global history is an all-encompassing, all-engrossing subject, pun intended. For most history teachers and students it is far too unwieldy a subject, without a clear organization, time sequence, or integration of cultures. And there are too many strange names to learn to pronounce!

Many of the reasons for this perception are justified, such as the vast quantity of material to grasp. But we are also blinded by the three evils of history instruction: *ethno-centrism*, *egocentrism*, and *econ-centrism*. Roughly translated, that means we have trouble grasping histories that are not about *us*, *our* people, and what *we* can get out of it.

How to overcome fragmented and biased views of world history as well as give students a sense of its deep and inherent mystery is what this book is about. We are the world and the world is interconnected with us, and our understanding of it can be greatly strengthened, as we suggest in this and the next chapter. There are two sets of ideas that we would like to propose: first, that we as teachers need to control the three "blinders" mentioned above; second, that we also need to be positive and adopt novel methods for teaching the world.

Instead of thinking about the world in segmented, isolated, nationalistic terms, why not look at the globe and its peoples as connected, on the move, sending ideas and beliefs to each other almost constantly long before history records began to be kept. Human beings are remarkable throughout history for their restlessness and inventiveness. Isolation and lack of change are unusual rather than the norm, often the product of political pressures or value decisions within a culture. Rarely do societies purposely cut themselves off from others. Rarely do groups opt out of the system, whatever the system is or was at the time. Trade, travel, migration, conquest, and exchanges of ideas, customs, products, art styles, and institutions are much more typical than the maintenance of boundaries.

The Problems of Teaching World History: The "Blinders"

World history is a fascinating subject but fraught with difficulties in its conception and presentation. Why? Because we are all part of a culture, time, and place that has socialized us into a particular context: an identity and society that is "ours." Outside of that society, people are "others." Of course, they have much the same problem: to them we are "others" as well. Viewing people as others may be helpful on occasion, but generally promotes the view that *we* are normal and fine, and *they* are somehow strange, exotic, or perhaps evil. Diminishing the humanity of others also helps us to ignore suffering and poverty in other lands, while allowing our government to do things that we certainly would not approve of at home.

First, this attitude is the root of what is sometimes termed *ethnocentrism*, thinking about everybody else as "outside" of our culture and experience. We call this one of the big three human problems, thinking about our culture as best and others as exotic, foreign, strange, etc.

Worse yet, we have our own personal identities as part of our family, job, neighborhood, state, organizations, nation, etc. We tend to see the world as composed not only of "us" and "them," but also as "me" and "they." Just who *are* those strange people who moved in two doors down our block? Foreigners have invaded my sports club? You don't speak English? What is the world coming to?!

Second, the personal is the root of what is sometimes called *egoism* or *egocentrism*. As individuals, understandably, we are focused on *ourselves*, *our* feelings, what is best for us, what *we* love. Me, myself, and I are the center of the world. Self-centeredness is normal, but for really developing an understanding of world history, we need to go outside of ourselves to try to grasp why others feel differently from how we do. This applies to our own nation's history as well, particularly in extending personality and human-ness to the less fortunate and conquered, the minorities and subcultures in our own country.

The third, and final, part of the syndrome is self-interest, or what I call *econ-centrism*. This might best be translated as "what's in it for me?" Our sense of gain, making a living, getting ahead, or being left behind, motivates a lot of our attitude toward the world. Although reasonable, focusing exclusively on our own well-being, and that of our society, diminishes our ability to open up to global realities about economics and occludes our grasp of the economic system that governs the world. As the current "meltdown" illustrates, countries and companies who thought they were independent of the system are suffering too. This is a lovely illustration of a "one-world" structure to economics, and understanding this aids in making better personal and national decisions.

A big problem with ethnocentrism as a syndrome is that it stresses home and self, nation and person, over interpersonal global, world, or international perspectives. There is not too much room left for "others," and we're not even talking yet about helping anyone, contributing to international agencies, or becoming a good world citizen!

To summarize, the "blinders" may be described as appearing in at least three forms of what we are calling *centrisms*:

1   *Ethnocentrism:* looking at the world from the point of view of our nation or culture as the *center* of the globe, and the *best* there is over everyone else.
2   *Egocentrism*: looking at the world from our own self-centered, narrow perspective.
3   *Econ-centrism*: looking at the world from *our* perspective and self-interest, from *our* history alone.

So where do we go from the three "blinders" to teaching world history in exciting ways that engage our students' attention, reasoning, and, perhaps most importantly, empathy? In the next section we discuss the "embracers," several ways of looking at world history by adopting new approaches that connect and illuminate aspects of global evolution.

Perspectives for Teaching the World: The "Embracers"

For a start, we are calling for a simple kind of empathy in which you, teachers and students, can step out of your roles and "stand in others' shoes," if only for an instructional period or two. Move outside the personal, national, and financial boxes to think about where ideas are coming from, how we developed and how we have constructed ourselves as citizens of local, national, and world communities (if we have), and whether we can empathize with people from other times and places, however distant and unlike our own. Let's see how things look to others, from other perspectives, from other ideologies.

In our view, multiple perspectives are basic to being a great world history teacher because they are mind-opening, sometimes mind-boggling. But there has to be a beginning, and that is the recognition in ourselves that we are ethnocentric, egocentric, and econ-centric. However, to understand even a small portion of world history, you must expand to outside sources, preferably from the people, time, and places we are studying. Examples abound: for instance, why not read the work of an ancient Egyptian rather than just a text; why not read or look at the artwork and ideas of a "barbarian" from the early Middle Ages in Europe; why not take a close look at what our enemies think of us? Now, with the World Wide Web available, we can find almost anything we want—we have no reason to stay locked within the box of our own culture.

How we get from all of this self- and cultural-centeredness to understanding the world is what this book is about. It is about the mystery of understanding as well as the mystery of analysis. To be an excellent detective we need practice at looking beyond ourselves to the evidence, listening to others' perspectives, and taking a "flyover" look at the whole event or problem at enough distance so that we can make sense of it, hopefully. And we need to maintain an open-mindedness and sense of empathy, or at least humility, in understanding other perspectives before we come to any conclusions about one or more aspects of world history. In other words, as teachers we will approach the evidence, the documentary and the secondary interpretations offered us, with caution, working to analyze and understand the primary before applying historians' theories and explanations.

We propose to help you learn how to hold ethnocentrism, egocentrism, and econcentrism at bay while you acquire suggestions and examples that will assist you to make teaching world history great fun, explore deep mystery, and build multiple connections.

To accomplish these goals, we will offer you a series of "advance organizers" for teaching the world. Throughout the book, we will provide you with both primary data for you and your students to interpret and secondary expertise to apply as well as supplemental reading and resources to pursue if time and inclination allow. Each chapter focuses on a thematic idea, an approach to mystery teaching, and one or more imbedded issues to struggle with in the classroom.

Three Structures for Teaching World History as Mystery

A first set of suggestions is for *themes* or *big ideas* that can run throughout any course, and help you connect the disparate pieces, events, and personalities of world history. A second set of suggestions is for *pedagogical approaches* to teaching the world, ways of constructing lessons, units, and courses to fit your curriculum. A third set of suggestions is for *historical issues*, persisting questions that are imbedded in history, but especially in world history approaches.

For example, our first chapter focuses narrowly on the mystery of Stonehenge built on a theme of human development—the formation of groups—and suggests a mystery approach of discovery, playing archeologist, while raising issues of inferring purpose, motive, and action from artifacts we don't fully understand, even now. Thus, theme, pedagogy, and issues are integrated into a modest, but complete, trail of historical detective work. Each theme, pedagogical strategy, and issue may be treated quickly or deeply, but all demand attention to didactic, reflective, and affective questions and objectives for high-quality history lessons.

A final word: categories are artificial. They define and divide in ways that help us think about our teaching and world history, but may also blind us to other issues and problems that fall between the cracks or are subsumed into one of our big categories. So, as you read this book, you need to think about places in which our proposals, explanations, and arguments fall flat, or miss the mark, or, still more seriously, omit an option or issue of importance that you thought of and we forgot about.

Throughout, the authors invite you to read and react, acquire and reject ideas, and add some of your own to the stew. Teaching the world needs all the thought and assistance it can get from you and your students!

Creating a Sense of Mystery about the World

A major way of teaching about the world is to view history as open to an examination of primary sources, to comparison and contrast of alternate explanations, and to theories purporting to integrate and connect examples to historical analogs. Thus, teachers can promote world history as a mystery to be solved by struggling with raw evidence, competing viewpoints, and theories about what drives people to take action.

Most artifacts, events, and personalities in history have already been professionally interpreted and reinterpreted many times over, leaving us, as students of history, with a lot of conclusions that may or may not reflect the range of evidence used to build these ideas. We really don't know how the historian or social scientists or critics got to where they are unless we take a look for ourselves at some of the original documents and artifacts upon which they based their interpretations.

We are arguing that, for novices, for students who we want to interest in history, making events into mystery stories is a good way of attracting and sustaining attention, even, or especially, for students who don't particularly care about the past, or the present, but who do care about friends, sneaker brands, and what they can buy. Any topic, we assert, from the sublime to the ridiculous, can be viewed as a mystery, and we can use this sense of the unknown to build excitement in trying to reach conclusions of our own.

Levels of Mystery in History

There are several important techniques for creating a sense of mystery about world history, all of which take advantage of a range of problems, from "leaps into the unknown" to philosophical disputes. These techniques are largely drawn from developmental and cognitive psychology research which indicates that student motivation grows out of involvement, discovery, and personal challenges to solve problems (e.g., Bruner, Gardner, Vygotsky, and others). Based on educational psychology and philosophical foundations of education, we can construct problems, or what we call "manufactured mysteries," for students to work at solving. We can also use raw data from history that itself offers real mysteries, unsolved questions and a clash of theories and interpretations. As teachers, we can use these problems, questions, and issues to

Mystery Packet: Stone Tools

Examine the stone tools shown here (Figures 1.1–1.3). Could you guess where they were made? Are they made largely of the same material in the same way? How do you think they were manufactured? Who made them? And for what reasons?

Figure 1.1 Front and Back Views of a Hand Axe.

Figure 1.2 Stone Arrowhead or Hand Axe.

Figure 1.3 Stone Arrowhead.

The hand axes in Figure 1.1 come from Spain and are dated to 350,000 years ago. The tools shown in Figures 1.2 and 1.3 come from the Midwestern United States and were made by Native Americans—they are probably not more than a few thousand years old.

Here's the mystery: how did stone tools of "roughly" the same style and make cross so many years and territory? Could it be that human migrations, trade, and connections made for a "global" world long before history as well as after history?

good effect in our classrooms, stimulating thinking and feeling and action. And we can also create mysteries of our own, even if the materials available offer only settled answers.

These techniques form the basis for our roughly hewn set of three categories or levels of inquiry for mysteries that we call minor, medium, and major problems.

Minor mysteries tend to focus mainly on piecing evidence together, and discovering missing parts and inconsistent data, and deciding what can be known with some degree of certainty versus what "unknowns" will probably have to be guessed at or extrapolated from what we actually have in our possession. Very difficult puzzles and unknowns may slide into more complex mysteries, particularly if they suggest or include analysis of causes and effects or multiple overlapping or conflicting viewpoints. Most of the arguments here are evidential and inferential, leading students to draw conclusions about what sort of data they would love to have to solve the problems they encounter.

Medium mysteries tend to focus on problems in analyzing why events occurred, zeroing in on causes and consequences, particularly from more than one interpreter or eyewitness, raising issues of inference and meaning but on a higher level than solving a puzzle. Mid-level mysteries may also engage students with multiple viewpoints, either at the primary source level or in conjunction with secondary sources. A complex comparison of first-hand eyewitnesses with secondary experts, such as historians, is part of medium mysteries, raising questions about which sources agree and/or disagree on one or more points of evidence and/or reasoning, and for what reasons. Dilemmas may cause students to feel that, at best, the problem is only partially "solvable" through evidence, and that reasoning and inference are equally crucial to drawing conclusions.

Major mysteries build on puzzles and unknowns, bring up many viewpoints, and often cause debates, but add another layer of complexity focused on philosophical and ideological stands by eyewitnesses, observers, and historians. Data, evidence, and reasoning are applied in a major mystery to building a synthesis or theory that seeks to explain and predict (successfully or unsuccessfully) an entire problem or issue. For example, based on evidence and reasoning about heroines and heroes, would students predict that human beings are still just as prone to propaganda as they have been in the past, or have they developed greater sensitivity to being "led on"? Added to synthesis and prediction, however, major mysteries include a consideration of how people feel about an event or person in history as "right," as examples of moral values, as expressions of universal or eternal historical questions. This is, in effect, a philosophical argument that admits of no easy answer based only on research but requires a sorting out and ranking of values and issues linking past and present to future: no easy task.

Techniques for Turning History into Mystery

We suggest *five techniques* to use as springboards and planning guidelines for mystery historical inquiry.

1. The Puzzle: Parts and Whole

In this technique, a few pieces of a puzzle are missing, and it is up to us as historical detectives to try to find the missing elements or puzzle them out by interpolating logical possibilities. For example, we know a lot about the Barbarians who attacked the Roman Empire but we know very little from their point of view, their own view of their lifestyle.

However, we do have considerable writing by Romans, Greeks, and others portraying the Barbarians and their customs and cultures, which we can sift for reliable evidence, filtering out the biases and hostilities that creep into "enemy" texts. After this filtering and study, we can identify with some assurance that pieces to the puzzle are missing and what *probably* would be accurate knowledge about those neglected Barbarians against whom so many prejudices were projected. This is a great opportunity for us to fill in gaps in knowledge by extrapolation from the pieces we do have, as well as a fine introduction to the mystery of prejudice, bias, and generalizing by hostile eyewitnesses.

2. The Known and the Unknown

In this technique, we pose problems to students on subjects in which there are a great many theories or interpretations but for which the evidence is missing or unavailable, and we really don't know the answers. For example, Bronze Age peoples built megaliths and monoliths, and stone henges all over Europe, but we really don't know the reasons why. They follow a pattern, but there are many interpretations, for example astrological, astronomical, social, religious, cultural, all, some, or none of which may be relatively correct. Because the people who made the henges can't be interviewed and left no written records in any language we know, we just cannot be sure how to definitively solve the unknown. So, that is great, because what we don't know is maddening but leads to a lot of hypotheses and careful thinking about artifacts and archeology and builds a sense of mystery and attachment to the prehistoric henge builders.

3. The Soluble and the Insoluble

In some historical cases, we know a great deal about an event from many sides and view-points. Each gives us a rich and varied perspective on an event, say the causes of World War I, from national, political, historical, cultural, and other views, but the more we know, the more insoluble grows the dilemma of pointing out "an answer" that is correct and true above all others. A good example of this is many cases of women in world history, about whom we know a great deal, yet who still appear as a distinct minority in most textbooks and volumes of primary source documents. And there doesn't seem to be much of an overall scheme or theory that explains the status and problems of women in history, either as half or more of humanity, nor in relation to males in social networks. What we, at best, conclude is that there are many perspectives and explanations, of varying reliability, that we may merge, synthesize, and compare, but which in the final analysis provide us with a range of factors to choose from and rank order as "causes." Endless wrangling and reinterpretation may yield better factor analysis but never a definitive conclusion, because a serious conclusion demands a theory that fits most or all of the facts available, and so far that theory, or any other theories, have not been definitively settled upon by most historians or observers. This makes for great lesson planning in building a mystery of "factors" for our students.

4. Prediction and the Unpredictable

In this technique, we can call upon students who have already studied a problem, asking them to make historical predictions about the future. In effect, we are playing crystal ball gazers but our predictions are based on sound evidence, knowledge of previous historical patterns, and a good understanding of current knowledge on a given topic. Our chapter on secret societies presents both primary and secondary documentation about the rise, purposes, and character of secret societies, from the Serbian Black Hand to Al-Qaeda, challenging readers to step outside their prejudices and understand why such groups develop in certain kinds of historical conditions, and to predict when they may occur. For example, we don't really know (as of this writing) what the outcome of the second Gulf War will be, but we could predict that the United States will not "win" and at best will be able to withdraw gracefully from Iraq. Why? Because we have pulled together an interpretation of the Iraq situation from history, news reports, social science analysis, many-sided viewpoints, and other sources, collated and synthesized these into a "gestalt." But, of course, we may be wrong because there are always errors in knowledge and events are subject to a great deal of unpredictability. But this makes fortune-telling exciting, doesn't it?

5. The Philosophical and the Ideological

In this technique, we call upon students to use their knowledge, skills, and understandings to fuse their values into taking a stand or position about the moral and ethical choices made in world history, reviewing past examples, drawing and testing analogies, and applying one or more philosophic viewpoints to the cases or examples we are arguing about. We may promote debate about views of humankind, and the beliefs and ideas that motivated people to make decisions, bad, good, or indifferent. We can draw students into debates about matters of definition that have emotional components, for example just who or what is a good or a great or a lousy leader, or what are the key factors in viewing someone in history as truly heroic, or do the grievances that drove people to join secret societies justify terror and violence? Major mysteries grow out of big questions about criteria, empathy and sympathy, hero worship and condemnation, great philosophies of history and society, such as those proposed by Hobbes, Locke, Rousseau, Hegel, Marx, and other thinkers who attempted to make sense of history and society as a whole. Morality and value issues make for stimulating argument, particularly when issues of historical analogy and moral relativity arise as part of the discussion (e.g., Can we really judge the past? Weren't past values different and not comparable to our own, or are there universals after all?). Students may disagree strongly with a thinker's position but that is all to the good as that motivates them to study the ideas presented and to acquire important decision-making skills that should be useful in making choices in a democratic republic.

Themes/Big Ideas in Teaching the World

A way of organizing "the world" is to view people and events through general topics we can call *themes,* which are concepts, big ideas drawn from history and the social sciences to give us a viewpoint when looking at the evidence of human events. A theme orients your perspective so that you tend to see history through a particular pair of lenses for the time being. These take in a lot of territory, but give us both a content and methodological structure, for example the procedures and content or knowledge of a social science or school of history, including history, anthropology, psychology, sociology, economics, political science, and so forth. You could combine fields, or draw a major idea out of one or more of them to serve as a focus for your investigation.

For example, you might want to review five or six cases combining environmental studies (geography) with history, collecting information on such varied topics as the state of ecology in the Roman Empire and during the Industrial Revolution. Or you might link trade and taxes (economics) with political changes (political science and history). Or if you are in a very creative mood you might go so far as to link artistic and clothing styles to periods (history) before, during, and after major revolutions to research correlations between what seem to be unconnected human activities such as art and clothing styles and political ideologies. We might want to look at heroines/heroes in history as a big, perhaps "eternal" theme that easily cuts across time and space, raising questions and issues about the people we look up to and emulate as inspiring in different fields and at different times.

Some suggested paired themes or big ideas might include:

- setting (ecology) and technological development (economics);
- interaction (trade) and imperial expansion (political science);
- diffusion (anthropology/art history) and intellectual history (history);
- movement (migration/culture) and patterns of social change (sociology);
- identity (psychology and philosophy) and class structure (sociology);
- power (political organization) and wealth (economics);
- heroism and gender (literature, humanities, philosophy, and political science).

Issues in Teaching the World

Whereas a national history has a more or less well-known sequence, with a clear beginning and set of eras, world history seen as a whole presents quite a few problems in coordination. Nations are relatively new phenomena. Time periods have been artificially devised within empires, faiths, and nations, but become a confusing mess when attempts are made to correlate these with each other. Our whole sense of time has been shaped by modern viewpoints and attitudes that emphasize the present and shorten historical perspective. We tend to stress change and progress rather than basic human values and the eternal aspects of the human condition.

As the philosopher of history Sylvaine Agacinski has put it,

> Modern consciousness is one of *passage* and *the passing*. From now on we think that everything *arrives and passes*. Nothing permanent gives things any kind of anchor against time. The movements that sweep the world along cannot even be unified, being too numerous and distinct and following different rhythms. Does this increase in flux still leave us a time that is truly ours? Can *passage* make an epoch, or does it compromise even any possibility of present. It is all the more necessary to speak of *modern times* in plural, since permanent facts seem lacking, those stable forms that would trace the outline of an unchanging landscape, capable of giving modernity a face. Thus, it must have many of them, and if it designates an experience of *passage* and of *passing*, of movement and of the ephemeral, of fluctuation and of the mortal, modernity does not renounce eternity alone it also renounces a unique form of eternity and of history.
>
> . . . passing is no longer a moment in a continuous history directed toward an end—a single step on a ladder that needs to be climbed to attain the final moment—but a *one-way passage* to which one blindly commits oneself.
>
> . . . From its beginning, philosophy has identified being with permanence, timelessness, whereas passing, the ephemeral, is cast out into nonbeing and stripped of all value. Thus, the relationship of the eternal to the temporal is analogous to that of being and appearance, the intelligible and the sensible.
>
> (Agacinski, 2000, pp. 11–13, italics in original)

So, do we want to focus on the *passing* or the *eternal* questions of history?

When viewing world history, the teacher needs to think outside the box of *passing*, of nation and person, and view events cross-culturally, from different areas, time zones, and multiple perspectives, as potentially *eternal*. In our view, this means that we can think about a case, example, local event as passing, but also as related to the eternal, long-lasting, and persisting questions of history, such as race, gender, leadership, and heroism, questions that have existed from time immemorial. Even if you don't agree, we think that eternal or persisting historical questions have enormous power to motivate interest and promote debate. To assist your thinking, we propose that you view areas across national borders, taking in regions, continents, whole sections of the earth. Ecological concerns, for instance, do not respect boundaries. Pollution of the sea and waterways spills across borders and boundaries and cannot really be studied within one place or nation alone if these conditions are to be analyzed and understood.

In addition, the histories of both India and China are very ancient and each has its own chronology and calendar system, different from that of each other and those from the West. Dates and places don't mean the same thing, and the concepts of medieval and Renaissance periods, for example, have little or no meaning in a comparison of Europe with the Middle East.

Timetables must be collated, compared, and coordinated in some meaningful way, or you, the teacher, like us, have to resort to a world calendar to make sense of years and holidays, as these vary by culture, region, and religion. This in itself can be an interesting mystery: Just what *were* the Emperor of China and the King of Persia doing when Augustus became the "father" of the Roman Empire, and were they in touch with each other in any way?

In much the same way we navigate across boundaries and time periods, we can also ask provocative and unexpected questions of the people we meet in history, people who might be called heroines or heroes, or villains and villainesses. Instead of looking only at status, usually important people, we can also examine the lives and conditions of ordinary working people, the poor and outcast, or role models such as mothers and wives, workers, and community activists. We can seek information about gender roles, race, class, and caste, through art, music, literature, and artifacts as well as through formal documentation.

Time zones can also lead to questions of comparison and diffusion between and among cultures across wide stretches of time and space.

Problems or issues (drawn from the same "big ideas" as our themes) we should be aware of and use to generate questions would include the following:

- borders and boundaries;
- classifying eras and time periods;
- race, class, gender;
- origins and evolutions;
- context and comparison;
- viewpoints/perspectives.

Approaches to Teaching the World

There is a wide variety of course structures or approaches that teachers can use to organize a world history course, and the strictly chronological is one of them. But that also places you in the position of aligning time periods and cultures with a Western perspective, which usually means emphasizing Western history *in comparison* with other histories, but with a sharper focus on the "insider" history in contrast to the "outsider" history. America in the world is also an insider/outsider approach. Both maintain a sense of *sequence* for students but tend to diminish a two-way search for connections between and among peoples and events. For each plus in this course structure, there are also minuses.

You might call this approach "The West and the Rest," which is probably a common classroom reality in the way the world is presented as most of us know a lot more about our own and related cultures than we do about those in other continents and climates. This is the basic approach most of us learned and reproduce, but we will argue that, if it ever was suitable for a global approach, it is much less so now in the current state of the world with the World Wide Web, international terrorism, and instant news exchanges. Yes, despite all of this wonderful communications and trade technology, we know very little about the interior landscape, the mental maps, or the value orientations and sacred beliefs of most of the rest of the world, especially from *their* points of view.

So we suggest other ways of organizing a world/global history course, using goals and structures that place an emphasis on at least a balanced if not equal representation of all or most cultures and viewpoints, with a good deal of attention to others' views of their own history, of us and our history, and of the world as a whole. Most of these courses place a strong emphasis on drawing connections, building multiple perspectives, and linking histories across boundaries and barriers. These more world-oriented, global approaches include:

- *Diffusion, adaptation, and amalgamation*—looking at world history as a series of inventions, exchanges, adaptations, and syntheses, for example the evolution of agriculture, the growth of cities, the building of empires, the creation of trade networks, the spread of inventions and industrialization. This is provocative but somewhat limited in scope to trade and borrowing, a sort of Columbian Exchange but worldwide.

- *East meets West, West meets East*—looking at history as a series of contacts, both peaceful and violent, between peoples from different regions and cultures, in which they learn from and take over customs, ideas, populations, languages, etc., across great swaths of territory and from a wide array of cultures, faiths, and political powers. Interesting, but concentrates on only two or three of the themes we have discussed with a central concern for contact and exchange.

- *Regions/cultures and geographies*—looking at history in terms of core areas, geographic units, that form bases for important and influential cultures and systems, which grow from unknown origins into powers that can and do influence surrounding regions, and then other parts of the world as well, slowly forming a world system of interlocking and overlapping economies. Certainly broadens our horizons out of the West and the Rest, but tends to "box" each region and culture into a self-contained whole implying that they are unique and homogeneous entities, which regions never were nor are at the present.

- *Home, nation, international; or local to global, global to local*—looking at history in terms of how we got where we are, how world trade, economics, politics, and culture impacts on us, and how our own culture and society impacts on others, for example the spread of jazz, dance styles, foods, medical practices, consumer tastes, and how these interact to create local economies, tastes, demands, and tensions between daily lifestyles and high-level policies and practices; global warming, nuclear proliferation treaties, oil prices, and other matters would fit into a local to global view of the world. A more up-to-date and eternal view of global with an emphasis on more recent historical periods, favoring study of the "modern" world over the distant or near distant past.

- *Global (integrated) systems (holistic perspectives)*—looking at history in terms of themes and ideas, strategies and issues, that unite cases and examples across time and space, drawn together to test a theory of empire, such as a comparison of empires, Greek, Roman, British, Ottoman, and American, to learn more about how they develop, prosper, organize, and decline; or perhaps a view of wars, big and small, WWI, WWII, Greeks and Persians, Romans and Gauls, Spaniards and Incas, British and Indian and African, etc., to test a theory about the causes and consequences of wars on conflicting political powers. Difficult but provocative and working toward a more "eternal" view than a passing view, drawing examples from across cultures, times, and places into a theoretical whole seeking to explain human politics, economics, and culture. This is the one to aim at in our opinion although it may cause you both strategic and conceptual problems before you get the whole machinery working well in world history classrooms.

Eternal Values and Moral Relativism

A last problem with world history is that crossing cultures, boundaries, time zones, systems of thought, and political powers creates a whole series of moral and ethical questions. We have dilemmas of judging right from wrong, power from justice, freedom from slavery, and we are faced with making decisions in unfamiliar contexts, times, and places where values were seemingly quite different from our own. Even the way that terms are defined is called into question.

We are also faced with the realization that core values themselves are culturally bound, and may vary greatly between times and places. Ancient Babylonian laws, for example, were harsh and draconian in comparison with most American laws, yet there runs within American society a tendency toward strong punishment, particularly during crime waves, or during periods of moral righteousness. We like tough guys too, on occasion, but also grow tired and suspicious that they may be demagogues or dictators in disguise, not unlike our ancestors the Greeks and the Romans (at certain periods).

Societies can shift allegiances, and change attitudes: what was right at one time may be viewed as wrong at another time. What is seen as wrong in one place is the exact opposite in another, and yet there also seem to be fundamental human problems and issues that crop up with regularity in almost every society, albeit in somewhat different forms, with somewhat different emotional attachments or rejections. Ethnocentric and superior attitudes allowed Spaniards to mistreat Incas and their subjects, resulting in a modern nation that still shows strong divisions between European, mestizo, and indigenous traditions five hundred years later.

In teaching world history, questions of morality become critical because a powerful society may develop and encourage the portrayal of a rival or dependant as being inferior in terms of values, not civilized, not ethical, different, exotic, perhaps repulsive. This negative image may be used as a pretext for invasion or plundering on the grounds that the "other" is just not of the same level as the invader. Since time immemorial arguments about might and right have gone on, and they continue into the most recent presidential election with respect to economic recession or depression, the war in Iraq, and a whole host of side issues about nuclear proliferation, religious freedom, terrorism, global warming, and treaty recognition, with projections of superiority and arrogance.

If only we had made better choices, and not been so ethnocentric, so econ-centric, so egocentric!

Viewing different customs and cultures as valid in their own right has led to accusations of moral relativism, the idea that every belief is subject to context and situation, that there are no universals. However, we would like to submit that a *method* of cultural relativism in which we try our best to interpret, empathize with, and appreciate another's culture, another's viewpoint, does not mean that we believe in relativism as a truth. This would mean that all value systems are equally defensible and effective: the Nazis, the Assyrians, the Belgians in the Congo, slave owners in the American South, etc. We propose that, for world history, we give other value systems a chance to speak for themselves through informants rooted in their societies before we pronounce a quick and easy judgment. But that doesn't mean that we cannot in passing make judgment, defend our viewpoints, applauding or condemning specific acts, state policies, or more general and pervasive mores and beliefs about leadership, race, gender, and heroism, proposing a standard of measurement for all time, for eternal use applied to eternal questions of world history.

In fact, throughout our book about teaching world history as mystery, we plead with you, the reader and teacher, classroom heroine/hero, to *hold off on judgment* until hearing the evidence, studying several perspectives without taking sides right away, until at least an attempt is made to stand in someone else's shoes for a while. Then we can leap to judgment, at least having briefly empathized with those we did not know, outsider views, alternate philosophies, and a stronger body of evidence to support our conclusions.

Allowing ourselves an attitude of empathy toward other cultures, peoples, times, places, and personalities deepens our understanding, and may actually lead us to develop and test "universal" values that may stand up across many cultures and time zones. So the last element of our approach to world history is the examination of values, both "ours" and "theirs," in a context of empathy and understanding before we make judicial rulings on who is right and who is wrong. Let's take our students into a "Court of Last Resort" where, after studying the facts of a mystery, they make their own interpretations and judgments, providing, of course, they play according to the rules of evidence and reasoning to defend their views.

We hope to help us all move toward a view of world history that draws upon many cultures, times, and places, integrating and connecting as we go along, to form a whole, a gestalt, that opens minds and hearts to both *passing* people, places, and events and *eternal* questions, themes, and persisting issues for humankind.

References and Further Reading

Agacinski, S. (2000) *Time Passing: Modernity and Nostalgia*, New York: Columbia University Press.

Bruner, J. (1961) "Learning by discovery," *Harvard Educational Review* 31 (1): 21–32.

Christain, D. (2005) *Maps of Time: An Introduction to Big History*, Berkeley: University of California Press.

Crosby, A. W. (1998) *Ecological Imperialism*, Cambridge, UK: Cambridge University Press.

Daniels, H. and Cole, M. (eds.) (2007) *The Cambridge Companion Volume to Vygotsky*, Cambridge, UK: Cambridge University press.

Davis, M. E. (2005) *How Students Understand the Past: From Theory to Practice*, Walnut Creek, CA: Altamira Press, Rowman & Littlefield.

Diamond, J. (1997) *Guns, Germs, and Steel: The Fates of Human Societies*, New York: W. W. Norton.

Dunn, R. E. (ed.) (2000) *The New World History: A Teacher's Companion*, New York: Bedford/St. Martin's Press.

Gardner, H. (1993) *Multiple Intelligences: The Theory into Practice*, New York: Basic Books.

Gunder, F. A. and Gills, B. K. (1993) *The World System: Five Hundred or Five Thousand Years*, New York: Routledge.

Kant, I. (1986) "Idea for a Universal History from a Cosmopolitan Point of View," in Ernest Behler (ed.), Lewis W. Beck (trans.), *Philosophical Writings*, New York: Continuum.

Mazlish, B. and Buultjens, R. (eds.) (1993) *Conceptualizing Global History*, Boulder, CO: Westview Press.

Spier, F. (1996) *The Structure of Big History: From the Big Bang until Today*, Amsterdam: Amsterdam University Press.

Waldman, M. R. (2000) "Re-imagining World History," in R. E. Dunn (ed.), *The New World History: A Teacher's Companion*, Boston: St. Martin's Press.

Vygotsky, L. (1978) *Mind in Society: The Psychology of Higher Mental Functioning*, Cambridge, MA: Harvard University Press.

White, H. (1975) *Metahistory: The Historical Imagination in Nineteenth-Century Europe*, Baltimore: Johns Hopkins University Press.

two
Looking at World History Anew

There is no history but world history . . .

(Leopold Von Ranke, cited by Andre Gunder Frank in H-World@msu.edu,
November 12, 1995)

The mark of the modern world is the imagination of its profiteers and the counter-assertiveness of the oppressed. Exploitation and the refusal to accept exploitation as either inevitable or just constitute the continuing antinomy of the modern era, joined together in a dialectic which has far from reached its climax in the twentieth century.

(Wallerstein, 1974, p. 233)

Teaching the world is, in our opinion, the most fascinating and mind-expanding challenge in social studies instruction, providing almost limitless opportunity to explore unfamiliar faces and events, as well as test provocative ways of thinking about the past, present, and future. Yes, it is a bit frightening, but with proper humility we can all approach the world's history as a voyage of adventure and discovery. Think of yourself as an explorer of olden times traveling into uncharted (at least for us) territories where we get to meet a lot of new folks. If we want to heighten the adventure, we can try meeting the new folks on their own terms rather than ours alone, meaning looking at the world from others' viewpoints, standing in their shoes (if they have any!) and immersing our-selves in their cultures.

Put aside egocentric and ethnocentric concerns, and dive into new and unfamiliar world views. Travel back and forth across time zones, geographic regions, mental spaces. Let go of biases and prejudices, if you can, and try to enter other cultures. Stop worry-ing about coverage, as it is quite impossible anyway, and go for depth, for documentary evidence, for social, political, and historical theories that attempt to explain the patterns and evolution of humankind and the human effects on planetary ecology.

Why is this important? Well, because we are on that planet right now and it is appear-ing increasingly interconnected. But perhaps we are also increasingly alienated from the earth and each other. Although the internet is among the most important advances in ages, humankind still seems rooted in the problems, issues, and customs of the past, unable to reach out from one parochial history to another. In a word, although we can communicate across the globe in seconds, we still don't play well with others or under-stand their concerns. And we have lost a good deal of sense about our earth, not really knowing in a deep, behaviorally changing kind of way that it is in big trouble in terms of pollution, food supplies, and energy.

World history, much more than other courses, permits the teacher great flexibility in choice of topics, materials, questions, themes, and structures. Mysteries abound, and hold great potential for creating interest in students, provided we choose thought-pro-voking key questions to guide our thinking and course of study.

To truly develop a *world* history, we argue that teachers and students need to look at the world anew—not as a collection of separate entities, cities, nation-states, regions, groupings, cartels, etc., but as inter-related, interlocking, interactive components of a sin-gle system of communication and exchange. We propose a view of the world as dynamic, nervous and energetic, and keen on travel, migration, and borrowing in transformative ways.

And here perhaps is the mind-blowing part: we propose, in line with the work over the last few decades by world historians and social scientists, that *the world has always been like this, connected and interactive, but moving at a slower pace.* Only in unusual circumstances have human societies achieved isolation and status quo. Even our distant ancestors moved around a good deal, and obviously exchanged ideas and goods—other-wise the making of fire, stone tools, and languages would never have achieved worldwide distributions well before there was any written history.

So instead of looking at world history as discrete, distinct units, we ask you to put on a new pair of glasses and systematically investigate possible links, exchanges, connec-tions, relations, diffusions, and fusions. Rather than examine one atom at a time, seek out configurations, relations, patterns, and evolutions.

For example, the United States is often taught as though it is a unique, exceptional state, outside whose borders (with the possible exception of England) nothing particu-larly influential occurred. From a world history point of view, the United States is a very successful nation but one of very few original ideas at all. We challenge you, our readers, to research one truly *original* idea invented in the United States, one that was not based on an idea born elsewhere. Our anthem is stolen from England, the hamburger from Germany (just look at the name!), apple pie from somewhere in Europe, the idea of democracy from ancient Greece, and that of a republic from ancient Rome.

So start peeling the onion of world history, researching layer by layer the forces of change and influence, and also examine the surfaces as well—how wide the net of influences was cast, and which links were most important. And seriously examine the ways in which we think about ourselves in history. This becomes crucially important in the classroom. If you think of history as one thing occurring after another, or as "great men" (women, where are you?), or as dates, names, and places, then you will not have much chance to present world history as mystery. Shift to studying people, places, and events through a prism of linkages and influences, going back and forth in time to identify causes and consequences of actions.

This is no easy task, we know, but it is most worthwhile, mind-expanding, and compelling in creating a different kind of world history course, one that may help students grasp the world they now live in.

You Decide

What kind of world view is shown in Figure 2.1? Is the world all there? Is anything missing? How did Posidonius see the world two thousand years ago? What did he get right and what did he not get so right? Why?

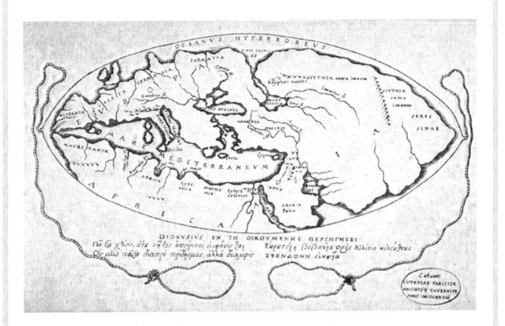

Figure 2.1 World Map according to Posidonius (150–130 B.C.E.), Drawn by Seventeenth-century Cartographers.

Inviting Inquiry in World History

To teach world history well, you may feel that you must know a great deal about the world and be able to translate that knowledge into exciting, accessible lessons for your students. You need a way of presenting the past that students find inviting—but there is way, way too much to cover, and too many strange names and places and ideas to render sensible. Immediately, problems jump out at you:

- How can I teach about a big, complex world of history when I only know some of its slices and fragments?
- How do I explain events that seem long ago and far away to young people first coming to terms with themselves as citizens of an interactive globe?
- What conceptions of the world will help me communicate the past to students in an engaging way?
- Which topics are most valuable to teach about and how do I connect these to other topics and still meet local, state, national, and professional standards?
- Why teach the world's history as a whole, and how do I justify this choice to administrators, colleagues, parents, and students?
- What philosophy of teaching is best suited to my class and to my overall goals?

Let us try to help you. First, we need to review world history and take a new view of the subject. This means trying out a new pair of lenses with multiple perspectives that permit us to see connections, make comparisons, and identify local contexts (and ourselves) as part of interactions between places, times, cultures, and peoples. We need to view ourselves, and our histories, in a world context—not as unique, or having newly sprung from the head of Zeus, or as condensations of many histories, regions, or self-centered stories about us. World history may be defined as

> [T]he story of connections within the global human community. The world historian's work is to portray the crossing of boundaries and the linking of systems in the human past. The source material ranges in scale from individual family tales to migrations of peoples to narratives encompassing all humanity.
>
> (Manning, 2003, p. 3)

Manning argues that there are two paths to world history, one "internal" and the other "external," the first seeking explanations through global linkages and connections beginning with local examples; the second using a "big picture" approach and many disciplines to understand worldwide patterns of change and development. Both of these histories have increasingly drawn upon sciences and arts outside history to enrich and expand our picture of historical evolution.

Here lies one of our first problems as teachers: how to teach world history on a personal as well as global level. One of the criticisms of world history is that it is too broad, abstract, and massive for students to grasp. Narrative history (history as story) is much easier to understand, perhaps, but as teachers we need to balance the personal and global, providing both broad summaries of people, places, and events as well as detailed inquiry into artifacts and documents from the past.

In this chapter, we will provide you with a brief overview of the transformation of world/global history as a subject that has occurred over the last several decades. This change is evidenced by the success of William McNeill's *Rise of the West* (1963), which places Europe firmly in the vortex of global communication and trade and argues for transnational movements during the first century, when contacts were made between Han China and Rome by way of Persia.

William McNeill expanded world history by borrowing from many disciplines (including science) to write *Plagues and Peoples* (1976) on the relationship between historical events and diseases. His idea of a cause-and-effect relationship between Europe and the world laid the groundwork for others to take up. During the '70s and '80s and beyond, the field has diversified to include all sorts of topics, methodologies, and interests that were at best marginal several decades before. Phillip Curtin (1969, 1984, 1989), for one, devoted considerable attention to trade and migration, disease and empire, particularly in Africa.

New paradigms for world history began appearing, notably in the work of Immanuel Wallerstein (1974, 1980, 1989), a sociologist who argued that European expansion and exploration led to a fully functional world economic system by the sixteenth century. Many adopted, mimicked, and debated the idea of a modern world one-economy system, a fine example being Braudel's (1973, 1981) work connecting capitalism and civilization, with special emphasis on material culture and economics. Crosby (1986) branched out to connect imperialism and ecological change, noting how the world is being "used up" through intensive exploitation in agriculture, mining, and energy resources.

As the new world views began to spread, historians developed more of a sense that proof was needed to support narrative (Stavrianos, 1998). First college and then secondary school textbooks began to shift ground to include new research, wider viewpoints, and the incorporation of many primary sources within secondary narratives.

By the 1990s, historians and social scientists were borrowing freely across disciplines, shifting from traditional narrative storytelling and biography to more "scientific" inquiry, often explicitly revealing sources of evidence to readers. Food history, social history, gender studies, regional (area) studies, technological development, cultural topics, and new approaches to methodology exploded across the field and have now become commonplace. Studies have jumped across time periods and geographic units to test theories of interconnection, for example that Asia was a big factor in "making" Europe what it is today (Embree and Gluck, 1997). Area studies began to appear, demonstrating that, even long before European expansion, trade, commerce, culture, and religions were spread across Asia by monks, merchants, and armies—contributing to a rich civilization in many areas (Chaudhuri, 1990). Some scholars took a more thematic view, many with a keen interest in empires, their rise and fall (Kennedy, 1987), and judgments about imperial benefits (Chua, 2007). Other scholars focused on production and consumption (Arrighi, 1994) and ecological exchanges (McNeill, 2000; McNeill and McNeill, 2003), comparing and contrasting regimes and documenting the efflorescence of flora and fauna across the world (Ponting, 1991; Fernandez-Armesto, 2001). Ambitious efforts have been made to demonstrate cross-cultural connections, at least in the Old World, going back at least four thousand years (Bentley, 1996). Recent arguments for pushing back the "world system" idea into the five-thousand-year range or more have been made (Frank and Gillis, 1993). The world is a "new" place: nervous, migratory, commercial, on the move and interconnected on many levels, not at all static, rigid, or impermeable. The scope and overview of world history is getting bigger and smaller at the same time, with precise local studies linked to large-scale explanatory theories (Spier, 1996). This means that there are many great books out there on history and the social sciences to apply to the classroom.

World History Organizations

World historians now have quite a large organization, the World History Association (WHA), that promotes instructional change as well as research. Social studies and history educators, through their organizations—principally the National Council for the Social Studies (NCSS) and the National Council for History Education—have often joined forces to try to modernize world history teaching to take into account the latest research and the most provocative theories (Appleby, Hunt, and Jacobs, 1994). There are a bewildering variety of ideas available now about what to teach, how to teach, how to organize courses, and even how to think about history itself as a subject. We will provide a history of world history teaching to help you understand where we are coming from and to better inform your own teaching.

We argue for a conception of world history as truly global, meaning that we will be willing to look at prehistory and history as interactive, as portable and porous (with open boundaries), and eventually as interconnected and integrated. Some people find the "one world" history both annoying and worrisome because we think of our nation as the center of the universe, as different from the "others," and maybe as "better" than the others. We have (in a very characteristically human way) privileged our interests and ourselves over all the rest. This ethnocentric view is satisfying but unfulfilling because it obscures our own connectedness. "Centeredness" is a defensive posture, a kind of tariff system in which incoming material is filtered out in a way that leaves us isolated. But it does help us to care less about the rest of the world, whose actions can be quite upsetting. It also helps promote both a healthy and an unhealthy feeling of nationalism, much like that in many other ethnocentric regions. Here again, connecting peoples, places, and events improves our overall understanding not only of the world but also of ourselves, who, after all, have a place in the world—we influence it and are influenced by it.

Once you see yourself as part of the world, a new perspective on teaching world history can develop. After all, we are carrying with us a great deal of historical baggage that has influenced us and shaped us, but of which we are mostly unaware. Quite a while ago, a noted historian and troublemaker, Karl Marx, observed that:

Men make their own history, but they do not make it as they please; they do not make it under self-selected circumstances, but under circumstances existing already, given and transmitted from the past. The tradition of all dead generations weighs like a nightmare on the brains of the living.

(Marx, 1852, trans. 1963, p.1)

Viewing history worldwide can be frightening as there is far, far too much to take in, and teaching this vast mass of material is impossible. We are going to state this again quite clearly: *impossible!* So don't try to "cover" the world, or even most of it. Rather, be selective and shrewdly choose examples that provide context, suggest comparisons, and encourage connections.

Give your brain a chance to "free associate" and link ideas, places, and events that are not customarily brought together in most world history texts. Choose topics that provide rich and entertaining primary sources, particularly sources accessible to most students. Our first principle is to *choose topics that focus on and develop a theme or big idea*, rather than try to cover! cover! cover! a host of dates, names, and places that students are unlikely to recognize. Choose topics that encompass "elegant ideas," especially ideas that link local contexts with world citizenship—such as cultural diffusion, migration, contact and conquest, trade and exchange, faiths and fashions, race and gender issues.

Herein lies our second principle, and that is *engagement with students through a methodology we call "mystery."* Teaching world history as mystery is really about returning history to its rightful place as a deeply fascinating and satisfying form of inquiry. In history as mystery, both teachers and learners investigate primary sources of evidence (much like professionals), comparing and contrasting these materials as a prelude to testing them against conclusions drawn in the classroom and by expert historians and social scientists. It is a rediscovery of the "messiness" of primary sources *before* historical interpretations, to build a basis for analysis and judgment.

In short, just as early Protestants upset the religious and political apple cart by insisting on reading the Bible for themselves, we will invite you to read history and make your own interpretations. As a third principle, we will not each set up our own storefront church, but compare our conclusions—based on evidence and reason—with those of experts: historians, sociologists, archeologists, political scientists, economists, humanists, and other thinkers who have had the time and skill to probe deeply into the subjects we are studying. This does not mean we have to bow down to the experts if we don't agree with their conclusions. A recurring issue in historical inquiry is that all of us are human and fallible and may come to incorrect conclusions because of our biases—not to mention lack of evidence. We define the evidence of history as including artifacts, art, music, literature, historical documents, diaries, letters, official announcements, film—in sum, the total range of human production, serving as potential sources for investigation.

Rethinking Views of the World

Next, we need to rethink the world, and that has become easier because the last four or five decades have seen the rise of many eminent world historians and social scientists whose research has prompted new ways of looking at history. There has also been development in social studies education, with growing concern that children and youth have a poor grasp of global connections. In fact, one of the standards for educational attainment set out by NCSS is recognition of global connections. A clear set of guidelines has been proposed by a trio of authors (Collins, Czarra, and Smith, 1998, p. 311–17) in *Social Education* (the journal of the NCSS), calling for three broad themes:

I.   Global challenges, issues, and problems
II.   Global cultures and world areas
III. Global connections: the United States and the World

The NCSS lays out knowledge objectives, skill objectives, and participation objectives, all based on a set of objectives developed under the auspices of the U.S. Department of Education in 1968. We particularly like this sample:

[Knowledge:] Students will know and understand that cultures cross national boundaries.
[Knowledge:] Students will know and understand that there are universals connecting all cultures.
[Skills:] Students will be able to state a concern, position, or value from another culture without distorting it, in a way that would satisfy a member of that culture.
[Participation:] Students will demonstrate an appreciation for universal human rights.

(Collins, Czarra, and Smith, 1998, p. 311)

Thus, the call for drawing global connections and for integrated world history has been developing for decades, but implementation in the classroom is much harder to achieve. One of the major aims of our book is to give teachers and students a framework, and examples, to implement this more global approach.

There has been an outburst of great change and vitality in the study of history, and there now seem to be many histories. This change began in the 1960s and has been growing ever since. The many different histories contrast often in focus and methodology, offering rich new findings and insights for our lesson planning and teaching, but it is difficult to get a grip on the totality of news and views.

Traditional history, still thoroughly respectable and enjoyable, tends to concentrate on narratives, telling a story based on expert research on a particular topic, usually of limited scope. World narratives by their very nature are difficult to pull off because of the volume and complexity of the data, although there are many historians who have attempted this feat. For our purposes, the narrative story in the classroom usually comes in the form of a textbook that is chronologically driven, and offers summaries of people, places, and events. Textbooks and expert historian narratives provide useful overviews but don't give a great deal of contact with primary sources, tending to offer answers rather than mysteries.

Sweeping changes in historical subjects and methods have grown out of conceptions of what is important in history, and out of the ease with which large amounts of data can be handled using computer research and data-crunching programs. For example, websites have proliferated and contents ballooned to such an extent that the amounts of information are truly amazing and awfully hard to make sense of without an interpretive framework or theory.

Ideas about history have also expanded to a wide range of related disciplines including all social sciences and most of the arts and many sciences. Environmental history, for instance, draws upon traditional storytelling and scientific method, whereas gender history has integrated sociological and anthropological techniques and findings to explain the role of women in world history. Economics has been widely used for decades by historians who seek to explain events from financial and trade factors rather than political alone.

In fact, there are groupings and branches to the history discipline now that might be arguably characterized as the following:

- narrative history;
- economics, politics, and economic history;
- sociology and social history;
- biological, medical, and environmental history;
- gender studies and feminist history;
- cultural history and literature.

Each of these draws from many of the same disciplines for inspiration, and many different disciplines, producing a rich and heady mix of the arts, sciences, social sciences, and history (Foucault, 1970). Each has a somewhat different focus and interest and some have been much more influential than others, for example social history seeks to illuminate the lives of ordinary people and has produced many interesting studies of commoners, the poor, slave life, and popular entertainment. Economic history and historians have applied many theories, capitalist and Marxist, to the understanding of world history, enriching us with more comprehensive views of booms and busts, for example, than we had before, views of the world as a unified economic system. Science has play a big role in histories of disease, for example the Black Death, or AIDS, presenting population and demographic conclusions about the rise and fall of human populations in different eras (Diamond, 1997). Feminist theory begun in the '50s and '60s has led to a discipline of its own, shedding light on the treatment of women in world history, along with complaints about unbalanced treatment that we are still debating how to change and correct (Firestone, 1977).

The arts, popular culture, film, forms of entertainment, and other aspects of human productivity provide another rich resource for historians, leading to studies of the ways in which cultural products and values have moved around the globe, for example Hollywood-style movies or Hong Kong Kung Fu films (Vansina, 1984). Applying literature and literary modes to analyzing historical writing or to enriching our understanding of the past has also grown, resulting in many wonderful young adult historical novels and children's books that can form part of a history course, K–12 or K to infinity (White, 1973).

Vast surveys combining historical and scientific method have led to comprehensive reviews of environmental history, discussing topics such as food, agricultural production, depletion of resources, and cultural adaptation to change (McNeill, 2000). Whichever disciplinary hat is worn, a different and enriching view comes into focus. History and the disciplines provide a many-faceted set of methods and guidelines for investigating history, of which one is the narrative method we still associate as the historian's main tool. To keep abreast of this intellectual ferment, historians must be expert in several fields at once, combining, rearranging, and testing theories drawn from other disciplines.

Developments in World History Courses

World history has gone through many changes, beginning with histories that were largely national in scope, that is the history of the world from a largely German or French or American point of view, moving back and forth only as other peoples' histories impacted upon or were impacted on by "us." For many years, students took courses in the history of "Western civilization," often quite well organized and presented as this is the history that most elementary and secondary teachers know best. Lovely, but just what is "Western" and what is "civilization" a world historian might ask (Braudel, 1998).

This Eurocentric bias still persists in some textbooks but has given way to what are called "area studies" organizing world history into a series of boxes, "East and West," that usually results in a strange mix of national and regional units, for example Japanese, Chinese, and Indian history, or East Asia, or the Middle East. Area studies still hold sway in many communities because it seems easier to organize material into distinct units with a beginning, middle, and end, allowing the teacher to focus on one area at a time. This, however convenient, is rather unrealistic in the sense that it overlooks the heavy cultural borrowing, centuries of political interference, and economic ties between and among these peoples. It also treats each culture as unique and distinct, which they are and are not at the same time. And some areas seem to have been left out of the curriculum almost entirely, such as South America, Africa, or Oceania (where is that?)

Another model, "global studies" or "world studies," seeks to supplant both the "Western civilization" and the "area studies" models, viewing each as having disadvantages that outweigh advantages, mainly in reinforcing ethnocentric boundaries and views and in creating "boxed" mentalities in which each group of people is viewed as separate and somewhat isolated from the others.

A brand new web-based, with-it program called World History for Us All represents one interesting attempt to come to grips with the problems of teaching the world. To do this, these historian educators organize their course around "three essential questions" and "seven key themes," as follows:

> How has the changing relationship between human beings and the physical and natural environment affected human life from early times to the present? . . .
> Why have relations among humans become so complex since early times? . . .
> How have human views of the world, nature, and the cosmos changed? . . .
> (World History for Us All, n.d.)

Why each of these is or should be an essential question for history is itself a good question, but note the effort to escape event- and personality-driven history for a largely environmental and interactive framework. Their seven key themes reinforce a thematic and conceptual stance toward world history in the classroom:

> Key Theme 1: Patterns of Population
> Key Theme 2: Economic Networks and Exchange
> Key Theme 3: Uses and Abuses of Power
> Key Theme 4: Haves and Have-Nots
> Key Theme 5: Expressing Identity
> Key Theme 6: Science, Technology, and the Environment
> Key Theme 7: Spiritual Life and Moral Codes
> (World History for Us All, n.d.)

One of the early issues among historians was integrating past histories so that they could be viewed as connected and interactive regionally and globally rather than as a series of discrete social entities that grew up isolated and alone. Immanuel Wallerstein (1974) proposed that the last five hundred years have been global in nature because exploration and discovery put virtually all peoples in all continents in touch with all others for better or worse through complex networks of trade, conquest, diffusion, and migration. Gunder Frank (1998) went one better than Wallerstein by arguing that the "Old World" of Afroeurasia was interconnected at least five thousand years ago with the New World being added after 1492.

More recent work has argued that people have been restless and inquisitive for perhaps 500,000 years, moving all over the face of the earth, albeit rather slowly, eventually populating nearly every environment and corner, and diffusing their tools, ideas, and social organization across the entire globe. We would add that taking a long view of worldwide history gives a newfound respect for our ancestors, and also a wonderful teaching tool in the sense that we, us, I, you, the students, are all part of a "great chain of being" inheriting (consciously or unconsciously) many attitudes, ideas, techniques, foods, and beliefs held over from long, long ago. In effect, we are carrying a vast quantity of baggage with us that we take for granted but which represents the accumulated developments and adaptations of many ancestors, cultures, and peoples across time and space.

We strongly favor teaching world history as interconnected and integrated, rather than as separated and cased into little national boxes or time periods. Viewing world history as a series of encounters, interactions, and connections gives both teacher and student a sense of where they came from that they might not have had before. Who we are, why we act as we do, now grows out of a series of historical connections and developments that fuses disciplines, history, and other subjects into some sort of "whole."

So, you (we) (us) really need to study history as true mystery to find out how we got here and why we take action in our current context. By viewing ourselves in world history, not apart from it, we may also develop a much healthier understanding and perhaps respect for those who came before us, building a better base of knowledge and skills for us to refine and redevelop. These past folk are perhaps less strange and unfamiliar once we connect their beliefs and actions to our own, discovering that there are patterns to human history that invite comparison and contrast, and may lead to new and surprising conclusions.

Collecting knowledge for its own sake is not a bad goal, but we would prefer collecting knowledge for the purpose of making sense of history as connecting past, present, and future action, trying to discover patterns in human motivation and belief, coming to grips with our own feelings and values, all of which are connected to a distant and not-so-distant past that has supplied us with most of the basics we still struggle with in our daily lives.

You Decide

Is the map shown in Figure 2.2 a new view of the world to you? What do you notice looking at this map as opposed to a standard up-and-down map. What is the point of focus? What areas are furthest out or closest to the center? Do you notice connections or relationships that you usually don't on a regular school map? Explain.

Figure 2.2 Dymaxion Map of the World.

Frameworks to Teach World History

Global/world studies is still in its infancy in some ways, and a lot of problems have to be worked out dealing with basics such as chronologies themes, geographic units, and essential questions. Meanwhile, we argue for two major components of teaching the world:

1 an emphasis on wide, cross-cultural, time-leaping comparisons and contrasts between times, places, people, and cultures;
2 the presentation of interconnected or interactive perspectives between and among primary and secondary sources.

The scope and structure of lessons, units, and courses should be open to experiment using examples, considering, testing, rejecting, and accepting examples as analogs, giving care and attention to detail. Arguing analogies is itself an interesting and thought-stimulating process in history, for example is the second Iraq War like the first one, or is the United States similar to or different from the Roman or the British Empire?

Interestingly, whatever "frame" or big idea is accepted, and several can be used simultaneously if you like, quite a different curriculum and questions emerge into consciousness. Sometimes this is referred to as "privileging" one set of viewpoints or topics over another. We think that there are several basic frames for teaching and learning world history, for example:

1 *Spatial*: Viewing people, places, and events across geographic or cosmological space, for example not just listing, but linking together, the ever-favorite River Valley Civilizations lesson, for example did Indus Valley people trade with Mesopotamia, who traded with Egypt, who traded with the Niger/Mali folks?
2 *Temporal*: Viewing people, places, and events across two or more time zones, or thinking about time itself as an idea, for example studying the sequence of related revolutions, the American, French, Russian, and Chinese, thinking about how time changed the dynamic of each as they adapted to both persisting and novel conditions, or how about comparing the Hebrew, Chinese, and Mayan calendars?
3 *Thematic*: Viewing people, places, and events regrouped and reorganized under thematic ideas such as gender, heroism, revolution, or wealth. Alternatively, you might employ more offbeat affective ideas such as love and marriage, ecological systems, popular entertainment.
4 *Dynamic*: Viewing people, places, and events from a kinesthetic lens, as morphing and changing across different times, within different spaces or settings, or under the influence of different ideas and values. This could include demographic developments, within and between groups, broad regional shifts, or even personal biographies and autobiographies of changes within one's own lifetime as reported in a diary or memoir.

Checking it Out: Big Questions in Teaching World History

As you can observe, once the new glasses are adopted—those for seeking out connectivity and interaction—world history begins to look a great deal different from how it did when everyone was neatly placed in their own little boxes. Building teaching aims around big ideas reinforces the new mindset and promotes essential and exciting questions.

Like all good history, world history needs a system of quality control, that is, the application of *evidence, reasoning,* and *theory*—all three—as components in checking to see if the cases and examples really work with the big ideas, and give us reasonable, defensible results. Historians and social scientists have professional scholarly responsibilities to fairly and systematically examine evidence allowing both for error and for fallibility, that is, keeping conclusions open to retesting in the light of criticism, new data, and alternate theoretical explanations. For school classrooms, it is fun to draw conclusions, but it is also fun to re-examine evidence and debate alternate explanations, both from students and from secondary sources. Playing off primary and secondary sources is a favorite history/mystery technique that we offer to you on a regular basis.

To put it simply, evidence, facts, and data are necessary to draw conclusion and make judgments. However, in any mystery situation, we may not have enough evidence, or the right kind, and we may find out that some of it was faulty or biased or both. Oops! So the *first* big question is: *Is our data accurate and balanced?*

Our second question focuses on historical and social science interpretations of the data. Once conclusions have been made, we need to check for reasoning. We need to determine if our experts, or ourselves, have been logical and fair, if there are enough reasons behind an explanation for most people to accept it. Thus, the *second* big question is: *Is our reasoning fair and logical in using data?*

A third way of testing data and reasoning is to go over both primary and secondary sources in search of agendas, hidden or public, that authors, artists, composers, and filmmakers build into their work. This can be quite important in some situations and perhaps less so in others, but is always useful because it gives us insight into the orientation and goals of the source. For example, if a deeply believing rebel is the author of a view of revolution, then her or his account may be overtly sympathetic to the underdog, and disdainful of the former leadership group. This doesn't necessarily change our conclusions, but it can be very important if that is all we study, indicating that we need another piece of evidence from a contrasting or competing source. Thus, we need to ask a *third* vital question: *Is the data shaped by a particular viewpoint or belief?*

Historians, social scientists, eyewitnesses—everyone in fact—report using language, line, form, sound, expression (in whatever media). How an historical account is presented and in what form may strongly influence our assessment. Some forms can be more emotionally powerful than others, and some structures are designed to impact our understanding and/or our emotions more powerfully than others. For example, a professional historical account aiming at objective reporting may offer a much more accurate story of events than a dramatic, highly selective novel or play, but we may find the literary style and format a great deal more enjoyable. Films as popular entertainment have this power to influence by combining many media (music, art, story, and character) so that we often fall prey to thinking about historical characters based on film, which is really not very accurate at all. For example, there are numerous film portrayals of Queen Cleopatra, and in nearly all of these she is shown as very exotic, sexy, and attractive as well as sly, conniving, and cunning. She is also usually "Egyptified," although she was quite Greek in origin and lifestyle and authentic busts show her in standard Greco-Roman styles. So, a *fourth* big question is: *How does style and presentation affect our interpretation of the data?*

Once we start analyzing the style and form of historical presentation, we are ready to think about *theory*. We need to think about the eyewitness, or historian, or social science expert, or filmmaker providing us with a synthesis: an organizing principle to make sense of the evidence. We might want to inquire if the story has a plot and meaning that grow out of a larger idea, an idea so big that it shapes goals, selects evidence, provides interpretations, and wraps it all up for us in a neat package (perhaps too neat!) We need to review our evidence and *how we learned about it and drew conclusions from it*, considering if these are our own answers or if the compilers and presenters have drawn us into accepting particular outcomes. A powerful philosophy may illuminate events but may also close off other possibilities and give predictive power to one interpretation of history, for example a liberal or conservative or Marxist or Hegelian viewpoint that explains not only what happened and why, but also what is likely to happen in the future. Do not misunderstand, please—we are not opposed to applying big-scale historical philosophies, but we do prefer to be aware of them as good detectives, and consciously rather than inadvertently accept their rules and conclusions for good reasons. So, we come to a *fifth* key question: *Are our conclusions shaped by an overall philosophy of history so powerful that it explains the data and predicts outcomes?*

Last, often overlooked in discussions of primary and secondary sources, is the moral, ethical, and affective dimension of history. We must think about the feelings, moods, and psychological states expressed in or exhibited by the evidence, the eyewitnesses, and the experts. Let's face up to the emotional aspects of history and talk about it both analytically (as in our search for ideology and philosophy) and also affectively—as human feeling, as decisions about what we like and dislike, as judgments of right and wrong, and as overall ethical perspectives on positive and negative actions in history, actions with ethical choices that affect our lives in the here and now.

All sources, whatever their attempts at objectivity, we argue, make some sort of explicit or implicit value judgments about the past, judgments that affect our interpretations as teachers and students. This emotional component, in our view, can make for very exciting classroom conversations, but it should be recognized and managed frankly and openly. We would much prefer sources that honestly lay out their attitudes and methods for us, but that doesn't always happen, so we must guide our students to be the detectives of emotion and judgment in the reporting of historical people, places, and events. We should also be bold enough to make our own judgments on the judgments of others, and allow others to make observations and criticisms of our judgments. Thus a *sixth* question comes into view: *Can we recognize, develop, and defend feelings and judgments about the past?*

Six Big Questions to "Check Out"

1 Checking evidence for accuracy.
2 Checking interpretations for reasonability.
3 Checking for ideological and philosophical agendas.
4 Checking for methods and styles of presentation.
5 Checking for proof, plausibility, and predictive power.
6 Checking for ethical, moral, and value positions.

Deductions

Finally, as this section is all about checking sources, testing conclusions, and detecting values and decisions within sources, we think that a great way to wrap up a course in world history as mystery is to "hold court" on the cases we studied. Was Napoleon really a hero? Why are there fewer women than men in world history books? What are the reasons for secret societies arising? How can we draw conclusions from artifacts alone? What forms of communication are most influential and powerful? Carefully defending interpretations and conclusions, teachers and students must test judgments with evidence and logic, while still keeping minds open to alternate explanations when confronted in our examinations.

We have provided an overview of historians' thinking about how to conceptualize world history, how to organize its myriad topics so that it reflects interaction and a wide scope for human action as well as local and national narratives. Roughly beginning in the second half of the twentieth century and continuing into the present, world historians and social scientists have offered provocative new ways to structure world history, giving us many hats to wear for interpreting both primary and secondary sources: sociological, anthropological, economic, ecological, cultural, feminist, and scientific as well as historical. World history has become much more eclectic in its organization of the past, pushing far back into time the connections and migrations that characterize human cultural evolution. Many of these new ways of thinking about world history are available to us in making decisions about the content and methods of instruction.

World history can be studied as cutting across time, comparing and contrasting events in different places, developing themes and big questions about categories of events, tying together methods, narratives, and case studies to test a wide array of theories. It can cover topics ranging from development and underdevelopment to economic systems, ecological conservation and destruction, the rise and fall of empires, relationships between humans and diseases, the exchange and exploitation of food systems, and overarching philosophies of history that promote a view of the *whole* of human existence and beyond. We have a rich mix of topics to choose from in addition to the traditional narrative form.

With all the new research into content also come new methods for teaching history, including our favorite and subject of this book, history as mystery. Teaching history as mystery, in our view, connects perfectly with the increasingly global approach to world history in two vitally important ways. First, teaching the world as mystery can take advantage of detailed studies of relatively small topics that may nevertheless make excellent mysteries in ways not thought of before. For example, the origins of food—its evolution and adaptation across cultures—presents an easy way to get into questions about world interaction, from big-scale events such as the Columbian Exchange to small-scale investigations of bread, salt, bananas, wine, coffee, chocolate, and many other favorite food products. In this book we have created a mystery around pizza, which actually comprises at least three separate pieces of detective work: on bread, cheese, and tomatoes.

Second, teaching the world as mystery can apply many of the "big" ideas proposed by world historians to explain, organize, and debate a slice of history using different lenses—chronological to be sure, but also thematic, regional, literary, gender- and issues-oriented, and philosophical. You now have a number of decisions to make about what you will teach, how to organize a unit, and what techniques of pedagogy you will employ to invite engagement from students.

We believe that mystery is a powerful way of engaging students because it places a premium on using primary sources to test narrative summaries (secondary accounts) and on using the resulting conclusions to check historical theories and methods of investigation. This has great potential to entice students into becoming historical detectives who have to develop, analyze, and synthesize a body of data, eventually judging the worth of their own conclusions with guidance and by comparison with professionals and experts.

Choices for conceptually organizing the teaching of world history include:

- standard chronological sequence (then to now);
- reverse chronological sequence (starting now and going backwards);
- area and regional perspectives (using geographic and cultural units of analysis);
- themes (big ideas, concepts, and essential questions as focal points);
- issues and controversies (making ethical, moral, and emotional judgments);
- integrating evidence, interpretations, and value judgments (creating a "big picture" of world history by testing a historian's view).

A note on making connections. World historians have been debating globalization for a long time. Even in the ancient past, some historians such as the ancient Greek Herodotus and the Roman Tacitus tried to write about faraway people and places, as well as their own cultures. In recent decades, historians such as Braudel, Wallerstein, and Gunder Frank have argued that global change, travel, diffusion, and exchange took place five hundred, one thousand, or more than five thousand years ago. Present-day historians still read the ancient, a connection across time as well as space.

We invite you and your students to also make these connections!

References and Further Reading

Aberth, J. (2007) *The First Horseman: Disease in Human History*, Upper Sadle River, NJ: Pearson/Prentice Hall.

Anderson, C. C., Niklas, S., and Crawford, A. R. (1994) *Global Understanding: A Framework for Teaching and Learning*, Alexandria, VA: Association for Supervision and Curriculum Development.

Ankerl, G. (2000) *Coexisting Contemporary Civilizations: Arabo-Muslim, Bharati, Chinese, and Western*, Geneva: INU Press.

Appleby, J., Hunt, L., and Jacobs, M. (1994) *Telling the Truth About History*, New York: W. W. Norton.

Arrighi, G. (1994) *The Long Twentieth Century: Money, Power, and the Origins of Our Times*, London: Verso Books.

Bentley, J. H. (1996) "The cross-cultural interaction and periodization in world history," *American Historical Review* 101: 749–70.

Bentley, J. H. and Ziegler, H. F. (2005) *Traditions and Encounters: A Global Perspective on the Past*, 3rd edn, New York: Oxford University Press.

Braudel, F. (1973) *Capitalism and Material Life, 1400–1800*, New York: HarperCollins.

Braudel, F. (1981) *Civilization and Capitalism, 15th–18th Century* (three vols, trans. S. Reynolds), New York: Harper & Row.

Braudel, F. (1998) *Memories and the Mediterranean* (trans. S. Reynolds, 2001), New York: Borzoi Books/ Alfred A. Knopf.

Brown, C. S. (2007) *Big History: From the Big Bang to the Present*, New York: The New Press.

Buchsmann, R. F. (2007) *Oceans in World History*, New York: McGraw-Hill.

Chaudhuri, K. N. (1990) *Asia before Europe: Economy and Civilization of the Indian Ocean from the Rise of Islam to 1750*, Cambridge, UK: Cambridge University Press.

Chomsky, N. (1994) *World Orders Old and New*, New York: Columbia University Press.

Chua, A. (2007) *Day of Empire: How Hyperpowers Rise to Global Dominance—And Why They Fall*, New York: Anchor Books.

Clossey, L. (Spring, 2005) "World history textbooks and their others," *World History Bulletin* XXI (1): 19–21.

Collins, H.T., Czarra, F., and Smith, A. F. (1998) "Guidelines for global and international studies education: Challenges, cultures, and connections," *Social Education* 62 (5): 311–17.

Crosby, A. (1971) *The Columbian Exchange: Biological and Cultural Consequences of 1492*, Westport, CN: Westport Press.

Crosby, A. (1986) *Ecological Imperialism: Biological Expansion of Europe, 900–1900*, Cambridge, UK: Cambridge University Press.

Curtin, P. (1969) *The Atlantic Slave Trade: A Census*, New York: Madison.

Curtin, P. (1984) *Cross-Cultural Trade in World History*, Cambridge, UK: Cambridge University Press.

Curtin, P. (1989) *Death by Migration: Europe's Encounter with the Tropical World in the Nineteenth Century*, Cambridge, UK: Cambridge University Press.

Dal Lago, E. and Katsari, C. (eds.) (2008) *Slave Systems: Ancient and Modern*, Cambridge, UK: Cambridge University Press.

Diamond, J. (1997) *Guns, Germs, and Steel: The Fate of Human Societies*, New York: W. W. Norton.

Duchesne, R. (2006) "Asia first?," *Journal of the Historical Society* 6 (1): 69–91.

Embree, A. and Gluck, C. (1997) *Asia in Western and World History: A Guide for Teaching*, London: EastGate Books.

Embree, A. T. and Gluck, C. (eds.) (2001) *Asia in Western and World History*, Armonk, NY: M. E. Sharpe.

Fernandez-Armesto, F. (2001) *Civilizations: Culture, Ambition and the Transformation of Nature*, New York: Simon & Schuster.

Firestone, S. (1977) *The Dialectic of Sex: The Case for Feminist Revolution*, New York: Cape.

Foucault, M. (1970) *The Order of Things: An Archeology of the Human Sciences*, London: Tavistock.

Frank, A. G. (1998) *ReOrient: The Global Economy in the Asian Age*, Berkeley: University of California Press.

Frank, A. G. and Gillis, B. K. (eds.) (1993) *The World System: Five Hundred Years or Five Thousand?*, New York: Routledge.

Gonick, L. (1990) *The Cartoon History of the Universe*, vols 1–7, New York: Doubleday.

Gonick, L. (1994) *The Cartoon History of the Universe*, vols 8–13, New York: Doubleday.

Gonick, L. (1997) *The Cartoon History of the Universe III: From the Rise of Arabia to the Renaissance*, New York: Doubleday.

Gran, P. (2009) *The Rise of the Rich: A New View of Modern World History*, Syracuse, NY: Syracuse University Press.

Hanvey, R. (1976) *An Attainable Global Perspective*, New York: American Forum for Global Education.

Hegel, G. W. F. (1899) *The Philosophy of History*, New York: Colonial Press.

Hodgson, M. (1993) *Rethinking World History: Essays on Europe, Islam, and World History*, Cambridge, UK: Cambridge University Press.

Kennedy, P. (1987) *Rise and Fall of the Great Powers*, New York: Random House.

Landes, D. (1999) *The Wealth and Poverty of Nations: Why Some Are So Rich and Some So Poor*, New York: W. W. Norton.

McNeill, J. R. (2000) *Something New Under the Sun: An Environmental History of the 20th Century World*, Aldershot, UK: Allen Lane Press.

McNeill, J. R. and McNeill, R. H. (2003) *The Human Web: A Bird's Eye View of World History*, New York: W. W. Norton.

McNeill, W. H. (1963) *The Rise of the West: A History of the Human Community*, Chicago: University of Chicago Press.

McNeill, W. H. (1976) *Plagues and Peoples*, New York: Anchor Press/Doubleday.

Manning, P. (2003) *Navigating World History: Historians Create a Global Past*, New York: Palgrave Macmillan.

Marx, K. (1852) *The Eighteenth Brumaire of Louis Bonaparte* (trans. 1963), New York: International Publishers.

National Council for the Social Studies. (1994) *Expectations of Excellence: Curriculum Standards for the Social Studies*, Washington, D.C.: National Council for the Social Studies.

Pomeranz, K. (2000) *The Great Divergence: China, Europe and the Making of the Modern World Economy*, Princeton, NJ: Princeton University Press.

Ponting, C. (1991) *A Green History of the World: The Environment and the Collapse of Great Civilizations*, New York: Penguin.

Ponting, C. (2000) *World History: A New Perspective*, London: Chatto & Windus.

Ponting, C. (2007) *A New Green History of the World: The Environment and Collapse of Great Civilizations*, New York: Penguin.

Spier, F. (1996) *The Structure of Big History: From the Big Bang Until Today*, Amsterdam: Amsterdam University Press.

Stavrianos, L. (1998) *The World to 1500: A Global History*, 7th edn, Englewood Cliffs, NJ: Prentice-Hall.

Stori, C. (1990) *The Art of Crossing Cultures*, Yarmouth, ME: Intercultural Press.

Tattersall, I. (2008) *The World from Beginnings to 4000 B.C.E.*, New York: Oxford University Press.

Vansina, J. (1984) *Art History of Africa: An Introduction to Method*, London: Kegan Paul Press.

Wallerstein, I. (1974) *The Modern World System I: Capitalist Agriculture and the Origins of the European World Economy in the 16th Century*, New York: Academic Press.

Wallerstein, I. (1980) *The Modern World System II: Mercantilism and the Consolidation of the European World Economy, 1600–1750*, New York: Academic Press.

Wallerstein, I. (1989) *The Modern World System III: The Second Era of the Great Expansion of the Capitalist World Economy, 1730–1840s*, New York: Academic Press.

White, H. (1973) *Metahistory: The Historical Imagination in 19th Century Europe*, Baltimore, MD: Johns Hopkins University Press.

World History for Us All (n.d.) Online. Available at http://worldhistoryforusall.sdsu.edu (accessed March 1, 2009).

Wright, R (2004) *A Short History of Progress*, Toronto: Anansi Press.

three
Stones that Speak
Of Megaliths and Monoliths

Of all the earth-works of various kinds to be found in England, those about which anything is known are very few . . . Within them all lie the secrets of time before history begins, and by their means only can history be put into writing: they are the back numbers of the island's story.

(Allcroft, 1912, p. 20)

People usually just step on them or pass them by, but stones can speak. Stones talk to us.

They tell us of the past—their builders, a style of life long lost, and maybe a sense of a culture and society. Stone has a wonderful quality: it lasts through the worst weather and most difficult periods. Once, in certain regions, stones were the ubiquitous building and tool-making material: arrowheads, fences, towers, houses, tombs, and structures we don't really understand.

Ancient Europe was a place of stone and wood, earthworks and mud. There are many remains across Europe of solitary or groups of stones set upright to attract attention (or so we think), as well as circles and barrows of stone edifices, villages, and markers, and, of course, the most famous pile of ancient stones, Stonehenge of England. These artifacts were created during the third and second millennia before the Christian era (four to five thousand years ago). A long time ago, and without any recorded history. We have only the archeological remains and our imaginations to go by, and the latter can often be a mystery in and of itself.

You Decide

Rock Art from Sweden

Humans have carved designs in rocks for thousands of years. Figure 3.1 shows one from prehistoric Sweden, a few days' journey from Stonehenge. What do you think the rock painting describes, symbolizes, means? Were our ancestors telling us something or just involved in a bit of graffiti? Is a story being told? How can we interpret artifacts without the benefit of words? What features of daily life are shown? How are people drawn? What are they doing? Are any symbols employed in the rock art? Was it art or was it communication or both?

Figure 3.1 Rock with Carvings, Found in Sweden. Photo: Iris Zevin.

The Mysterious Stone "Henges" of Europe

Stones are not very impressive to us nowadays, as we are used to skyscrapers and huge stadiums, but we still take notice of the more mysterious examples, such as England's Stonehenge, the subject of volumes of discussion as to its building, intent, meaning, and function.

But these most famous of stones are just the tip of the iceberg in terms of mystery, as there are other, perhaps more elaborate, leftovers of forgotten ages spread around England, Ireland, Scotland, France, Italy, Sweden, Sardinia, Malta, and other places. Numerous earthworks, tombs, stone circles, the remains of markers, lines, mazes, rock art, paths, or roads, and other indications of the people of the late Neolithic period and the Bronze Age dot Europe. Most of these date from prehistoric or just barely historic times (meaning since the advent of writing), about five to three thousand years ago.

What makes these stones a delightful mystery, a real unknown, is that we are not completely certain who the folks were who constructed them, or for what purpose they were constructed, and we are not always clear on the ages of these finds. So that gives us three good questions (at least) to pose to our students: purpose, age, and makers. We might also add to these questions of reconstruction and culture. We are all so used to explicit statements of aims that not having these is a great burden in understanding the past, when there were undoubtedly pretty good planners and engineers—who didn't leave us their blueprints.

They may have had blueprints, but these may not have been written down. Or if they were drawn in some way, they have not survived the ages. Fortunately, however, the present societies in which these stones are located have often respected, revered, or even feared them, and thus left them largely untouched. Now we can take a look and decide for ourselves. However, many of the stones have been destroyed, recycled, or incorporated into newer buildings by people in need of raw materials. In the case of Stonehenge, the original source of the sarsen stones (limestone blocks)—crags thirty miles away—has been largely mined over and changed by development. So we do not know the precise origins of the large stones that make up the Stonehenge.

We therefore invite you and your students into a minor, or maybe a medium, mystery—a mystery of missing information and partial discoveries, overlaid by a good deal of theorizing and romanticizing about the past. Yet it is also a way to teach archeology—analyzing the art, architecture, and culture of peoples *without writing*—as well as a way of understanding the lifestyles of our ancestors, those who preceded the historical peoples we read about in our textbooks. Please keep in mind that, for the purposes of this book, you are receiving only a taste, a sample, a selection, of the vast amount of information available about the famous Stonehenge and its cousins that dot much of Western Europe. We are indebted to scholars whose work we have drawn from, particularly Burgess (1980), Chippindale (2004), and Renfrew (1983), and we look forward to continuing studies of our mysterious ancestors from the Neolithic and Bronze Ages.

Mystery Packet: Views of Stonehenge

Figure 3.2 Victorian-Period Watercolor Drawing of Stonehenge. Portrait owned by Jack Zevin.

In what way does the artist present Stonehenge in Figure 3.2? Is it nicely reconstructed, or as a ruin? Is one ring of stones shown, or two or three? Why are some of the stones leaning far over while others are standing? What part do the gathering clouds play in the overall design and mood? Why draw the shepherd and his sheep entering from the front? How realistic do you think the old drawing was, and what if that is all you have to go on?

Figure 3.2 shows a romanticized portrait of Stonehenge. Compare it with the "real" portraits in Figures 3.3 and 3.4. In what way do the photographers present Stonehenge? Is any person or animal or thing included? What are the angle and mood of the photos? Do you feel that the photographers have captured the "mystery" of Stonehenge? Why or why not? How does this compare with the painting? Are the photographs like the painting in showing how the stones are formed and situated? In what ways are the painting and the photographs alike or different? Which medium do you think may have portrayed Stonehenge more accurately? Why? Is either medium "objective" or "subjective"? Explain your viewpoint.

Figure 3.3 Stonehenge Lives! Druids Gather to Celebrate Summer Solstice. Photo: Stock Photo (May 1, 2004), Corbis.com.

Figure 3.4 Early Photograph of Stonehenge (1853). Photo: R. Sedgfield.

Look at Figure 3.5. How does the artist present Stonehenge? How does Stonehenge look compared with how it looked in Figures 3.3 and 3.4? Which of the photographs do you think is "truest" to reality? How can you tell? Can you guess when, why, and how the photo in Figure 3.5 was taken? Can you give it a likely date: the 1900s, 1920s, 1940s, 1960s, yesterday? Are the planes close, in the foreground, or farther back, or directly over the stones? How do you investigate a ruin, object, or remain from long ago? How can you remain objective about it? Are photos objective? What have you studied that gave you the most reliable clues to the real meaning and purpose of Stonehenge and which gave you the least? Explain what sorts of evidence you find most valuable in archeological and historical inquiry, and why.

Figure 3.5 Planes over Stonehenge (image in public domain).

Note: The Edwardian postcard in Figure 3.5 is not an unaltered photograph. Photographs of the airplanes were cut out of the magazine *Flight* and added to the original photograph. This may be considered an early, non-digital example of "Photoshopping."

The Past as Baggage

A second, and perhaps equally important, mystery regarding ancient monuments concerns our abiding need to project (our own) current beliefs upon them, often obscuring (pun intended) their probable meaning by giving one that serves current conceptions.

You Decide

- Can a mystery be solved even if part of the data is subjective? What if the mystery object or document is surrounded by hundreds of years of speculation, controversy, and theorizing? Does that make the problem harder, or easier, to deal with, and why?
- How do you feel about these issues, and how would you describe and portray Stonehenge in as objective a manner as possible?
- If you found more drawings and/or photographs and films of Stonehenge, would each have the same problems, or would some be more objective than others, and how could you tell? What are your standards for accuracy and "objectivity"?

For example, we imagine people of long ago as nationalities like ourselves, or we count them as representatives of our culture, or we see them as progenitors. Artifacts in the United Kingdom become British or Scottish, French artifacts become French or Celtic or Gaulish in some way, and Irish ruins hearken back to the days of the druids and dragons. In short, we seem to want to claim the past for our country and culture and deny it to others, even though the evidence for it belonging to us is pretty slim. The political identification of people who lived four or five thousand years ago is very hard to determine, but was probably not part of anyone's current (or imagined) national constructions. Worse yet, the archeological site becomes an *icon*, an image of the past that is popularized and used in advertising, as a tourist attraction, and for propaganda, all of which changes its interpretation in people's minds. Perhaps it was "tribal" (a word I dislike intensely for its inherent putdown of what are often large national groups and for its connotations of the primitive). Perhaps it was a village culture organized into chiefdoms, or some sort of larger organized political entity. We simply don't know.

For some of you, teaching about Neolithic and Bronze Age peoples is a way to rehabilitate the under-represented cultures that preceded the Greeks and Romans, and who probably made up most of Europe well before the first Greeks knew they were Hellenes, or the first Romans got out from under their Etruscan overlords. Maybe these folks were the ancestors of the Celts, maybe not, or maybe partially so. Their burials and skeletons

You Decide

Can we recreate the past?

Yea, verily, the past can *never* be recovered, says the wise old sage. Do you agree or disagree and why?

resemble both earlier and later European peoples, but a full assessment of culture is quite difficult to do from pots, stones, tools, and bones. Art helps. So does clothing and weaponry.

So many authors persist in claiming these ancient peoples as Celtic, and books on the subject are divided between England, Ireland, France, Scotland, and so forth, with very few offering a cross-national view of the time period, implicitly treating Stonehenge as a precursor of Celtic (preferably their own) cultures (the egocentric bias!) These pre-historic folks are often collectively known by the name "Celts" and *may* have been the forebears of the builders of most of the stoneworks we will examine in this chapter.

Background: The Stone Makers and Earth Movers of Neolithic Europe

Across Europe today you can find a variety of remains dating back to the Neolithic period ("new stone age") and the Bronze Age, the points in time when people learned how to improve stone tools followed by the ability to smelt metals, making beautiful artifacts of bronze and copper, silver and gold (followed much later by iron making) (Table 3.1). At the same time, our ancestors in the Middle East were sending each other letters on papyrus and clay tablets, organizing cities, cutting canals into the earth, and creating the first known empires. Nevertheless, the European and Middle Eastern peoples may have been in touch now and then through trade networks.

But this is where Europe was, building cozy farms and villages, setting up stones, creating earthworks, and drawing designs on a number of artifacts, pots, weapons, and other materials. Most easily accessible to us are the stones and other artifacts left in the British Isles, as these have been studied and popularized in the language we inherited as Americans, and are relatively easy to visit. Artifacts come in types and styles, many of which have been labeled and defined in ways that may or may not be true to their actual functions. So be careful of your conclusions and your projections.

First, there are the large and dramatic circles of stone, the most familiar example of which is Stonehenge. But there are larger and more complex arrangements as well, for example Avebury Plain is larger and contains many more stones in its circle. These stones are set upright, unless of course they have fallen down. There are also some nice stones

Table 3.1 Time Line (with due humility, based on recent historical thinking by experts)

Neolithic period (5000 B.C.E.–2500 C.E.)	*The New Stone Age:* Henges, stone circles, monoliths
Bronze Age (2500 B.C.E.–700 C.E.)	*Invention of metallurgy:* Stone circles, rows, barrows, copper and bronze weapons and armor (~ 2000 B.C.E.)
Iron Age (700 B.C.E.–43 C.E.)	*Invasion by the Romans!* Hill forts, Celtic earth designs, Pictish peoples, and druidism

Source: Based on the work of Colin Burgess (1980) *The Age of Stonehenge*, London: Castle Books.

in Brittany at Carnac and other places, if you wish to venture further afield from dear old England.

Second, there are sets of stones set up with walls and a large (sometimes huge) slab on top, which seem like shelters or homes, but which have usually been called burial tombs. Depending on local cultures, these have been termed *dolmens*, *quoits*, or *cromlech*. An area called the Burren in western Ireland contains quite a few well-preserved remains of "forts" and dolmens. Farmers have destroyed or rearranged many of these, and their original settings or structures may have been altered, further contributing to the uncertainty of our interpretations. In some cases, materials have been returned or discovered and a reconstruction attempted, particularly at tourist sites. These reconstructions may or may not be just as the ancients intended.

These stone structures have distinctly different designs. Usually the items seen as tombs consist of several large stone slabs, whereas the structures seen as homes consist of many small stone slices arranged as walls—circular or square—an entrance, and some sort of chimney or hole to let smoke rise out from the hearth. The holes suggest a home because that is where people usually do their cooking.

Third, there are earthworks—sometimes in the shape of animals, sometimes in the shape of humans, sometimes as mazes or designs, and every now and then as large fortresses, ring upon ring of walls within walls, raised up a story to several stories high at key locations in a geographic area. A place called Maiden's Castle, for example, in Dorchester, southern England, covers 120 acres and has a mile and a half circumference rising several stories high, with curious openings or baffles at each end. Some thought of this as a fort (and used it as such for a while), and others have conceived of it as a religious ceremonial center, but its original purpose is open to conjecture.

Fourth, there are drawings, designs, and inscriptions on some of the stones that give clues to the people who lived then, and provide us with a sense of the art styles that were favored, some of which have carried over into historical and even present times, and which are usually viewed as "Celtic" in form and style. Or perhaps the Celts took over earlier peoples' styles, passing them on to us, but you will get the chance to decide for yourself.

Fifth, there are what we might call "behavioral leftovers" that may intrigue you, ideas and customs that seem to predate historical writing and modern religions such as Christianity and Judaism, and hearken back to customs we might call "pagan." These customs are rooted in the bond between people and earth, hunting and agriculture, usually known locally in a community, but seldom practiced outside or in the large cities that characterize most modern and historical cultures. For example, in parts of England, people still, or have until recently, celebrated spring with maypole dances, May Day or horn dances (wearing antlers), or danced the dance of the "Green Man," a fine fellow covered with wicker and leaves looking much like the Jolly Green Giant. Wicker Man is also a tradition (even a film) in which some villages burn a "wicker man" made of a twig frame sometimes ten to twenty feet high each spring as a symbol of renewal and the burning of sins, starting anew, or "turning over a new leaf." We tend to overlook the meaning and message of such customs, but many scholars and observers feel that these date to the distant past of our agricultural village ancestors, who worshipped the earth and its cycles, and who turned to much-beloved Druids, or priests of the earth, for guidance and ceremony. But it is a "stretch" to assume that the ancients of the fourth millennium B.C.E. did the same thing, or that we are still doing what they did. Don't you agree?

A little theory is in order here. We would argue that no matter how old or distant or "strange" an object, artifact, report, written or unwritten, happens to be, it can speak to us if we apply good sound historical principles to its interpretation, avoiding the three historical mystery evils to which many people succumb: ethnocentrism, econ-centrism, and egocentrism. In other words, look at the object in its own right, imagining what the folks then would have done with it. Become sympathetic to the artifact. Let yourself be drawn back into time, separated from current meaning and intention. What, after all, did people have to work with and know how to work with three, four, or five thousand years ago? Rocks, mud, wood, bone, and a bit later metals, but certainly no email.

In this context, we would also argue that all of us have historical memories that have been passed down to us by our parents, families, schools, cultures, and societies, most of which we don't think about at all, but which are based on deep human beliefs and emotions rooted somewhere in the past. Some of this is evident in language, life cycles, and weather cycles, some in customs, food habits, enjoyment of animal pets (why do we need dogs anyway?), social arrangements, and ceremonies. Do we know why we buy a dozen eggs, and not ten? Why do many of us like to stand on a hill and watch the clouds go by? What does it mean to "turn over a new leaf"? Why do we celebrate May Day? Where do pancakes, blini (look it up if you don't know), flapjacks, and hotcakes come from? What is the purpose of building a maze and why do people enjoy mazes? The ancients can help us answer many of these questions, and you can add pertinent ones of your own linguistic leavings, verbal mystery clues, traces on the tongue.

From an archeological point of view, thinking about the past—listening to stones that speak—can help us connect with the way life may have been lived then by analogies to basic, unchanging human needs. Matters of life, sustenance, burial, faith, power, security, economics, entertainment, and ritual still concern us, although the forms and maybe the functions may be quite different—or maybe not so different after all!

What the Stones Tell Us

Let's take a look at some of the finds in Europe—especially England, but also France, Germany, Ireland, and Scotland—that offer us a basis for solving questions of form and function, style and meaning.

Let's also look at some of the interpretations given to a famous example such as Stonehenge, and to other places, which may or may not stand up to historical thinking and concordance. First of all, the term "Stonehenge" has been liberally applied to public circles or ovals, but some are ditches and others embankment enclosures, all lumped together by most writers and observers. Many of these circles include stones set in the earth, raised up, topped off, and other variations. All seem to be set out in the open, usually on a plain, and are often the sites of burials.

Archeologists have attempted to classify the sites according to their design, with Class I sites representing a single bank with an internal ditch and one entrance. Class II sites have two opposed entrances, but there are many variations on these patterns, as some, like Stonehenge, have external ditches. The major difference in classification seems to grow out of circles that include free-standing stones or stones with an embanked ring of some kind, and circles that have stones set at the inner edge of a ring bank and are associated with what are sometimes called "ring cairns," stones set at the edge of earth embankments. For many observers, even scholars, this is a fine distinction, but maybe Figure 3.5 above will help you figure out the differences.

Others sometimes contain more than one continuous circle, others are in sections or we see a ring of pits, and still others have no visible remains of entrances. There are estimated to be at least a hundred or more such sites that have been discovered in the British Isles, and aerial photographs have produced new examples. There are maps of the sites, which, according to the investigator, cover the less romanized portions of the British Isles, which is interesting in itself. The size of the rings can vary greatly, from nine or ten meters to about five hundred meters in diameter, with the famous Stonehenge coming in at around one hundred meters. Stones can vary from a few feet high like those at Avebury, not too far from Stonehenge, where there is a very large but not high and numerous stone ring, to single stones perhaps fifty tons in weight, so there is great variation.

These sites are frequently burial places, with the smaller ones almost always including burials, and the larger ones, most in the south of England, including remains of hearths and timber buildings, now decayed. Rings of pits, posts, and stones are fairly well measured out but some are irregular, and many are surrounded by banks of earth, slightly raised, so as to provide a view of the center of the circles. Some, including Stonehenge, have yielded cremation cemeteries, with a variety of urns set in the earth embankments, sometimes within the henge and at other times outside the circle.

Despite the fame of Stonehenge and other cherished sites, a good deal of the surrounding areas has not been excavated, or has been developed and plowed over, and we are therefore missing a good deal of evidence concerning settlements or cultures outside the dramatic places. In short, we are not always sure if there was a community near or surrounding each site, or if the sites were set apart from local populations.

Stonehenge and most of the ruins like it date from the third millennium B.C.E. for early and simple examples, and continue through more elaborate and better-designed examples dating to about the second millennium B.C.E. Thus, some of the oldest rings date to about 2800–2500 B.C.E., and some of the "newer" examples date to about 2200–2000 B.C.E. The building of stones circles and earthen embankments also coincides with

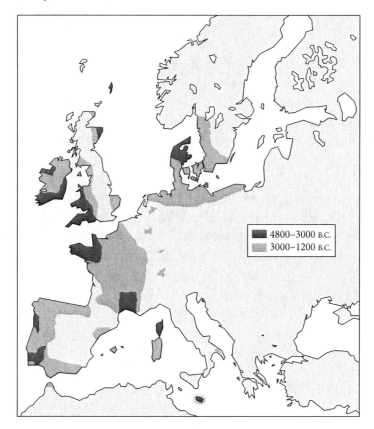

Figure 3.6 Map of Megalithic Architecture in Western Europe. Source: Modified from original by Tharkun Coll/Creative Commons.

what archeologists have termed "grooved" and "beaker" ware (pottery), which is associated with specific periods in British archeological reckoning.

In addition to stone circles, there are many examples of "cursus" lines or monuments and "barrows" around Europe, especially in the British Isles (Figure 3.6), usually consisting of parallel banks or lines of earth and external ditches perhaps forty to eighty meters apart, usually in straight lines that run for up to several miles across country. Barrows are smaller but set up in straight ditches or topped with slabs of stone. Most are contemporary with Stonehenge, but many have not been fully excavated and less is known about their function than about the larger, more dramatic stones.

What was life like in the British Isles and parts of Europe in the third and second millennia? Well, there is evidence, already noted, of stone circles, smaller rings, single stones, barrows, and burial cairns. These may be called public monuments of some kind, but there are also the remains of stone villages—earthen compounds containing burials, pottery, and foodstuffs (not always recognizable). Some time during this period there was the development of metal working, and the later sites during the second half of the third millennium contain rather elaborate weapons, helmets, jewelry, and assorted items—perhaps used for pinning clothing together or for cooking. Spear points, knives, arrowheads, and axes—first in stone, and then in bronze—appear throughout the period, often with sleek decorations, accompanied by changes in pottery styles, particularly the growth and spread of "beakers" (as they are called) (Figure 3.7). These beakers are almost always found with burials, and were very common for hundreds of years, adding to but not necessarily supplanting older styles of pottery design.

Questions for Discussion

- How big are the beakers? Do they have similar shapes? Wide mouths, or narrow? Were they probably meant for drinking, storage, or serving, and how can you decide?

- Do their designs mean anything or are they probably esthetic? Can we tell? Why decorate a beaker? What might decoration tell you about the people of the time? Did they have an esthetic sense?

- Why would people cremate their relatives and community members and place their ashes in beakers?

- Do we still follow the same customs? How do ours differ?

- What do the beakers tell us about these peoples' technology? Production? Consumption?

- If beakers were produced over a long period of time, does that imply stability?

Do these artifacts help you construct hypotheses about life in the second millennium before Christ, the time of the building of Stonehenge? How so?

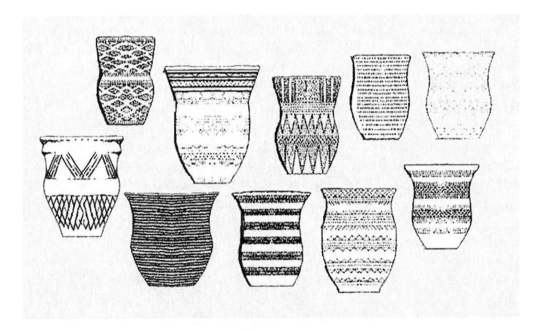

Figure 3.7 Beakers of Different Styles Ranging from 3000 to 2000 B.C.E. Based on an image in Colin Burgess (1980) *The Age of Stonehenge*, London: J. M. Dent.

Agriculture dates back to the fifth millennium B.C.E. and was thus fairly well developed by the third and second millennia, with evidence of neatly fenced-in fields throughout the British Isles and Western Europe. Cattle, sheep, goats, and pigs, as well as dogs, were raised in most communities, with the greatest amount of bone seeming to be from cattle, according to archeological finds. Farms tended to take the shape of what are called "Celtic field systems" (there's that persistent claim again), that is, usually rectangular fields about a quarter of an acre to an acre and a half in size, not large, set off by an earth bank and small marker stones. The main crops were wheat and barley, emmer-type grains of Middle Eastern origin, which did not change much until the first millennium B.C.E. There is evidence of earlier agriculture continuing into the time when barrows were built, small tightly defined areas, with stones all round, of small plots of rich earth in which varied crops were grown, perhaps vegetables.

There are plenty of interpretations of Stonehenge and many other artifacts (all of them quite free and easy with generalizations), which is great, considering that the folks left us no writing, few pictures, and a lot of deteriorated artifacts. In addition, over the years, people have taken stones as building materials for homes and castles in England, France, Ireland, and Scotland, leaving us with incomplete remains of what may once have been great circles or pathways or forts or playing fields.

In any case, scientists have noted that there were at least four Stonehenge designs on the same site, and that these developed over a very long period of time, growing in elaboration and style—to read in (always dangerous) our own artistic notions about tastes and design. The makers were not satisfied apparently with the work of earlier folks, or new designers were hired. The original design and two remakes are reproduced in Figure 3.8, beginning about 2800 B.C.E. continuing on to about 2000–1500 B.C.E., a span of a thousand years or so.

The earliest ring is basically a ditch and an embankment with a sort of opening or entrance. They have what are called *Aubrey holes*, named after the important antiquarian of the mid-seventeenth century, Mr. John Aubrey, who measured and recorded many facts about Stonehenge, including its ring of holes, which probably had posts set up in them.

Hundreds of years later, at approximately 2100 B.C.E., a set of bluestones (large megaliths from the west side of Salisbury Plain) were set up well inside the older ring, and some sort of "altar" stone (there we go analogizing again) was set up at one end of this double half-circle. Outside, the entrance was made more presentable, and a stone set up near its opening. A moat or ditch was constructed around the perimeter. Oddly, the inside circle was dismantled before it was finished. Design problems? Perhaps there was a change of ministers or leaders or priests? Budget collapse?

In a third phase (estimated at about 2000 B.C.E.), an interior circle of sarsen stone (very large slabs) was set up and, within that, a horseshoe-shaped ring of bigger stones, with tops set up on them, sometimes called *trilithons* or three-sided tower stones. The so-called altar stone seems to have been moved elsewhere and there were a few other minor

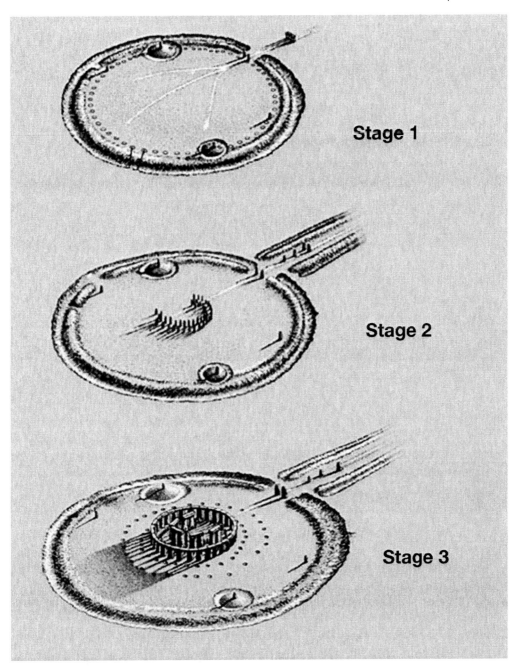

Figure 3.8 Stonehenge in Three Stages.

alterations in the design by the inhabitants of the community. (By the way, archeologists love to give fancy names to their finds, thus enriching our language but not necessarily strengthening our interpretations or solutions of ancient mysteries.)

Somewhat later still, but we are not sure how long after these changes, a new bluestone circle was erected, the altar set up again, and the horseshoe dismantled—but we have no idea why. Stonehenge has remained like that ever since, with considerable damage from wind and rain and weather, as well as from people scavenging for building materials, but with enough left over for passers-by to be impressed and eventually leading to preservation and partial reconstruction.

Questions for Discussion: Chart of Different Stonehenge Designs

- How would you describe the shape of the different Stonehenge designs? How could the stones have been erected? Why is there an entrance, as far as we can tell?

- Were there probably designers and engineers in charge? What could be the reasons for the rebuilding and redesign? Why are there outer embankments and inner stones?

- What are the reasons for building large structures? How many people would it take to create a large project? How highly motivated would people have been to carry out these projects?

- If there were many stone henges and similar stone monuments all over England, Ireland, France, and other places, how might that alter your interpretation of their probable purpose? Of human communication patterns four thousand or more years ago?

- What is your overall interpretation of Stonehenge's design and purpose? How much more information and what kinds of information would you need to support your ideas?

Burials and other artifacts of daily life were found in the vicinity of Stonehenge, thus implying that there was a community present nearby. Of course, we do not know how extensive it was or if it drew upon a series of villages, a tribal confederation, or a kingdom of sorts.

The famous Stonehenge is only one of many in Europe, and there are other larger rings in England, for example Avebury, that cover a good deal more territory and used up more earth in their construction. There are also numerous *menhirs* or single standing stones which dot the landscape in France, especially in Brittany and Normandy, as well as in other parts of the continent. Ireland still holds what many feel are gravesites, dolmens, tombs, and single or multiple stones, as well as earthworks in the form of hills, walls, domes, tombs, and other shapes—the purpose and function of which are long lost to us. Some say the greatest mystery of all is deciding just why the stones were set up at great cost by people who are usually viewed as "tribal" in character. The organization necessary for carrying and setting up a ring of stones of this size would be considerable and implies either a highly organized and fairly populous community under some sort of leadership, or a deeply felt set of shared values that led many to contribute their time and labor to the project—or both. (If you don't believe this, try moving thousands of nice neat bricks for fifty miles or so and stacking them, or digging up tons of earth to make a mound ten feet high. With the school board's permission, maybe you can try this in the schoolyard as an archeological experiment. No, just kidding!)

So then, what do you make of Stonehenge and the other materials presented? What do you think the original designers had in mind? And how would you explain all of the effort that went into their construction—not to mention the construction of numerous tombs, posts, single slabs, barrows, burials, circles, and earthworks throughout Western Europe at the time?

Mystery Packet: Theories of Stonehenge

Theory One: Astronomical Theory—The Observatory and the "Clock"

Professor Gerald Hawkins, using a Harvard/Smithsonian IBM computer, analyzed the settings, stones, and post holes of Stonehenge and developed a theory that the purpose of the structure(s) was to serve as an astronomical "clock" to chart the movements of the sun, moon, and stars (Hawkins and White, 1965). In Hawkins' research, 165 items—stones, holes, mounds, field sizes, etc.—were plotted on a computer graph and aligned with the planets and brightest stars, and then with the rising and setting of the moon and the sun. According to Hawkins, there was a "total sun correlation," and "almost a total moon correlation too." He used the earlier discoveries by Aubrey of holes set in the ground around the center to argue that these functioned as computer predictions of eclipses of the moon, which related to a recurrent cycle of about one-third of the fifty-six stones. Hawkins claimed that the chances for such a system of alignments was one in a million, and argued that Stonehenge was a "Neolithic computer" of sorts. This theory was widely published in journals and newspapers, finally resulting in a full explanation in book form.

Critics, such as the archeologist R. J. Atkinson (1966), argued that the idea had problems. First, several of the holes used for sight lines may have been irregular pits and not humanly constructed. Second, many of the sight lines taken as significant were a few degrees out of line, according to precise measurements, which may have resulted in a loss of moon or sun events. Third, the famous Aubrey holes had been covered over in ancient times, and could not have functioned as tally points as the larger station stones stand over the filled holes. Thus, Stonehenge could not have served as a "computer" and an observatory at the same time.

Theory Two: Esthetic Theory

Many who have studied Stonehenge and other prehistoric artifacts of the period view the arrangements of the stones as pleasing in an artistic or esthetic sense. Observers have often felt that the stones have an inner beauty and express a sense of awe and wonder. Some in the past have gone so far as to develop an artistic interpretation of the stones, with the famous poet William Blake being perhaps the most outstanding. Blake states in his book *Jerusalem: The Emanation of a Giant Albion*:

> All things Begin & End in Albion's Ancient Druid Rocky Shore and the sons and daughters of Albion walk beneath a vast trilithon, twenty times taller than the trees round its base, or measure out a lintelled temple that twists a snake's tail across the plain . . . The Nature of my work is Visionary and Imaginative; it is an endeavor to Restore what the Ancients called the Golden Age.
>
> (Blake, 1952, pp. 173–4)

This has been updated by more modern writers who argue for "the existence in prehistoric times of an active science of spiritual physics, whereby the functions of the mind and body were integrated with currents of the earth and powers from the cosmos" (Screeton, 1974, pp. 13–14).

Theory Three: Mathematical/Spiritual Theory

Alfred Watkins (1970), a miller and amateur photographer who studied Stonehenge, proposed a theory that it was part of an ancient British system of tracks and paths he labeled *leys*, which represented a visionary approach to networking communities in prehistoric times. He envisioned these as fanning out across the entire countryside, marked by ridges, beacons, barrows, and other points of passage that represented pagan worship. Two of the most important and noteworthy leys go right through Stonehenge, estimated at about twenty miles or so in length and connecting to other important sites dating to prehistoric times. Watkins viewed ancient surveyors laying out "old straight tracks" using staffs like those of men in prehistoric hill drawings, some of which can still be seen.

Critics have pointed out that many of the lines occur by chance and represent different time periods, most of which cannot be determined to belong to the era of Stonehenge with any accuracy. Straight lines are not, or were not, necessarily the quickest routes in ancient times between two points, and it is unlikely that any paths created then followed modern mathematical or engineering principles; they probably followed the contours of the earth. Finally, many of the lines actually are imperfect if studied in detail, and may have shifted with time and use, so certainty eludes us according to these scientific skeptics.

Theory Four: Celts and Druids Theory (Back to the Future Nationalism?)

Among the first historians to show an interest in Stonehenge and Neolithic ruins was John Aubrey, a seventeenth-century scholar born in 1626, who tells us that "I was inclin'd by my Genius, from my Childhood to the Love of Antiquities; and my Fate dropt me in a Countrey most suitable for such Enquiries" (Aubrey 1979, p. 81). He developed a project for a book titled *Monumenta Britannica*, which was to catalog the remaining ruins and artifacts of bygone ages throughout England and which become more and more ambitious. Aubrey followed relatively modern research methods of fieldwork, direct observation, planning, and measurement and surveying, and became enraptured with several sites including Stonehenge. He saw this as an ancient stone circle built according to "algebraical" methods. Because of the manner and monumental qualities of their building, he viewed these as temples of some sort, most likely built by the legendary Celtic Druids of the pre-Roman peoples. He proposed (with avid support from others) that these were likely to be the aboriginal temples of native British people, and added on a theory of their origins:

> That the Druids being the most eminent Priests (or Order of Priests) among the Britaines: 'tis odds, but that these ancient Monuments (sc.Aubury, Stonehenge, Kerrigy Druidd, etc.) were Temples of the priest of the most eminent order, viz Druids.
>
> (Hunter, 1972, p. 159)

He never actually excavated the area, as King Charles II had requested, nor did he finish his great project of reviewing all of the prehistoric sites in the British Isles.

However, Aubrey's work was carried on by a doctor, William Stukeley, who spent many a summer (1721–4) at Avebury and Stonehenge, surveying, measuring, and observing in great detail. The work of Stukeley led to many discoveries—ditches, burials, barrows—adding a great amount of detailed knowledge, from which he concluded that the builders had produced

> "a fine design for the purpose of running," calling it a *cursus*, as it seemed a *hippodrom*, a running track for the "games, feasts, exercises, and sports" of the ancient peoples and designed "to render this more convenient for sight," it is project on the side of rising ground, chiefly looking southward toward Stonehenge. A delightful prospect from the temple, when this vast plain was crouded with innumerable multitudes! . . . A huge body of earth, a bank or long barrow, seemed "the plain of session, for the judges of the prizes, and chief of spectators."
>
> (Stukeley, 1723, pp. 41–2)

Questions for Students

(Form a student committee and discuss each possibility, voting for each one as most or least likely. Extra credit for giving reasons and sharing them with other committees.)

- Was Stonehenge an observatory?

- Was Stonehenge a ceremonial center?

- Was Stonehenge a political object?

- Was Stonehenge a memorial?

- Was Stonehenge a sports stadium?

- Was Stonehenge a public works project?

- Was Stonehenge erected for some other purpose?

Explanatory theories come in a variety of forms. The popular theories have themselves changed with time and the accumulation of evidence.

Teacher's Background Information: Theories of Stonehenge

At one time, Stonehenge was seen as the product of Celtic peoples who used it for religious worship with astronomical orientations, that is, star watching as part of prophecy and prediction. Celtic druids and their flocks were imagined parading into the stone circles carrying symbols of nature, and singing lovely chants, perhaps holding torches and marching slowly through the entranceway. This theory is still popular today.

Then, somewhat later, much more credence was given to Stonehenge and its like being astronomical observatories aligned with certain stars and constellations and used to tell time and season. Much effort was put into measuring alignments with stars and star systems, and into measurements between and among posts, stones, lintels, and so forth in a attempt to demonstrate their application to astronomical movements in the skies above England.

More recently, archeologists and other observers have dealt with these ancient artifacts from a socio-functional view, inferring political, social, and economic relationships from the building and maintaining of these monuments for long periods of time. From their review of the research, ideas have developed about the stability and size of the local population, and their probable organization into some sort of alliance of chiefdoms, with a combined power and allegiance significant enough to organize many millions of man hours to construct burial and ceremonial sites of this type.

With the discovery of many "beaker" burials with cremated remains, and "inhumations" (i.e., body burials) in and around Stonehenge and other similar stone circle sites, there is a renewed effort to interpret these ruins as burial centers for important people—leaders or revered holy figures. The burials have led to reinterpretations of many sites as places to honor the remains of important or not-so-important people of the past, with the implication that the people then had notions of afterlife and religion.

Several social scientists and historians have also taken second and third and fourth looks at this period and concluded that Stonehenge and probably Avebury (as well as various sites in France and Spain composed of concentric rings of stone) were for ceremonies that drew crowds of spectators, and were not isolated or solitary affairs set aside exclusively for the highest and mightiest. These ideas grew out of very careful analysis of the rings and earthen embankments surrounding the large stones, all of which are somewhat raised in height, which has led to the theory that observers could stand or sit up at an angle to the center, gaining an improved viewpoint. Thus, our feelings about the drama and romantic qualities of some of these places are confirmed, but perhaps in a different way from how we may have originally thought: the ceremonial center for burials, services, an expression of faith, astronomical observation, augury, or all of the above involve participation by many people.

Then, of course, we have those who feel that none of our ancestors was capable of much and that visitors from outer space, time travelers, or peoples from the Middle East—who had superior engineering and technological skills—must have directed the locals in developing their designs and dragging all those terribly heavy stones to the plains of Salisbury to set them up in a dramatic circle. There are strange signs on some stones and beakers that may represent a "Stargate" situation, in which representatives of a higher power helped our ancestors.

You Decide

Always be careful of great big theories! Match theory to data as much as possible, and pay attention to detail, to reasonability, and to the criticisms of other people, especially those who do *not* favor your own pet ideas. Think about historical and archeological theorizing when there are no written records, no historical documentation, or very little. How much easier does that make it to theorize? How much harder do we have to work to reach definite conclusions? What do you think? Which theory do you subscribe to as the top one? Which theory do you personally prefer?

Summary and Conclusions

Mysteries in history, such as Stonehenge and life in the second and third millennia, are real in the sense that we are missing a great deal of evidence that would help us test, revise, and strengthen our hypotheses. Archeological problems are generally "real" mysteries, and not manufactured at all, because we are dealing with a distant past usually without writing and sometimes even without much imagery, symbolism, or art to use as guides to formulating interpretations.

Yet because of, or in spite of, the uncertainties involved in drawing conclusions about archeological data, discoverers, researchers, observers, visitors, believers, and exploiters are completely willing to "manufacture" new mysteries in which ancient findings are put to work as tools of tourism, national pride, ethnic claims, and new age religion—raising questions about the underlying reasons for the appeal of certain sites to the rampant human imagination.

Not every place or time grips the soul as strongly as certain popular icons, of which Stonehenge is one good example. There are plenty of others in the form of the Egyptian and New World Pyramids, the Mona Lisa and the Sistine Chapel ceiling, and the Great Wall of China. Just why certain sites become popular icons is not at all clear, although the press, TV, and films help bolster the images in our minds. Not all images command the imagination, as some are far more attractive than others, and this too is part of the human mystery. Stonehenge, a great and ancient circle in England sitting out on a windswept plain, perhaps draws us because of its design and drama, and perhaps because *we* need to read into it a religious meaning, an astrological message, or an awe-inspiring monument to the past. Freud might look upon this as an effort to satisfy our deepest psychological need for linkages to the primitive and the primordial libido—tying us to an impressive distant past in which the ancients were so motivated as to assemble a memorial large enough to commemorate events or people we know little or nothing about, but would like to share and imitate to this day.

Megaliths and monoliths, large stones singly or in formation, have been found across a vast area in Europe and parts of Asia, speaking to a cultural idea that traveled across considerable distances and times. Although we have no written records from the Neolithic and Bronze Ages, stones, objects, pottery, art styles, and other material objects lend support to the theory that peoples of that time exchanged ideas and techniques within a system of "international" trade.

Wouldn't it be fun to go back into time to interview the builders, or write an imagined play in which they explain and show off their work? Wouldn't it be fun to worship, play, and meet in ancient Stonehenge? Commune with the stones: what will you feel and find out? Hold an ancient stone that people shaped and see if you gain insights into the prehistoric past of humankind.

References and Further Reading

Ablanet, J. (1986) *Signes sans Paroles*, Paris: Carnet Press.

Allcroft, A. H. (1912) *Earthwork in England: Prehistoric, Roman, Saxon, Danish, Norman, and Mediœval*, London: Macmillan.

Ammerman, A. J., and Biagi, P. (eds.) (2003) *The Widening Harvest: The Neolithic Transition in Europe: Looking Back, Looking Forward*, Boston: Archeological Institute of America.

Anderson. W. and Hicks, C. (1990) *Green Man*, New York: HarperCollins.

Atkinson, R. J. C. (1966) "Moonshine on the Stonehenge," *Antiquity* 40. 212–16.

Aubrey, J. (1665–1693, reprinted 1980) *Monumenta Brittanica*, Quarto series, Vol. II, in two parts, Bodleian Library, Oxford.

Aubrey, J. (1979) *Rings of Stone*, London: Frances Lincoln.

Blake, W. (1952) *Jerusalem: The Emanation of a Giant Albion*, London: Stuart Piggott.

Blake, W. (1968) *The Druids*, London: Thames & Hudson.

Bord, J. and Bord, C. (1975) *Mysterious Britain*. London: Granada Press.

Bord, J. and Bord, C. (1980) *The Secret Country*, London: Granada Press.

Burgess, C. (1980) *The Age of Stonehenge*, New York: Barnes and Noble Books.

Burl, A. (1979a) *Rings of Stone*, London: Frances Lincoln.

Burl, A. (1979b) *Prehistoric Avebury*, New Haven, CT: Yale University Press.

Burl, A. (1989) *The Stonehenge People: Life and Death at the World's Greatest Stone Circle*, London: Barrie Jenkins.

Burl, A. (1999) *Great Stone Circles: Fables, Fictions, and Facts*. New Haven, CT: Yale University Press.

Castleden, R. (1994a) *Making of Stonehenge*, London: Routledge.

Castleden, R. (1994b) *Stonehenge People: An Exploration of Life in Neolithic Britain*, London: Routledge.

Childe, V. G. (1979) *The Dawn of European Civilization*, London: Garnstone Press.

Chippindale, C. (2004) *Stonehenge Complete*, London: Thames & Hudson.

Cork, B. and Struan, R. (1984) *The Young Scientist Book of Archaeology*, London: Usborne Publishing.

Cornwell, B. (2004) *Stonehenge, 2000 B.C.*, New York: HarperCollins.

Delaney, F. (1993) *The Celts*, New York: HarperCollins.

Duke, K. (1996) *Archaeologists Dig for Clues*, New York: Harper Trophy Book.

Gibson, A. (2005) *Sickles and Circles: Britain and Ireland at the Time of Stonehenge*, London: Tempus Publishing.

Hadingham, E. (1976) *Circles and Standing Stones*, Garden City, NY: Anchor/Doubleday.

Harvey, K. (ed.) (2009) *History and Material Culture: A Student's Guide to Approaching Alternate Sources*, New York: Routledge.

Hawkins, G. S. (2001) *Beyond Stonehenge*, London: Allen, Hubert, and Associates.

Hawkins, G. and White, J. B. (1965) *Stonehenge Decoded*, London: Souvenir Press/Fontana.

Heggie, D. C. (1982) *Megalithic Science*, London: Thames & Hudson.

Hunter, M. (1972) *John Aubrey and the Realm of Learning*, London: Duckworth.

Knightly, C. (1986) *The Customs and Ceremonies of Great Britain*, London: Thames & Hudson.

Lowenthal, D. (1985) *The Past is a Foreign Country*, Cambridge, UK: Cambridge University Press.

Mithen, S. (1998) *The Prehistory of the Mind: A Search for Origins of Art, Science, and Religion*, London: Thames & Hudson.

National Geographic. (June 2008) *Secrets of Stonehenge*, Washington, D.C.: National Geographic Society.

North, J. (1997) *Stonehenge: Prehistoric Man and the Cosmos*, New York: Simon & Schuster.

Pitts, M. (2000) *Hengeworld*, London: Century Publishers.

Renfrew, C. (ed.) (1983) *The Megalithic Monuments of Western Europe*, London: Thames & Hudson.

Richards, J. (1991) *Stonehenge*, London: Batsford/English Heritage.

Ross, S. (1991) *Ancient Scotland*, Edinburgh: Lochar Publishing.

Screeton, P. (1974) *Quicksilver Heritage*, London: Thorsons.

Slade, M. (2000) *Burnt Bones*, New York: Signet.

Society for American Archeology. (2000) *Teaching Archaeology: A Sampler for Grades 3–12*, Washington, D.C.: SAA.

Stukeley, W. (1723, 1740) *Memoirs*, vol. 3, London: Society of Antiquaries.

Sykes, H. (1997) *Celtic Britain*, London: Cassell Paperbacks.

Tattersall, I. (2008) *The World from Beginnings to 4000 B.C.E.*, Oxford, UK: Oxford University Press.

Todorov. T. (1984) *Theories of the Symbol* (trans. C. Porter), Ithaca, NY: Cornell University Press.

Watkins, A. (1970) *The Old Straight Track*, London: Garnstone.

Wolf, D., Balick, D., and Craven, J. (eds.) (1997) *Digging Deep: Teaching Social Studies through the Study of Archaeology*, Portsmouth, NH: Heinemann.

four

Rome Lasts!
A Mystery of
Durability and Power

The burden of the proof is on the party affirming, not on the party denying.

(Emperor Justinian)

In this chapter we will present a mystery that runs counter to what most teachers teach their students about the Roman Empire: that it fell—wham! We strongly believe that most people have a "mental map" of Rome that includes a great many inaccurate and false ideas. One of the primary ideas is that the empire fell with a heavy thud somewhere in the vague and distant past between the classical age and the medieval period. We might argue that Rome and its empire never really fell at all. We could argue that Rome lived on as the Byzantine Empire for a while and then as the Holy Roman Empire almost to modern times. Many Roman symbols and ideas are part of the United States, for example the eagle, government architecture, diplomacy, and warfare.

Your conclusion depends a lot on how Rome and empire are defined. Just what do you mean by "falling"? How might Rome be compared to more recent empires? Each decision is highly debatable, and that is good for classroom discussions.

The history of Rome is extraordinarily lengthy and complex, dating back to the pre-historic Bronze Age. Rome continues to modern times, now being a city of tourism, government, and religion that millions of people visit each year, mainly to see a past they probably don't understand very well. One need only trot over to the archeological museum to discover that settlement was extensive well before the idea of a state was born. We hope to help you help students illuminate an aspect of Rome that is often overlooked. Rome was probably one of the most stable and long-lasting states ever developed in world history, with few rivals.

Why was Rome able to last so long? Why do some empires last and others fall to decay? What character and resources, population and organization gave the Roman people and their leaders the ability to withstand invasions, economic crises, internal disputes, and warfare on several fronts? How did they maintain a highly organized life as a distinct state with its own culture, language, customs, and economy? For comparison and contrast, you could inquire about other empires, for example the British Empire, or the Ottoman, or, for the brave, the American Empire (if you agree with the idea).

Rome is probably a medium mystery because so much is known, but interpretations differ. It may grow into a major mystery because of imbedded deep value and historical questions that focus on the rise, continuation, and fall of imperial states in general. Study of any great society of the past or present raises issues of sampling by historians and social scientists, that is, we are privy to a sliver of the vast quantity of documents, records, images, sculptures, buildings, and points of view available. We must make decisions based on an abbreviated study. Scholars of the subject spend lifetimes investigating aspects of Roman life, slowly sorting through the evidence as guides to making generalizations. Some like to draw comparisons between Rome and other empires, which extends questions about durability across times and cultures.

In this chapter we will play the role of archeologists and historians, assessing Roman technology and government. Two sets of evidence will be presented for your investigation. First, images of Roman technology and related facts will tie in with a report on trade from a Roman historian. Second, a series of eight documents about empire and revolt against empire will complete our sample for investigation as historical detectives.

We must also remember to be open to revising our interpretations of Rome's character and longevity based on other views and new evidence. The problem of historical sampling is itself a "mystery" problem, that is, how do our choices about documentary evidence shape our understanding of a people, place, or time, and can we trust the conclusions we draw? What constitutes fair sampling in studying history is a general mystery question that we recommend for all inquiries.

For example, learning about the ancient Persians entirely from ancient Greek sources, which is mostly how we learn about them, gives us a very skewed and unsympathetic view. Learning about Rome only from patriotic Roman sources would likewise give us a very positive but probably unrealistic picture of the culture, so we need critics as well. In our sampler, sources are varied, including Greek, Jewish, and Roman historians (including a few who may be covert critics of their own regimes). We have tried to offer balanced sources in the sense that some are critical, some complimentary, providing classroom detectives with contrary agendas and views.

Rationale

Because there is so much material about Rome, and its history covers at least five distinct periods (prehistoric, Etruscan, Republic, Empire, Byzantium and beyond), we will present this mystery as a series of unfolding "factors" illuminated through primary sources. Each source, documentary and pictorial, will offer suggestions for both Rome's strength and vitality, and its problems and issues. Students act as investigators who must read, view, analyze, and synthesize each factor as a step toward developing an overall interpretation of survival power. Of course, students may disagree with questions we ask and materials presented, and argue that Rome really did fall: it isn't much of a mystery after all.

However, Rome's long life as a state, Republic and Empire, was based on a series of institutions, values, and decisions quite striking to consider. It was a highly organized system of control that lasted many hundreds of years. As an empire, Rome was a fine example of a multi-cultural, tolerant, and capitalistic state, rather like modern states and empires in many ways. We will provide documents that offer views of Roman technology, government, economics, and citizenship, factors from which students can make their own assessments. Most of our focus will be on early and middle imperial times because this gives us the opportunity to make comparisons with other large states and empires, using these as foils for discussion of the Romans.

There will be invitations to compare and contrast Rome with the U.S. and British or other empires to extend the mystery into other times and places. Testing empires can be thought-provoking, extending to other realms, morphing from a unit to a course.

The entire chapter is laid out as a "mosaic," each piece giving the reader/observer a different aspect and factor to consider. A checklist will be provided for assessing why states last rather than collapse.

To Do

Choose any empire in history you find interesting and want to learn more about and collect pictures, maps, and graphs of its assets. For instance, you might take a look at the ancient Persian Empire or Athenian; the Holy Roman Empire; or perhaps the Russian or French Empire. Does the empire you picked measure up to Rome?

Plan of Action

Students will be provided with a mosaic of documents, pictures, and maps providing external and internal views of the Roman Empire from the late Republic to the late Empire. Most of the materials date, however, from the late Republic, and early or middle imperial period. Please keep in mind that the focus of the inquiry is on why Rome and empire lasted. Students are asked to assess archeological features (roads, bridges, aqueducts, medical tools, etc.) that contributed to sustainability as well as hint at vulnerabilities. Rome itself investigated in depth would take at least a full year of study. We believe most teachers will be better served by a careful selection of interesting and informative primary source material.

Thus, the plan of action is to provide a portfolio of primary sources that will serve as the foundation for detective work. The portfolio of sources is set up for group investigation, as a major classroom activity. The plan could also be accomplished by individuals, but we are suggesting that groups of three or four students be given the task of first discussing the images of Roman technology, drawing conclusions that they can share.

The entire picture mystery packet should then be combined with the documents, much like adding tiles to a mosaic, so that a picture of Rome emerges from the accumulated inquiry. As a finale, lead the class as a whole in debriefing the material, debating conclusions and generalizations while recording these on an electronic blackboard, or traditional blackboard.

Therefore, groups will first investigate pictorial materials for clues about the level of technology common in the empire. Second, groups will read and assess the value of each document as a clue to the political system and values upon which Roman life was based. Key essential questions that run through all of the materials are as follows:

1   What kinds of technology did Romans achieve? What kinds of architecture were they capable of? Did they have transportation? Medicine? An economic system?
2   Which skills helped keep Rome powerful? Are there problems and issues? What factors probably contributed to growth of the Roman Republic and Empire? Which factors were most important?
3   Was the Roman economy large? Was there widespread trade? Was the economy varied and productive? How can you tell?
4   How do the documents contribute to a picture of Roman power and values? What conquests did the empire make? How did the conquered view the Romans?
5   How did the Romans view the conquered? Why?
6   Overall, from the evidence you have, would you judge Rome to be well organized or poorly organized? Give reasons for you evaluation.

Students will form groups, and each will receive a handout of their own primary documents for consideration and study, with a set of focus question to guide thinking. A checklist is provided for keeping track of decisions on each document and final judgments. Let's look at an example of a primary document, Aelius Aristides talking about empire. Why is he so taken with the power of the empire? Does he see it as basically good or evil?

The Economy of Empire

Can an empire, any empire, grow without trade and commerce? Here is a picture of Roman trade and commerce, presented by the historian Aristides.

Around [the Mediterranean] lie the continents far and wide, pouring an endless flow of goods to you. There is brought from every land and sea whatever is brought forth by the seasons and is produced by all countries, rivers, lakes, and the skills of Greeks and foreigners. So that anyone who wants to behold all these products must either journey through the whole world to see them or else must come to this city. For whatever is raised or manufactured by each people is assuredly always here overflowing. So many merchantmen arrive here with cargoes from all over, at every season, and with each return of the harvest, that the city seems like a common warehouse of the world. One can see so many cargoes from India, or if you wish, from Arabia Felix, that one may surmise that the trees there have been left permanently bare, and that those people must come here to beg for their own goods whenever they need anything. Clothing from Babylonia and the luxuries from the barbarian lands beyond arrive in much greater volume and more easily than if one had to sail from Naxos or Cythnos to Athens, transporting any of their products. Egypt, Sicily, and the civilized part of Africa are your farms. The arrival and departure of ships never ceases, so that it is astounding that the sea—not to mention the harbor—suffices for the merchantmen . . . And all things converge here, trade, seafaring, agriculture, metallurgy, all the skills which exist and have existed, anything that is begotten and grows. Whatever cannot be seen here belongs completely to the category of nonexistent things.

(Aelius Aristides, 1950)

You may innovate in creating questions and activities of your own along the way. We welcome new and different ways of handling historical sources. After all, crossing time and space is challenging!

You Decide

- What picture does Aristides paint of Roman trade patterns?
- Why does Aristides claim that "Whatever cannot be seen here belongs . . . to the category of nonexistent things"? Is he boasting or probably truthful? Why?
- What sorts of things are traded and from which places?
- Why are most goods headed in the direction of Rome?
- Would Rome be rich or poor in goods and services according to this account? Why?
- Does trade make a place rich and powerful or weak and isolated?
- How important is trade in keeping an empire together and prosperous?

Mystery Packet: Pictures of Roman Territory, Technology, and Manpower

Each piece of evidence shown in Figures 4.1–4.7 suggests the many ways in which the Roman Empire was built and maintained. Perhaps all empires need what the Romans developed? It is your task to form small groups and assess each piece of evidence as:

1 — important for building great empires;
2 — moderately important for building great empires;
3 — somewhat important for building great empires;
4 — not important for building great empires.

Figure 4.1 Roman Aqueduct Built c. 19 C.E. (Pont du Gard, in France). Photo: Armin Kübelbeck/Creative Commons (original in color).

Figure 4.2 Relief (Carving) of a Roman Harvesting Machine (image in public domain).

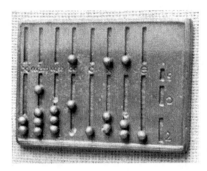

Figure 4.3 Reconstruction of a Ancient Roman Abacus (Counting Machine). Photo: Mike Cowlishaw/Creative Commons.

Figure 4.4 Carving of a First-Century C.E. Boat with Rudder (Steering Device) (image in public domain).

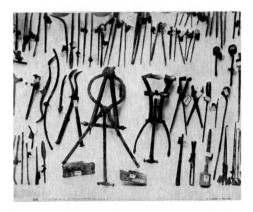

Figure 4.5 Medical Instruments Found at Pompeii. Photo: Giorgio Sommer (image in public domain).

Figure 4.6 The Appian Way, an Ancient Roman Road Still in Use, Connecting Rome to Southern Italy. Photo: Wikimedia Commons user Longbow4U/Creative Commons.

Figure 4.7 The Extent of the Roman Empire in 116 C.E. Can you identify the modern-day countries that were part of the Roman Empire? Based on map by Jani Niemenmaa/Creative Commons.

Discuss each choice, check off the agreed-upon decision, and keep a record of your reasons. For example, is territory important? Is the size of the army, manpower, important? Are aqueducts, fresh water supplies, important? Bridges? Roads? Mathematics? Medical tools? Glass making? Harvesting crops? Shipping? Money and coin system? Does each contribute to power? Trade? Travel? Well-being? Wealth? Do all empires need the same assets? Why or why not? Did the British Empire have the same assets as the Roman Empire? Does America have the advantages of Rome: More or less? Can you find a better empire?

Mystery Packet: The Pros and Cons of Empire

Let's investigate the arguments for and against Empire by Roman historians. Some justify and defend the Republic and Empire. Others speak through the mouths of the conquered, and seem to oppose its spread and control. As you share these documents, consider reasons for and against Empire. Think about how peoples from other lands react to invasion and interference from outside forces.

Compare the Roman historians defending Empire with those opposing it. What arguments seem persuasive to you, for or against? Which arguments seem very reasonable? Would you be willing to join a movement against Rome, or any empire, now or in the past? How would it feel to be on the winning side or the losing side?

Document One: Empire Seen From a Roman View

Praise of Rome by a Greco-Roman historian, Aristides, who offers up a rationale for empire:

> Extensive and sizable as the Empire is, perfect policing does much more than territorial boundaries to make it great . . .
>
> Like a well-swept and fenced-in front yard . . . the whole world speaks in unison, more distinctly than a chorus; and so well does it harmonize under this director in chief that it joins in praying this Empire may last for all time. All everywhere are ruled equally. The mountain people are lowlier in their submissiveness than the inhabitants of the most exposed plains. The owners and occupants of rich plains are your peasants. Continent and island are no longer separate. Like one continuous country and one people, all the world quietly obeys. Everything is carried out by command or nod, and it is simpler than touching a string. If a need arises, the thing has only to be decided on, and it is done. The Governors assigned to cities and provinces govern their various subjects; but among themselves in relation to one another, all of them alike are governed . . . (by) the supreme governor, the chief executive. They are convinced that he knows what they are doing better than they know it themselves. They fear and respect him more than any slave could fear his master standing over him personally and giving orders. None of them are so proud that they can sit still if they so much as hear his name. They heap up praise on him, bow, and utter a double prayer, to the gods on behalf of him, and to him on their own behalf. If they feel the slightest doubt about the subjects' lawsuits, public or private, or whether petitions should be granted, they immediately send to him and ask what to do, and they wait for a signal from him, as a chorus from its director. No need for him to wear himself out making the rounds of the whole Empire, or to be in one place after another adjusting the affairs of each people whenever he sets foot in their country. Instead, he can very easily sit

and manage the whole world by letters, which are practically no sooner written than delivered, as flown by birds.

(Oliver, 1953, p. 64)

Questions for Students

- Why does Aristides pray that the empire last for all time?

- How are commands given in the empire, and by whom?

- Who is the supreme commander of the empire and how great are his powers?

- According to Aristides, where are petitions and letters sent?

- Would you say the author gives a picture of a centralized power and command, or one that is democratic? Why?

- Do you agree or disagree with the statement, "The constitution is a universal democracy under the one man that can rule and govern best"?

- How would you describe this author's views: factual or propaganda? Why?

- Would modern empires use the same arguments as Aristides or different justifications? Why?

Document Two: Empire Explained to the Provinces

This document is a speech attributed to General Petillius Cerialis addressing the Gauls after putting down their revolt in 70 A.D. Note that Roman historians generally reported in their texts, without references, speeches by leaders that may have been accurate, or their own literary creations, or a mix. Stylistically these speeches follow Roman models but the speakers may well have been familiar with Latin and Roman styles, so it is hard to tell if these are truly authentic or invented. What do you think?

Gaul always had its kingdoms and wars till you submitted to our authority. We, though so often provoked, have used the right of conquest to burden you only with the cost of maintaining peace. For the tranquility of peoples cannot be had without armies, nor armies without pay, nor pay without tribute. All else is common between us. You often command our legions. You govern these and other provinces. There is no privilege, no exclusion. From praiseworthy emperors you derive equal advantage though you dwell far away, while the cruel ones are most formidable to those near them. Endure the extravagance and rapacity of your masters just as you bear barren seasons and excessive rains and other natural disasters. There will be vices as long as there are men. But they are not everlasting, and they are compensated by the intervals of better times. Perhaps you expect a milder rule . . . and imagine that armies to repel the Germans and Britons will be provided for less tribute than you pay. Should the Romans be driven out—which the Gods forbid!: What will result but wars among all these peoples? The good fortune and order of eight centuries has consolidated this mighty fabric of empire, and it cannot be pulled asunder without destroying those who sunder it. And yours will be the greatest peril, for you have gold and wealth, which are the chief causes of war. Therefore love and cherish peace and the city in which we enjoy an equal right, conquered and conquerors alike. Let the lesson of fortune in both its forms the good and the bad warn you not to prefer contumacy and ruin to obedience and security.

(Tacitus, 1931)

Questions for Students

- What does Cerialis say are the benefits of Roman rule? What do the Gauls get out of it?

- Why does he say that Romans have "to burden you only with the cost of maintaining peace"?

- What does the general mean when he says, "Romans driven out—which the Gods forbid . . ."?

- Why does he think the result of losing the Romans will be wars, many wars?

- Do you trust the general's views and arguments? Is this probably truth or propaganda? How can you tell?

- Would an American or British general talk to the Iraqi or Afghani peoples in the same way?

- Does conquest usually breed loyalty or opposition? Then? Now? (Think about the Vietnam War.)

The Costs of Revolt

Many peoples welcomed or submitted to Roman rule. Some opposed their rule quietly. On occasion, several peoples revolted against Roman conquest or Roman rule. There were vastly different points of view about facing Roman power. Several documents follow to suggest the issues and views of those opposed. One case concerns the Jews of ancient Israel. A second case reflects the views of Britons during the Roman invasion of their island. Who might you be sympathetic to: conquerors or conquered? Why? Why might people oppose interference in their lives now? Can you find a few interesting examples of revolts going on right now against outside powers, against empires?

Document Three: Advice to the Jews: Don't Do It!

Josephus Flavius, a Jewish historian and Roman noble, wrote this to his people, the Jews, before a great revolt against Rome in 66 A.D. that lasted four years until 70 A.D., concluding with the destruction of the Holy Temple, and dispersion (diaspora) of many of the Jewish citizens throughout the Empire.

Now I know that there are many who wax eloquent on the insolence of the (Roman) procurators . . . Granted that the Roman ministers are intolerably harsh, it does not follow that all Romans are unjust to you, and surely not Caesar, yet it is against them that you are going to war. It is not by their orders that an oppressive official comes from them to us . . . How absurd it were because of one man to make war on a whole people, for trifling grievances to take arms against so mighty a power! . . . Will you, I say, defy the whole Roman Empire? Look at the Athenians, the men who, to maintain the liberty of Greece, once even consigned their own city to flames . . .

Those men today are subjects of the Romans, and the city that was the queen of Greece is governed by order from Italy. Look at the Spartans . . . content to serve the same masters. Look at the Macedonians who . . . with Alexander scattered broadcast . . . the seeds of world empire; yet they submit to endure such a reversal of fate and bow before those to whom Fortune has transferred her favors. Myriads of other peoples, swelling with greater pride in the assertion of their liberty, have yielded.

And will you alone disdain to submit to those to whom the whole world is subject?

(Josephus Flavius, 1927/1928, pp. 348–61)

Questions for Students

- What problems does Flavius admit the Romans have presented to the Jews?

- According to Flavius, did others succeed in fighting Rome? Which examples does he give?

- Why does he distinguish between revolt against local officials and revolt against the Emperor?

- Do small powers win against great powers? Can you find examples in history where small powers prevailed? Where great powers won? What usually happens?

- Do empires have more power than nations or tribes? Why?

Document Four: Rabbis Argue about Empire

This excerpt from the Talmud (discussions on Jewish law) outlines an argument about the Roman state shortly before the second Jewish revolt against the Empire in 132–5 A.D. This revolt was very bloody and ended with all of the Jewish people sent away from their country to other lands within the Empire.

> Once Rabbi Judah and Rabbi Jose and Rabbi Simon were sitting, and Judah son of proselytes was sitting with them, Rabbi Judah began and said, "How excellent are the deeds of this nation (Rome). They have instituted market places, they have instituted bridges, they have instituted baths." Rabbi Jose was silent. Rabbi Simeon ben Yohai answered and said, "All that they have instituted has been instituted only for their own needs. They have instituted market places to place harlots in them, baths, for their own pleasure; bridges, to collect tolls." Judah son of proselytes went and reported their words, and they were heard by the (Roman) government. They said, "Judah who exalted shall be exalted; Jose who remained silent shall be banished . . . ; Simeon who reproached shall be put to death.
>
> (Hadas, Babylonian Talmud, Sabbath 39b, 1929)

Questions for Students

- Why did Rabbi Judah speak for the Romans?

- Why did Rabbi Jose remain silent?

- Why did Rabbi Simeon speak harshly about the Romans?

- Why was Rabbi Judah reported to the government?

- What did the government decide about each Rabbi? Why did they praise Judah, banish Jose, and condemn Simeon to death?

- Were the Roman officials fearful of revolt, fearful of Rabbis, fearful of a small country?

- What are the reasons why an empire might put down a revolt? Jail a dissident? Stop free speech?

- Are there any empires now (e.g., China) that permit free speech, free press, free assembly?

Document Five: Romans Conquer Jerusalem

A noted Roman historian also discusses the war with the Jews, the first war in 66–70 A.D. He begins by offering some explanation for the rebellion against Rome. Does his story fit with those by Josephus and the Rabbis?

> At Jerusalem Hadrian founded a city in place of the one which had been razed to the ground, naming it Aelia Capitolina, and the site of the temple of the god he raised a new temple to Jupiter. This brought on a war of no slight importance nor of brief duration, for the Jews deemed it intolerable that foreign peoples should be settled in their city and foreign rites planted there . . . At first the Romans took no account of them. Soon, however, all of Judea had been stirred up, and the Jews everywhere were showing signs of disturbance, were gathering together, and giving evidence of great hostility to the Romans, partly by secret and partly by overt acts; many outside peoples, too, were joining them through their eagerness to gain, and the whole world, one might almost say, was being stirred up over the matter. Then, indeed, Hadrian sent his best generals against them. Foremost among these was Julius Severus, who was dispatched against the Jews from Britain, where he was governor . . . He was able, rather slowly . . . but with comparatively little danger, to crush, exhaust, and exterminate them. Very few of them in fact survived. Fifty of their most important strongholds and 985 of their most famous villages were razed to the ground; 580,000 men were slain in the various raids and battles, and the number of those that perished by famine, disease, and fire was past finding out.
>
> (Cassius Dio, 1914)

Questions for Students

- What does Cassius say set off the war with the Jews?

- According to Cassius, how did the Romans handle the revolt?

- Given the numbers involved, if true, was this a big or little conflict?

- Was it costly to the Empire or easily done? Where did one of the best generals come from to fight the Jews?

- Should the Jews have revolted? Should, could, anyone revolt against a great power?

- In more recent history, have any empires been brought down by revolt? (Look up Gandhi in India, working against the British. Was that successful or not?)

Document Six: Queen Boadicea of the Britons Gives Rome a Bad Name

Rome invaded and conquered a great deal of what is now Great Britain, but met with resistance and revolts from the local Britons. In 61 A.D., many of the tribes and peoples united under a queen who led them successfully against the Romans, but only for a short time, as they eventually fell to Roman legions. In this speech, reported by a Roman historian, Queen Boadicea gives her view of the Romans and their goals of conquest.

Is she sympathetic to empire or opposed? How do you feel about her speech and her fate?

You have learned by actual experience how different freedom is from slavery. Hence, even if any one of you had previously, through ignorance of which is better, been deceived by the alluring promises of the Romans, yet now that you have tried both, you have learned how a great mistake you made in preferring an imported despotism to your ancestral mode of life, and you have come to realize how much better is poverty with no master than wealth with slavery. For what treatment is there of the most shameful or grievous sort that we have not suffered since these men made their appearance in Britain? Have we not been robbed entirely of most of our greatest possessions, while for those that remain we pay taxes? Besides pasturing and tilling for them all our other possessions, do we not pay a yearly tribute for our very bodies? How much better it would be to have to ransom ourselves every year! How much better to have been slain and to have perished than to go about with a tax on our heads! Yet why do I mention death? For even dying is not free of cost with them; nay, you know what fees we pay for our dead. Among the rest of mankind death frees even those who are in slavery to others; only in the case of the Romans do the very dead remain alive for their profit . . . We have . . . been despised and trampled underfoot by men who know nothing else than how to secure gain.

(Cassius Dio, 1914)

Questions for Students

- How does Queen Boadicea attack the Romans in her speech?

- What "alluring Roman promises" does she poke fun at and why?

- Why is the queen angry at the Romans? What does she see as the real reasons for Roman conquest and control? Do you agree or disagree?

- Do the queen's views sound like truth or propaganda? How can you decide?

- Do these reasons fit modern times as well as ancient times? Do these reasons fit any times and any empire? Why or why not?

Document Seven: Calgacus of the Caledonians (Scotland?) Argues for Union

Tacitus, a famous Roman historian, reported the words of Calgacus, a Caledonian chief, to Roman readers, during the period of conquest by the Roman Governor of Britain, Agricola, to take over the northern portions of the country in 83–4 A.D. Calgacus was probably what we would now consider a Scot or a Pict, and he explains the value of unity to the tribes of his region. But, alas, can tribes defeat an empire? How much union is required to defeat empire?

> Taught at last that a common danger must be repelled by union, the Britons had, by embassies and treaties, called forth the forces of all their states. Already more than 30,000 armed men were to be seen, and still there poured in all the youth and those whose old age was hale and vigorous, men renowned in war, each the bearer of decorations of his own. Preeminent among the many chieftains in valor and in birth was one named Calgacus, who is reported to have addressed the following multitude gathered round him and clamoring for battle.
>
> Whenever I consider the causes of this war and our present straits, my heart beats high that this very day and this unity of yours will be the beginning of liberty for all Britain . . . Now they have access to the farthest limits of Britain, there are no more tribes beyond, nothing but waves and rocks, and more deadly than these, the Romans, whose oppression you have sought in vain to escape by obedience and submission. Plunderers of the world, now that there are no more lands for their all-devastating hands, they search even into the sea. If the enemy is rich they are rapacious, if poor, they lust for dominion. Not East, not West has sated them; alone among all mankind, they covet riches and poverty with equal passion. They rob, butcher, and plunder and they call it "empire'; and where they make a desolation, they call it "peace."
>
> (Tacitus, 1931)

Questions for Students

- Why would Tacitus, a Roman himself, want to give attention to the words of a Caledonian chief speaking against the Romans?

- How far and wide does the chief say the Romans have conquered? Why does he think they want to conquer other peoples?

- Is the tone of the chief sad, angry, resigned, and/or cynical? Why?

- Does this speech ring true or false? Why?

- If you lived among the Britons at that time would you join the revolt or the Romans, or maybe neither one? Why?

- Is it easy to unite people against an enemy, or an empire? Are nations more easily aroused to revolt than tribes? Does revolt matter? What do you feel about Calgacus' speech?

- Can you find examples of leaders speaking out against invasions in the past, for example Chief Joseph of the Nez Perce against the U.S. government, or now, for example the Dalai Lama speaking for Tibet against China?

- Whose views can be trusted most: leaders of empires or leaders of revolts?

Document Eight: Citizenship: The Reward for Cooperation and Participation in Empire

The emperor and the Senate of Rome discuss Admission of Provincials to service in the Senate. One of the policies used by the emperors to cement loyalty was the extension of citizenship to other peoples in the Roman Empire. As the dominant people, Romans often suggested that everyone speak Latin, and, if educated, read and write Latin as well. Thus, Latin became the standard language throughout most if not all of the Empire. The speech indicates that citizenship was offered to those behaving well as subjects, and this included many rights and privileges not given to foreigners or slaves. The Gauls, among the first conquered, asked for citizenship, and, in this policy meeting, it is the emperor who defends the idea of citizenship for them and for all, while the noble Senators oppose the idea. What do you think: is citizenship for everyone? How do we feel about extending citizenship in the United States, or the European Union, to all immigrants, legal and/or illegal?

[W]hen the question of filling up the membership of the senate was debated, the leading men of Gallia Comata, as it is called, who had long before attained the rights of allies and Roman citizenship, sought the privilege of obtaining public offices at Rome. There was much talk of every kind on this issue, and a variety of arguments in opposition was expressed before the emperor. "Italy," some asserted, "is not so feeble that it is unable to furnish its capital with a senate . . . Let [the Gauls] by all means enjoy the title of citizens, but let them not cheapen the distinctions of the senators and the honors of the magistrates." The emperor was not impressed by these and similar arguments. He at once spoke out in opposition, and, convening the senate, he addressed them as follows: "[The experience of] my ancestors . . . induces me to employ the same policy in governing the state, namely that of transferring to this city all outstanding persons, wherever found. I am fully aware that the Julian family came from Alba, the Coruncanian from Camerium, the Porcian from Tusculum, and . . . , members have been brought into the senate from Etruria, Lucania, and the whole of Italy, that Italy itself finally was extended to the Alps, so that not only individuals but even regions and tribes were amalgamated into our state. We had stable peace at home, and our foreign relations were in an excellent state in the days when the people beyond the Po were admitted to citizenship, and when, under the pretext of settling our legion throughout the world, we reinforced our exhausted Empire by joining to ourselves the most vigorous of the provincials. Do we regret that the Balbian family came over from Spain, and others not less illustrious from Narbonese Gaul? Their descendants are still here, and are not second to us in patriotism . . . If you review all our wars, none was ended in a shorter time than that with the Gauls. Thenceforth there has been an unbroken and loyal peace. Mingled with us as they are now, in their way of life, in their culture, and by intermarriage, let them bring us their gold and wealth rather than keep it in isolation. Everything, members of the senate, which is now considered to be of the highest antiquity was once new . . . This practice, too, will establish itself, and what we are this day defending as the precedents will itself be precedent."

(Tacitus, 1931)

Questions for Students

- How does Tacitus report the meeting of the emperor and the Senate? Who is for and who against admitting "provincials" to high office?

- What exactly is the Senate? What is a "provincial'? Who are the Gauls?

- Why does the emperor want to offer seats to people from outside Italy? Why does he feel the Gauls should be first?

- What arguments does he offer to convince the Senate to expand?

- Do you think it is smart policy to admit people from all over the Empire to the Senate? Why or why not?

- How important was citizenship in Rome to people, both high born and low? Is this like or unlike U.S. policy toward making immigrants citizens? Is this like opening up the European Union? Is this like the creation of Soviet Republics?

- Does it help or hurt a state, a republic, an empire, to make many kinds of people citizens?

- Is citizenship belonging? Does it lower the risk of revolt or raise it higher? Why?

- If you were the emperor how would you decide on the Gauls? If you were the President of the United States, what would you tell the Senate our policy should be toward immigration? Citizenship for the few, the many, all? What is the power of empire? What might cause its downfall?

- What factors help an empire to last and last and last?

As the Republic morphed into Empire, many of the traditional values and symbols were kept alive in various ways as symbols of the culture, much as America keeps in touch with its base of Revolutionary-era laws and customs, founding fathers and mothers, culture heroes/heroines, and devotion to English as the basic language of the land whatever culture the citizens represent. Citizenship played a key role in the growth of the Roman Empire and its defense, as our documents suggest, along with policies that promoted the "Romanization" of the many conquered peoples and allies.

A major mystery you should discuss with students is why the Roman policies, what might be called an interesting mix of advantages and punishments, open-minded policies and tightly held ideas of patriotism and tradition, worked so well in keeping the Empire alive in a number of forms for hundreds and hundreds of years, diffusing many of these ideas and customs into the medieval and then into the modern world.

As a debriefing or finale to the students' investigation of the document package, we encourage discussion of the following essential or focal questions to wrap up this mystery:

1 What impresses people about a leader, a state, a country? What makes you want to identify with that nation or empire? Would you have identified with Rome if you lived in the Empire or would you have found it an uncomfortable place to live? Why?

2 Which of the documents and images you studied probably contributed most to strengthening the Roman self-image? Which sources suggest a weakening of their self-image? Which factors do you see as crucial or key to Roman survival: military, political, social, cultural, religious, or some other feature? Why?

3 How have the documents contributed to your image of the Roman Empire? Do you now see it as stronger or weaker than you did before? Why? What other information or sources might you want to look at to help better answer this question? Would you look more closely at political, economic, religious, social, cultural, or military types of sources?

4 What are the advantages and/or disadvantages of living in a very powerful state like Rome? Would your answer to this question change if you were a slave? A worker? Or a member of a conquered people or minority?

5 Do you see the organization, beliefs, and problems of the Roman state as like or

unlike those of the United States? Why? Would any empire or great power hold the values and beliefs of Rome? Would any empire or great power face the same problems that Rome faced, as far as you can tell from your reading and viewing? Explain!

Summary and Conclusions

Many conclusions are possible from studying our rich overlapping packet of documents and pictures. We have developed insights into the underlying strengths and weaknesses of Roman imperial life and the Roman state. Modest conclusions might include that Roman society projected a powerful set of values to its citizens and to the outside world.

Political power, military might, and economic and technical organization and skills characterized the expanding empire. It was held together by a sense of identity and nationalism (we might call it), and a stubborn sense of superiority. This sense of superiority was disseminated both within and outside the Republic and Empire. The Roman model influenced the many conquered peoples to become more and more like the Romans. Rome sealed this influence by offering benefits to its peoples that included safety and security, economic opportunity, language, culture, and above all citizenship. Incentives to adapt and assimilate or be conquered and destroyed were pervasive and persuasive to millions, as alternates were few and frightening.

Rome and Romans also exhibited less positive sides to its culture: its sense of entitlement, superiority, and arrogance, particularly of the upper-class elite. Class division was also apparent, with immense wealth in the hands of relatively few families, leaving most of the population as workers or farmers who were relatively poor.

The army could be both a positive force for security (*Pax Romana*, peace within empire) and building public works as well as a destructive force if challenged or opposed. Although the Empire promoted a sense of toleration, it also became increasingly insistent on tight political and economic control, sometimes sparking revolts, rebellions, or passive-aggressive reactions against the bureaucrats and military of the empire.

In some ways, Rome can be viewed as a "model" empire for discussions of durability and influence over a very long period of time. The symbols and signs of the Roman state have been carried over into many of the current world's cultures. Coinage (such as the American quarter) follows Roman examples and sizes. Latin still exerts an influence on all Western and Eastern languages and ideas, law codes, and civics. Many building styles descended from Rome, such as stadiums, temples, and public buildings (think of the New York Stock Exchange and the Capitol), dot the landscape of major American, South American, and European cities. And to this day, don't other empires still enjoy the civic life, including "bread and circuses"?

References and Further Reading

Adkins, L. and Adkins, R. A. (1994, reprinted 1998) *Handbook to Life in Ancient Rome*, Oxford: Oxford University Press.
Aelius Aristides (1950) *To Rome* (trans. and with an introduction by S. Levin), Glencoe, IL: Free Press.

Alfoldy, G. (1988)*The Social History of Rome.* Baltimore: Johns Hopkins University Press.

Moulton, C. (ed.) (1998–2005) *Ancient Greece and Rome: An Encyclopedia for Students* (four vols), New York: Scribner's.

Aurelius, M. (1964) *Meditations* (trans. Maxwell Staniforth), New York: Penguin

Avant, D. D. (2005) *The Market for Force*, New York and Cambridge, UK: Cambridge University Press.

Biesty, S. (2003) *Rome in Spectacular Cross-Section*, Oxford, UK: Scholastic.

Blacklock, D. (2004) *The Roman Army: The Legendary Soldiers Who Created an Empire*, New York: Walker.

Brunt, P.A. and Moore J. M. (eds.) (1967) *Res Gestae Divi Augusti: The Achievements of the Divine Augustus*, Oxford, UK: Oxford University Press.

Cassius Dio (1914) "Roman History, I and II," fragments of Books XII–XXV (trans. E. Cary), Loeb Classical Library vol. 37, Cambridge, MA: President and Fellows of Harvard College.

Corbishley, M. (1991)*What Do We Know About the Romans?*, New York: Peter Bedrick Books.

D'Ambra, E. (1993) *Roman Art in Context: An Anthology*, Englewood Cliffs, NJ: Prentice-Hall.

D'Ambra, E. (1998) *Roman Art*, Cambridge, UK: Cambridge University Press.

De Puma, R. D. (1988) *Roman Portraits: The University of Iowa Museum of Art, September 10–October 30, 1988*, Iowa City: The Museum.

Dillon, E. (1975) *Rome under the Emperors*, New York: Thomas Nelson.

Dowden, K. (1992) *Religion and the Romans*, London: Bristol Classical Press.

Dubois, M. L. (2004) *Early Civilizations: Ancient Rome*, Mankato, MN: Capstone Press.

Dupre, J. (2001) *Churches*, New York: HarperCollins.

Elsner, J. (1998) *Imperial Rome and Christian Triumph: The Art of the Roman Empire A.D. 100–450*, Oxford, UK: Oxford University Press.

Farnham, E., Foley, H. P., Kampen, N. B., and Pomeroy, S.B. (1994) *Women in the Classical World: Image and Text*, New York: Oxford University Press.

Ferguson, J. (1970) *The Religions of the Roman Empire: Aspects of Greek and Roman Life*, Ithaca, NY: Cornell University Press.

Fryd, V. G. (1992) *Art and Empire. The Politics of Ethnicity in the United States Capitol, 1815–1860*, New Haven, CT: Yale University Press.

Garnsey, P. and Saller, R. (1987) *The Roman Empire. Economy, Society, and Culture*, Berkeley: University of California Press.

Gazda, E. K. (ed.) (1991) *Roman Art in the Private Sphere*, Michigan: University of Michigan Press.

Gebhard, D. and Gerald M. (1993) *Buildings of Iowa*, Oxford, UK: Oxford University Press.

Grant, M. (ed.) (1988) *Civilization of the Ancient Mediterranean: Greece and Rome* (three vols), Riverside, NJ: Scribner's.

Grant, N. (1991) *Wars that Changed the World: Roman Conquests*, North Bellmore, NY: Marshall Cavendish.

Greene, K. (1986) *The Archaeology of the Roman Economy*, Berkeley: University of California Press.

Greene, K. (1992) *Roman Pottery*, Berkeley: University of California Press.

Hadas, M. (trans.) (1929) "Babylonian Talmud, Sabbath 39b," *Philological Quarterly* 8: 373.

Josephus Flavius (1927/1928) "The Jewish War, Books III–IV," in *Josephus: Volume II* (trans. H. St. J. Thackeray), Loeb Classical Library vol. 487, Cambridge, MA: President and Fellows of Harvard College.

Keppie, L. J. F. (1991) *Understanding Roman Inscriptions*, Baltimore: Johns Hopkins University Press.

Kleiner, D. E. E. (1992) *Roman Sculpture,* New Haven, CT: Yale University Press.

Kleiner, D. and Matheson, S. (eds.) (1996) *I, Claudia: Women in Ancient Rome*, Austin: University of Texas Press.

Kleiner, D. and Matheson, S. (eds.) (2000) *I, Claudia II: Women in Roman Art and Society*, Austin: University of Texas Press.

Lefkowitz, M. R. and Fant, M. B. (1982) *Women's Life in Greece and Rome: A Sourcebook in Translation*, Baltimore: Johns Hopkins University Press.

Levick, B. (2000) *Government of the Roman Empire: A Sourcebook*, London: Routledge.

Lewis, N. and Reinhold, M. (eds.) (1990a) *Roman Civilization: Selected Readings*, vol. 1, *The Republic*, 3rd edn, New York: Columbia University Press.

Lewis, N. and Reinhold, M. (eds.) (1990b) *Roman Civilization: Selected Readings*, vol. 2, *The Empire*, 3rd edn, New York: Columbia University Press.

Ling, R. (1991) *Roman Painting*, Cambridge, UK: Cambridge University Press.

Macdonald, F. (1993) *A Roman Fort*, New York: Peter Bedrick Books.

Macdonald, F. (1996) *First Facts about the Ancient Romans*, New York: Peter Bedrick Books.

MacDonald, W. L. (1982) *The Architecture of the Roman Empire, Vol. I: An Introductory Study* and *Vol. II: An Urban Appraisal*, New Haven, CT: Yale University Press.

Mann, E. (1998) *The Roman Colosseum*, New York: Mikaya Press.

Marks, A. (1990) *The Romans*, London: Usborne Publishing.

Morley, J. (1992) *A Roman Villa*, New York: Peter Bedrick Books.

Nash, E. (1980) *Pictorial Dictionary of Ancient Rome*, New York: Hacker.

Oliver, J. H. (1953) "Aelius Aristides, to Rome" (trans. S. Levin), *Transactions of the American Philosophical Society* 43 (4).

Payne, R. (n.d.) *The Horizon Book of Ancient Rome*, ed. C. Moulton, New York: American Heritage Publishing.

Pollitt, J. J. (1983) *Art of Rome c. 753 B.C.–A.D. 337: Sources and Documents*, Cambridge, UK: Cambridge University Press.

Pomeroy, S. (1975) *Goddesses, Whores, Wives, and Slaves*, New York: Schocken Books.

Potter, T. W. (1987) *Roman Italy*, Berkeley: University of California Press.

Ramage, N. H. and Ramage, A. (1995) *Roman Art: Romulus to Constantine*, 2nd edn, Saddle River, NJ: Prentice-Hall.

Reinhold, M. (1984) *Classica Americana*, Detroit: Wayne State University Press.

Richard, C. (1994) *The Founders and the Classics*, Boston: Harvard University Press.

Richardson, L. (1992) *New Topographical Dictionary of Ancient Rome*, Baltimore: Johns Hopkins University Press.

Rubinstein, C. S. (1990) *American Women Sculptors*, Boston: G. K. Hall.

Rutland, J. (1986) *See Inside A Roman Town*, London: Grisewood & Dempsey.

Scarre, C. (1995) *Chronicle of the Roman Emperors: The Reign-by-Reign Record of the Rulers of Imperial Rome*, London: Thames & Hudson.

Scullard, H. H. (1981) *Festivals and Ceremonies of the Roman Republic*, Ithaca, NY: Cornell University Press.

Shelton, J.-A. (1998) *As the Romans Did. A Sourcebook in Roman Social History*, 2nd edn, New York: Oxford University Press.

Stambaugh, J. E. (1988) *The Ancient Roman City*, Baltimore: Johns Hopkins University Press.

Tacitus (1931) *Histories Books IV–V, Annals* (trans. C. Moore and J. Jackson), Loeb Classical Library vol. 249, Cambridge, MA: President and Fellows of Harvard College

Turcan, R. (1996) *Cults of the Roman Empire*, Oxford: Blackwell.

Vermeule, C. (1981) *Greek and Roman Sculpture in America. Masterpieces in Public Collections in the United States and Canada*, Malibu: J. Paul Getty Museum and Berkeley: University of California Press.

Wallace-Hadrill, A. (1994) *Houses and Society in Pompeii and Herculaneum*, Princeton, NJ: Princeton University Press.

Ward-Perkins, J. B. (1981) *Roman Imperial Architecture*, New York: Penguin.

Wells, C. (1992) *The Roman Empire*, 2nd edn, Cambridge, MA: Harvard University Press.

five
Mythlabeled?
Or, Creating the Crusades

This is a new kind of—a new kind of evil. And we understand. And the American people are beginning to understand. This crusade, this war on terrorism is going to take a while. And the American people must be patient.

(George W. Bush, September 16, 2001, press conference)

Recent historians of the crusades caution against trying to apply that past directly to understand the present, particularly world events related to the attack on the World Trade Center on September 11, 2001. In a recent book, Christopher Tyerman warns readers that:

> the battles of the cross are held to presage the conflicts of European imperialism, colonialism and western cultural supremacism. Yet many of the supposed links between past events and current problems are modern, not historical constructs, invented to lend spurious legitimacy to wholly unconnected current political, social, economic and religious problems.
>
> (Tyerman, 2006, p. xiv)

In his view, the comparison to the crusades is a way of legitimating the current conflicts that the administration of George W. Bush lumped together under the phrase "war on terror." No matter what course of action one supports in the series of conflicts—against

Al-Qaeda, against fragmentary terror groups, against the Taliban, against poppy growers in Afghanistan, against Saddam Hussein, against Sunni militants, or with Sunni militias supporting the new Iraqi government against Sunni militias aligned with different groups aimed at destroying the current Iraqi government—and those conflicts often get subsumed under that one label, they are not the same as the medieval conflicts, and perhaps linking them all to crusading also creates false links among current events that ought to be seen as separate. Another historian provides a more pointed critique:

> For the West to label contemporary conflicts as crusades is to obscure the secular mandate of a just war and to ignore the fact that, in the Middle Ages, most westerners supported the crusades, while today there is tremendous opposition to military action.
>
> (Phillips, 2004, p. ix)

This author points out that, in October 2001, Osama Bin Laden announced that his goal was to unite Islam in the face of the Christian crusade, and suggests that using the term "crusade" reopens the "bitter legacy" of medieval conflicts. Both authors suggest that "crusade" as a term can frame the present in ways that obscure the complexity of many different struggles, and fundamentally misrepresents the past.

Despite those words of warning from the historical profession, in the aftermath of the attacks on the Twin Towers in September 2001 the temptation was quite strong to see what is commonly called the war on terror as fundamentally connected to the crusades, and even to view the American occupation of Iraq in similar terms. Speaking at the White House on the afternoon of Sunday September 16, just five days after the towers fell, President George W. Bush spoke without scripted remarks, saying, "My administration has a job to do and we're going to do it. We will rid the world of the evil-doers." He acknowledged that he could not complete this job overnight. "This crusade, this war on terrorism is gonna take awhile. And the American people must be patient. I'm gonna be patient." Just days after the attack on the towers, President Bush made the same connection that Bin Laden would make a month later: the struggle between the United States and Al-Qaeda would be a long one, and it was a crusade.

As quoted by Phillips, the point Bin Laden made was that this was a battle between Muslims and Christians, and the Christians were the aggressors. Perhaps this is what President Bush intended as well, although maybe Bush also meant that the crusades lasted on and off for five hundred years, and that he saw the attack on the Towers as the opening in what would be a long-lasting, multi-generational conflict. It is hard to know what the president meant, as the remarks may have come to his lips unbidden in informal remarks shortly after a shocking attack on American soil. But somewhere he picked up an image of the crusades that seemed to him, consciously or not, to parallel in some fashion the war on terror.

Viewing the Present through the Lenses of the Past, Viewing the Past through Historical Lenses

Whether or not we agreed with President Bush and his approach to Al Qaeda or Afghanistan or Iraq, his remarks should give us pause as historians and history teachers. They reveal the power of the historical act called *periodization*. Although this concept receives sustained attention during graduate seminars and at history conferences, for most middle or high school students it is buried deep in the historian's backpack, so to speak, far below the primary sources and interpretations and perspectives and supporting evidence, even below time lines. Historians frequently use this powerful cultural tool in the way that the 1930s radio hero the Shadow used his superpower: to cloud people's minds and make different parts of the past invisible. Historians create historical periods by highlighting certain events (and obscuring others) and tying disparate moments of the past together. For although there certainly were expeditions that left Europe in 1095 and later to recapture Jerusalem for the Christians and defeat the heathens, it is not absolutely clear that those expeditions hold the full meaning of a crusade. We will argue that perhaps there might not really be such a thing as the crusades, and that maybe we are all better off not teaching about the crusades as an event after all.

Although we have no hesitation in making up mysteries, this is a concern broached by the historians who study these events. To quote Tyerman again,

> historians organize the past to help them make sense of the evidence. In doing so they run the risk of becoming imprisoned by their own artifice. Between 1095 and, say 1500, there were scores of military operations that attracted the privileges associated with the wars of the cross.
>
> (Tyerman, 2004, p. 32)

In short, calling a series of events that took place over a great many years starting in the late eleventh century the crusades gives them a unity and implied common meaning—and this powerfully shaped the way President Bush saw the world. It had an equally strong impact on those who disagreed with him. Peter Ford's September 19, 2001, headline in the *Christian Science Monitor*, "Europe cringes at Bush 'crusade' against terrorists," suggests that Bush's remarks upset people around the world. Although they disagreed with Bush, Europeans, too, saw the crusades as real and with a fixed meaning. But what if that sameness of crusade is more historians' creation than report, more created than found, more interpretation than fact? How would our students ever know that such a possibility might even exist?

Strangely, this is something that (at least where we live—New York) teachers are supposed to make visible to their students. Buried in the state standards for social studies (New York State Education Department, n.d.) are mandates to teach students to "describe the reasons for periodizing history in different ways" in United States history, and even more ambitiously "to evaluate the effectiveness of different models for the periodization of important historic events, identifying the reasons why a particular sequence for these events was chosen." This sounds pretty dull. But whoever controls periodization controls the world! If the Dark Ages are a time of blackness when nothing worth mentioning happened, and they begin after the fall of the Roman Empire and end with the voyages of exploration, then we can skip hundreds of years of history. If someone writes a book about the crusades, or tells George Bush in school that there were crusades and this is what they meant, that periodizing will color the way he sees the world and shape his understandings.

When disagreeing with a characterization of past or present events—such as Bush or Bin Laden calling recent events a crusade—we attack the analogy as untrue, either because the present is somehow different from the past, or because the person making the analogy is not telling the truth about the past. This is how Phillips approached his warning about conflating past and present: just wars in the West are secular ones, not religious undertakings, and there was far more consensus in the West in support of any given crusade than there is in the contemporary world for the American invasion of Iraq or the detention center at Guantanamo Bay. Rarely do we turn to questions of periodization and say that those past events don't really all belong together, that it might be a mistake to refer to the existence of the crusades at all. We just accept the work of historians in periodizing an era or in connecting events. Our goal in this chapter is to create a minor mystery out of the habit of labeling a series of events as the crusades in order to shed light on this major culture tool wielded by historians.

When we tackle the creation of historical periods, we ask different questions from when we question an analogy directly. We might ask, "When did the last crusading event end?" Or wonder, "If the crusades are safely in the past, then maybe they are not part of our modern world. But what if they began and then they continued right up until the time of Napoleon? Does that make them modern?" This type of question does not automatically destroy the analogy proposed by George W. Bush. If the crusades continued through the time of Napoleon, perhaps crusading is not comfortably medieval and far away from us, but something that is also part of the world we consider modern.

More than addressing how we relate to the crusades—as part of a distant past or as relatively close to our current times—the standards point out that to periodize is to *interpret*, to *define*, to *explain*. Fundamentally, we want to start by asking, "Were there crusades?" Or, "What are the characteristics we are trying to explain when we place many events together under that term, and should all of those events get called crusading?" When we start this way, we hope to open up an interpretive problem for ourselves and for our students.

Having looked into the literature on the crusades, we find that they are much more complex than we had remembered. We have all kinds of material we'd like to present to students to show them a more complicated picture, one that is truer than the general impression most of them have in their heads. But instead of substituting our picture for theirs, we want to pose a problem that helps the students see how much any multi-century event is necessarily "made up" by historians. In world history, even suggesting that some multi-century development is significant may be utterly dependent on only one particular cultural perspective. From other points of view, the "crusades" didn't even occur. So we are trying to set up a mystery for our students that will allow them to get at this phenomenon of periodization, the tendency of historians to make the past manageable by taking all kinds of messy, individual developments and lumping them together in a single term.

A mystery of periodization allows us another indulgence: the chance to wallow in secondary sources. We love wild primary sources that force us to reconsider what we thought was true about the past, but primary sources are *not* where the action is in history. We spend far more time reading secondary sources, getting a broad historical perspective, understanding how historians and geographers and sociologists or anthropologists and even interdisciplinary thinkers are re-encountering the past. We get very nervous when students spend too much time with textbooks and then go directly to primary sources, and never see an actual bit of secondary historical writing. How are they supposed to write decent historical essays if the only secondary source they ever encounter is the textbook? How will they learn about historical arguments or interpretations if they never read any?

Should We Speak of the Crusades?

We now put away the soapbox and begin to focus on our mystery. Let us make this a minor one, a relatively simple matter to solve by allowing students to quickly arrive at their own conclusions. We don't care what they decide, as their opinions will all be perfectly acceptable. Should we ever use the word "periodization" with them? Maybe later. As we begin this study, we simply ask, "What and when were the crusades?"

There are various ways of getting at this, but a simple one to start with is the following observation:

> The word "crusade," [is] a non-medieval Franco–Spanish hybrid only popularized in English since the eighteenth century . . . In the Middle Ages there existed no single word for what are now known as the Crusades. While those who took the cross were described as *crucesignai*—people (not exclusively male) signed with the cross—their activities tended to be described by analogy, euphemism, metaphor or generality: *peregrinatio*, pilgrimage; *via* or *iter*, way or journey; *crux*, literally cross; *neotium*, business.
>
> (Tyerman, 2004, pp. 4, 13)

Whence did the concept behind the term "crusade" come from? Surely the things that we now call by this term must have something in common. The themes that inspired those who took part in a great movement that we, retrospectively, call the First Crusade were set out by Pope Urban II on Tuesday, November 27, 1095, when he preached at Clermont Cathedral in Auvergne. Examining his words should tell us what crusading was all about.

Unfortunately, we don't have a copy of his speech. Only three accounts of it survive, all written years later, after the Christians had already captured Jerusalem. The writers all tell of his speech from memories colored by that victorious ending, so whatever tentative or open-ended thoughts he might have expressed are gone. And the sources disagree. We have secondary summaries by historians of the elements that seem to have been in his speech according to these reports, from letters he wrote before and after, and by drawing on descriptions of his preaching in early 1096 just after Clermont. Urban II apparently called for people to undertake

> a penitential journey in arms to Jerusalem to recover the Holy Sepulcher and to "liberate Christianity" and the eastern Christians, the expedition earning warriors satisfaction of penance and remission of sin, signaled by a vow to enforce the obligation and the adoption of the sign of the cross.
>
> (Tyerman, 2006, p. 63)

Urban attached regulations designed to protect crusaders' property, to prevent husbands unilaterally abandoning their wives, to prohibit indiscriminate clerical and monastic participation and to ensure advice was sought from local priests (Tyerman, 2006, p. 67).

According to these sources, what Pope Urban II launched in 1095 had in common these elements:

- the journey in arms to Jerusalem;
- the liberation of Eastern Christians as well as the holy places;
- a grant of remission of sin and freedom from any other penance;
- the requirement that people undertaking this voyage place on themselves the sign of the cross.

This was a temporary action. Although they risked death, those who lived would be released from their vows when they reached Jerusalem. Anyone who stayed in the Holy Land would no longer be a pilgrim, and the majority were expected to return home in a few years' time. Let us apply these elements to the series of events that we call the "crusades," a term Pope Urban II never used, to describe events he never lived to see:

- *Crusade I* (1095–9)—Capture of Jerusalem by Western Christian armies.
- *Crusade II* (1146–9)—After Zengi, a Muslim general, captures Edessa from the Christians, Pope Eugenius III calls for a second crusade, which ends with a successful reinforcement of Christian rule.

- *Crusade III* (1189–91)—After the fall of Jerusalem, a crusade led by Frederick Barbarossa (Germany, Holy Roman Empire), Richard the Lionheart (England) and Phillip Augustus (France) departs for Palestine. After recapturing the ports of Jaffa and Acre, Richard negotiates a treaty with Saladin to allow Christians access to Jerusalem, but the crusaders never recapture Jerusalem.
- *Crusade IV* (1202–4)—Bent on recapturing Jerusalem, a group of Western nobility contract with Venice to build a huge fleet to transport their anticipated army to Egypt. Too few crusaders arrive to pay for the fleet. They sail off and first sack and capture the Christian city of Zara, an enemy of Venice. Later, after camping outside of Constantinople, the Eastern Christian city, the crusaders become involved in a dispute about who should be emperor, and end up sacking and looting the city and installing themselves as rulers. They never travel to Jerusalem.
- *Crusade V* (1217–22)—Crusaders capture the Egyptian city of Damattia, returning it to Egypt in a truce in 1222.

After you have rewritten your own definition, and decided how you want to account for the attack on Zara and the sack of Constantinople in 1202–4, consider the following paragraph from historian Jonathan Phillips. Can you tell, from this paragraph, if he thinks we should consider what is called the Fourth Crusade to be fundamentally part of the same idea as the First Crusade, or should we see it as something very different, perhaps so different that calling them both "crusade" is a problem?

> The outcome of the Fourth Crusade clearly represents a dramatic distortion of the basic idea of the Catholic Church fighting the infidel. Contemporary and modern historians alike have been fascinated by how a movement that began with the object of reclaiming the Holy Land for Christianity could, in just over a century, develop into a vehicle for the destruction of the most magnificent city in the Christian world.
>
> (Phillips, 2004, p. xv)

What do you think? Does calling it a "dramatic distortion" mean that it doesn't deserve to be called a crusade, that it is something different, or that somehow we have to see the preceding crusades as part of the same movement that sacked Constantinople— and does that change how we think about them?

To Do

Check the crusades described here against the general definition offered above. How can your definition include the Fourth Crusade? Is the Fourth Crusade an exception that proves the rule? Or is it something different, something that should not be called a crusade?

Other Crusades

Pope Innocent called for a crusade to conquer Spain from the Muslims. In 1193 and 1197, Pope Celestine issued crusade letters, and in 1197 said that people who had vowed to go to Jerusalem could go to fight in Spain instead.

To Do

Adjust your general definition of the crusades so that it can now include the fighting in Spain. How does it change your definition if crusading, still against Muslims, now includes battles outside the Holy Land? Does this mean that the Fourth Crusade is no longer an exception—it was outside of the Jerusalem area, but so what?— or that it still poses problems as it wasn't against Muslims.

More Crusading

In the Baltic Crusade (1199/1204–30), Pope Innocent allowed priests and laymen who had vowed to go to Jerusalem to go instead to the defense of the Livonian Church in the Baltic region, fighting the pagan communities around Riga. This produced a "perpetual crusade" until around 1230, when the Christians, particularly from northern Germany, had conquered Livonia (Riley-Scott, 2005, pp. 161–2).

The Danes launched a similar campaign in Estonia, competing with the Germans advancing from Livonia:

> By 1220 the idea of a perpetual crusade was taking root. The Crusaders were signed with the cross, were referred to as pilgrims and crusaders (*peregrini* and *crucesignai*) and enjoyed the full indulgence. Measures were taken to tax the Church on their behalf. Their crusades were justified as defensive aid to missions and were privileged in much the same ways as crusades to the East [Jerusalem].
>
> (Riley-Scott, 2005, p. 162)

You Decide: Define the Crusades

Please adjust your definition of "crusading" to account for crusades I–V to the Holy Land, including the Fourth Crusade that never got there, the crusades against Muslims in Spain but not in the Holy Land, and now the crusades in the Baltic against Pagans—crusades that lasted for decades. Can you come up with a definition that includes everything? If you can, is it still helpful?

Bonus: Notice that Tyerman translates *crucesignai* as "people signed with the cross," whereas Riley-Scott translates it as "crusaders." Is this an important difference? What different interpretations do the different translations support? Why might two experts end up with different translations of the same word?

More Crusades to Think About

The Albigensian Crusade—In May 1204 Pope Innocent granted the crusaders all of the indulgences promised, including remission of sins for participants, for those who took up arms against a break-away group in the south of France called the Cathars, who believed not in the Trinity but rather in two Gods, one material and one spiritual. This time the call was to suppress heretics.

Crusading in Italy—In 1239–41 Fredrick, the Holy Roman Emperor in Germany, had invaded Sicily and was reaching into northern Italy. Pope Gregory granted remission of sin to all who fought against Frederick in Italy and Germany, and allowed those who had pledged to go to Jerusalem to fight against Frederick instead. After Frederick died in 1250 crusades were called against his heir Conrad IV in 1253–4, and continued in southern Italy for at least another two decades.

Crusading in Finland and Norway—In the 1320s and beyond, fights on the border between Russian Orthodox Christians and Catholic Christians led to crusades over several decades to protect the Catholics from the Russian Orthodox Christians.

> ## To Do
>
> Adjust your definition of "crusades" so that it can account for these crusades against heretics, Catholics fighting over political boundaries, and Catholics fighting Russian Orthodox Christians over borders.

How Should We Teach the Crusades?

What, in the end, is a crusade? How can it possibly be so many things, or, if it is so many things, how much does it help us to say that they are all the same thing? Can you come up with a definition for this phenomenon? Can your students come up with a definition that accounts for all of these different wars? How about this one?

> The Crusades were wars justified by faith conducted against real or imagined enemies defined by religious and political elites as perceived threats to the Christian faithful.
>
> (Tyerman, 2006, p. xiii)

This is, to say the least, an extraordinarily broad definition that allows almost any, but not all, wars to be called crusades. Strikingly, it says nothing directly about Jerusalem, or Muslims, or any of the other elements that seemed so critical to us when we first thought about this topic. This problem has plagued the great historians who wrote multi-volume histories of the crusades. In an excellent overview of the historical writing, Jonathan Riley-Scott notes that:

> finding an acceptable general definition of crusading has always been so difficult that it has often been considered best to leave it well alone . . . Grousset in the

1930s, Steven Runciman in the 1950s . . . Setton in the 1960s never explicitly stated what they stood for.

(Riley-Scott, 2004, p. 308)

We find this striking enough to ask, as we have suggested your students ask, what do we understand better if we identify all of these activities as, in very important ways, the same? What do we clarify by claiming that European Catholics in 1096 who responded to a call to capture Jerusalem from the infidel are engaged in the same activity as those fighting the Muslims in Spain, sacking Christian (though not Catholic) Constantinople in 1204, killing European heretic Cathars in France in 1204, fighting pagans in the Baltics, and Russian Christian Orthodox in Norway and Finland, all the way to the fall of Malta in 1798? This is a historian's dilemma.

In some fundamental sense, nobody who took the cross and went to fight in Jerusalem in 1096 is likely to have imagined that their vows and actions would be used to fight against the German emperor in Italy, to attack Christians in Zara and Constantinople and Finland, or to slaughter Cathars in France. Yet the people who took part in those later actions did see similarities in these actions and claimed the mantle of the earliest people to take similar vows. Calling them all "crusaders" adopts a certain understanding that perhaps some later groups had, but may do an injustice to the earlier "people signed with the cross." What do we do, as historians and teachers, when we decide that something so diverse—battles against real or imagined enemies of the church, internal or external—is fundamentally the same?

You Decide

Does it provide an important interpretation and understanding when we call all of these different military campaigns crusades, or does it hide differences and reject interpretations that are more important?

Maybe we are better off distinguishing wars of expansion and inter-Christian warfare from battles to establish a Christian presence in Jerusalem? Perhaps we should drop any reference to crusades, teach about different wars or battles as they enter our curriculum, and examine Christian arguments for war alongside other justifications for war throughout world history. Whatever way you decide the issue, the important but obscure historical activity made visible is *periodization*—the way that historians shape meaning simply by defining and lumping together events under a name and giving it dates and numbers that it never had at the time. Crusades, Middle Ages, Golden Age of Spain— historians do it all the time and yet students rarely interrogate this way of shaping how we think about the past.

How about another consideration. Perhaps the crusades should be taught in a European history class, but not in a world history class, where a few battles might be mentioned and students might consider Christian attitudes toward just war or war in the name of Jesus without actually studying the crusades. This is a variation on the old question about a tree falling in a forest that no one hears. Is it really a sound if no one hears it? In this sense, it is quite possible to argue that, in world historical terms, the crusades never occurred.

There is no Islamic historiography of the Crusades as such. For contemporary Islamic narrators the Crusades were not much more than skirmishes which inflicted pinpricks upon the fringes of the Islamic world. Crusaders came and went: their activities might be laconically noted by chroniclers, but not dwelt upon . . . no Arabic word was coined to indicate that these intruders were engaged in a special and individual form of warfare.

(Fletcher, 2004, p. 84)

Carole Hillenbrand (1999) quotes J. P. Berkey, a historian of the Mamluks (Moslem rulers in the mid-thirteenth century), as pointing out that "The European Crusaders were in some ways the least of the problems faced by contemporary Muslims; more threatening . . . were . . . waves of Turkik and Mongol invasion and settlement" (p. 226). Hillenbrand collected a sweeping number of secondary and primary accounts in her book, *The Crusades: Islamic Perspectives*, and these perspectives can look quite different. To look at the period after Saladin and Richard battled, when so many more "crusades" lay ahead from the perspective of current Western historians, it is worth considering her assessment of the way that the Ayyubids (1193–1249), Saladin's successors, related to the "Franks" and the way that the "Franks" related to them.

Various factors contributed to the lack of a single-minded focus by the Ayyubids on *jihad* against the Franks. They were enthusiastic about the benefits of trade with the Franks and the wider world, using the Frankish ports. A common interest in the local defense of Syria and Palestine no doubt motivated both Ayyubids and Franks to unite on occasion against external aggressors, be they the Khwarazmains, Franks from Europe, or even Ayyubid rivals from Egypt.

(Hillenbrand, 1999, p. 224)

In other words, the Muslim world was not unified, and neither was the European world. The people we call crusaders—whose vows had expired when they reached Jerusalem—fought among themselves over control of different cities and kingdoms they established in the area, even after Jerusalem fell to Saladin. Ayyubids and "Franks"—the term derived from the large number of Frenchmen who came and that was simply applied to all the Europeans—could ally with each other against outsiders, and even against different alliances of Franks and Ayyubids. And in the middle of all of this the Mongols invaded, causing far more disruption around the world than any European effort to capture Jerusalem!

This doesn't mean that individual Muslims did not write about the Franks with hatred, or notice that there was a battle going on with Christians. The Mamluk sultan al-Ashraf captured an important city in 1291 and was praised by a poet in terms that clearly show the sense of a larger battle, even if they do not use the terms "crusade" or "crusader."

> Because of you no town is left in which unbelief can repair, no hope for the Christian religion! Through al-Ashraf the Lord Sultan, we are delivered from the Trinity and Unity rejoices in the struggle!
> Praise be to God, the nation of the Cross has fallen; through the Turks the religion of the chosen Arab has triumphed.
>
> (quoted in Hillebrand, 1999, p. 240)

Yet the Christian states established in the areas around Jerusalem also hosted Muslim notables, and often allied with small Muslim states against other small Christian states. Ten years after the capture of Jerusalem and then Aleppo in what we call the First Crusade, Tancred of Antioch allied with the king of Aleppo and faced a coalition of Turks, Arabs, and Christians. A contemporary historian comments, "It had decidedly not taken the Franj long to become full partners in the murderous game of the Muslim petty kings" (Maalouf, 1989, p. 72). This continued throughout the entire period that Christians held power in the area.

In February of 1130, Prince Bohemond II of Antioch, a Christian state, died in an ambush. His widow Alix seized power in the city and wrote to Imad al-Din, the Muslim ruler of the city states of Mosul and Aleppo, for support. The Christian king of Jerusalem, Baldwin II, encountered a messenger from Alix leading a pure white horse with silver shoes and fancy armor as a gift to Zengi. He hung the messenger and took Antioch from Alix (Maalouf, 1989, p. 116).

You Decide: Periodization

If Muslim sources noticed individual invaders and attacks, but referred to "the Franks," did not use the term "crusader," and in the overall scope of Muslim historiography made relatively few references to "the crusades," does declaring the crusades an important event become a Eurocentric act of periodization?

Would we better understand world history if we taught specific mobilizations, but subsumed crusading into different historical periods?

The Crusades in the Present

The idea of the crusades has appealed to more than one U.S. commander trying to ready his troops for a sustained battle with evil. On June 6, 1944, "D-Day," as Allied forces prepared to invade Normandy and push the Nazis out of France and into Germany, General Dwight Eisenhower issued this Order of the Day:

> Soldiers, sailors and airmen of the Allied Expeditionary Force!
>
> You are about to embark upon the Great Crusade, toward which we have striven these many months. The eyes of the world are upon you. The hopes and prayers of liberty-loving people everywhere march with you. In company with our brave Allies and brothers-in-arms on other Fronts, you will bring about the destruction of the German war machine, the elimination of Nazi tyranny over the oppressed peoples of Europe, and security for ourselves in a free world.
>
> Your task will not be an easy one. Your enemy is well trained, well equipped and battle hardened. He will fight savagely.
>
> But this is the year 1944! Much has happened since the Nazi triumphs of 1940–41. The United Nations have inflicted upon the Germans great defeats, in open battle, man-to-man. Our air offensive has seriously reduced their strength in the air and their capacity to wage war on the ground. Our Home Fronts have given us an overwhelming superiority in weapons and munitions of war, and placed at our disposal great reserves of trained fighting men. The tide has turned! The free men of the world are marching together to Victory!
>
> I have full confidence in your courage and devotion to duty and skill in battle. We will accept nothing less than full Victory!
>
> Good luck! And let us beseech the blessing of Almighty God upon this great and noble undertaking.

The battle against the Nazis was, in Eisenhower's view, a Great Crusade. The last line suggests that this means it would be a battle blessed by God, or perhaps more accurately deserving of God's blessing, as he asks for the blessing rather than bestowing it on the troops. He viewed the crusades, as Bush did, as a sacred military undertaking against evil.

Summary and Conclusions

It is possible to argue about whether this view of the crusades is "true." Surely the Greek Orthodox Christians who lived in Constantinople and suffered the destruction of the Fourth Crusade would disagree. The contemporary Muslim world views the crusades differently. The crusaders were also responsible for extensive violence in Europe. In 1096 crusaders converted some Jews and slaughtered others—men, women, and children—in

Speyer, Worms, Mainz, Cologne, Regensburg, and Prague. Anti-Jewish violence was associated with many crusades. The Jews exemplified a rejection of Jesus, yet they were living in the midst of Christians (Cohen, 2004). The great twentieth-century historian of the crusades, Steven Runciman, denounced the crusades as "one long act of intolerance in the name of God which is the sin against the Holy Ghost" (cited in Tyerman, 2004, p. 15).

One could have a mystery about the character of the crusades, perhaps setting out different views—Muslim, Jewish, Orthodox Christian, Pagan—against those of different crusaders. That approach, however, recognizes the existence of the crusades as a single undertaking. If some students concluded that the crusades were evil, they would in a certain sense be agreeing with Eisenhower and Bush that the crusades *were*, that five hundred years of battles over various goals in widely different locations deserve a related name. Bestowing that common name and purpose on those different battles is a historian's decision, an act of periodization, that has profound consequences for how people view the world. We suggest that a world history course is a perfect place to examine, as a minor mystery, the way historians lump together events as a powerful act of interpretation that often goes unseen, but one that can be held up and questioned.

References and Further Reading

Bush, G. W. (September 16, 2001) *September 11, 2001: Attack on America. Remarks by the President Upon Arrival the South Lawn 3:23 P.M. EDT; September 16, 2001*, The Avalon Project: Documents in Law History and Diplomacy. Online. Available at http://avalon.law.yale.edu/sept11/president_015.asp (accessed March 10, 2009).

Cohen, J. (2004) *Sanctifying the Name of God: Jewish Martyrs and Jewish Memories of the First Crusade*, Philadelphia: University of Pennsylvania Press.

Eisenhower, D. D. (1944) *General Dwight D. Eisenhower's Order of the Day*. D-day statement to soldiers, sailor, and airmen of the Allied Expeditionary Force, 6/44, Collection DDE-EPRE: Eisenhower, Dwight D: Papers, Pre-Presidential, 1916–1952; Dwight D. Eisenhower Library; National Archives and Records Administration. Online. Available at http://www.ourdocuments.gov/doc.php?flash=true&doc=75 (accessed March 10, 2009).

Fletcher, R. (2004) *The Cross and the Crescent: Christianity and Islam from Muhammad to the Reformation*, New York: Viking.

Ford, P. (September 19, 2001) "Europe cringes at Bush's 'crusade' against terrorists," *Christian Science Monitor*. Online. Available at http://www.csmonitor.com/2001/0919/p12s2-woeu.html (accessed March 10, 2009).

Hillenbrand, C. (1999) *The Crusades: Islamic Perspectives*, Edinburgh, UK: Edinburgh University Press.

Maalouf, A. (1989) *The Crusades Through Arab Eyes*, New York: Schoken.

New York State Education Department (n.d.) *Social Studies Learning Standards, Standard 2, Key Idea 2 (World History)*. New York State Learning Standards and Core Curriculum. Online. Available at http://www.emsc.nysed.gov/ciai/socst/socstand/soc22.html (accessed December 12, 2009).

Peres-Rivas, M. (September 16, 2001) "Bush vows to rid the world of 'evil doers,'" *CNN News*. Online. Available at http://archives.cnn.com/2001/US/09/16/gen.bush.terrorism/ (accessed December 12, 2009).

Phillips, J. (2004) *The Fourth Crusade and the Sack of Constantinople*, New York: Penguin.

Riley-Scott, J. (1982, 2005) *The Crusades: A History*, 2nd edn, New Haven, CT: Yale University Press.

Tyerman, C. (2004) *Fighting for Christendom: Holy War and the Crusaders*, New York: Oxford University Press.

Tyerman, C. (2006) *God's War: A New History of the Crusades*, Cambridge, MA: Harvard University Press.

six
The Possibilities
for Pizza
A Search for Origins

(In Napoli where love is king
When boy meets girl here's what they say)
When the moon hits your eye like a big pizza pie
That's amore!
(Famously sung by Dean Martin, lyrics by Harry Warren and Jack Brooks, 1952)

We believe that there is always room, in any history book or book about teaching history, for a bit of humor alongside some good detective work. Food history is an area that offers teachers a great deal of room for humor, hands-on research, and some serious sleuthing all combined into one. Along the way, you can conduct a good deal of work on the origins of our most popular foods, often with surprising results! And you can plan for a bit of eating with your students which, in the case of pizza, will undoubtedly render you quite popular.

Nowadays, in our globalizing world (no offense, but it has been "globalizing" for a long, long time), people, particularly youth, often easily lose track of where the foods they love have originated from. As a result of centuries, perhaps eons, of cross-pollination, diffusion, genetic engineering, and migration of cultures, some foods are strongly associated with one ethnic group or another, whereas other foods are almost totally forgotten or simply not considered. For example, if you poll most students about the origins of potatoes, corn, chickens, turkeys, oranges, apples, or other common everyday foods, they usually give answers that are not even close to their historical origins.

Some foods retain a lot of their original qualities whereas others have been trans-formed, adapted, and genetically engineered many times over. For example, bread, broadly defined, is found in nearly all world cultures in some form, although styles and contents may have changed a great deal over history and it has taken on many new shapes and ingredients, purposes and meanings. Apples, although products of genetic engineering to some extent, still retain their basic shape and purposes as well as symbolic meanings in both American and European cultures. In some instances, foods are the stuff of legends and stories, literature and iron chef performances; a lot of fun indeed!

Therefore, we are presenting a food mystery focused on the very popular pizza, which is actually composed of several different foods, each of which can be the subject of research and study: bread, tomatoes, and cheese. This is probably a minor mystery in the sense that we (sort of) know the origins of pizza, but many of its main features are shrouded in the historical past (we don't really know when bread was evolved, or cheese), although we do know the areas these foods originally started in. In the case of pizza itself, depending on how it is defined, there are many competing claims and counter-claims to evaluate so we will offer these for your study and judgment.

Perhaps the more important, medium mystery cooked in the pizza is an histori-ography question about the reliability of evidence. One theme running throughout this chapter will be to probe the veracity of web reports about the invention of pizza and its supposed origins. Students will be asked to judge which websites offer hard evidence for their claims, which are most reasonable given previous historical accounts, and which are motivated by some sort of commercial goals or nationalistic feelings.

Background Information and the Problem of Defining Terms

Food is very much a part of history, as much as and perhaps more important in a basic sense than who is ruling at the time, or which power conquered which other power. Many historians have investigated the history of food in recent decades, and this trend is accelerating with very detailed studies of particular foods and drinks. From the advent of agriculture and city life, food production has taken on greater importance and meaning because of the necessity of feeding masses of people in a reliable way. Even arguing that people, humans, go back "only" about three or four million years, for the vast major-ity of that time the way of life was centered on hunting and gathering from the wild. Populations were relatively small and likely organized in bands that lived off the land and sea. Only for a comparative minute, since about ten or twelve to seven thousand years ago, have human beings learned to domesticate animals and practice agriculture.

Most hunters now hunt for sport not for livelihood because we have a large, well-oiled production network to supply both our basic needs and specialized tastes. Although cooking, fire, goes back at least half a million years depending on which theory you subscribe to, most of that art was barbecue aimed at roasting or baking animal flesh, rather than the great variety we are used to since the Neolithic "agricultural" revolution.

Most historians and scientists see this revolution as beginning around twelve or fifteen thousand years ago in Southeast Asia, the Middle East, and Central America, at different times and rates of development, some of it controversial. Probably as more research is conducted, there will be an expansion of sites claiming to be the "original" places where the revolution began (Tannahill, 1988, pp. 19–41).

This brings us to a matter of language, as usually by "revolution" we mean rapid and startling changes in political regimes, or in technology. Well, the agricultural revolution, so-called, took a great deal of time, thousands of years, and is still under way in a sense with new ideas about cloning and food irradiation in mass-produced crops. The issue of language, or definition, will come up strongly in this mystery because of a problem: just what do we define as pizza? Who created the tomato sauce many of us take for granted on our pizza, or the cheese, and do we always have to have the very same cheese and type of tomato sauce? If someone makes a flat bread and places a tomato on top and adds some cheese, is that then pizza?

We have a world where styles and types of "pizza" have proliferated to such an extent that perhaps we cannot settle on a precise meaning of the label.

Debating Definitions

For both historical and classroom purposes, it is important to define terms. For example, how can we have a good argument over the origins of pizza and its deeper meaning when we can't agree on just what it is in real life?

Therefore, we propose that this mystery begins with a sample of quasi-pizzas and pizzas and a discussion of basic definitions. Most would propose that pizza is a round or rectangular body of dough, yeast risen (maybe), upon which is placed a slathering of some sort of tomato sauce, topped off by some sort of cheese. Even here we are heading into trouble because some pizzas are cheese filled, others covered with pesto and goat's cheese, still others oil and garlic, no cheese, no tomatoes, hold the onions, etc., etc.

But let's try to settle on a satisfactory definition so that we can pursue the mystery of pizza's origins. Thus, most folks who order a "slice" get a flat piece of bread with canned tomato and cheap cheese, and they are usually satisfied! Agreed?

If we can agree or at least achieve a majority vote on this matter, then we can proceed with our mystery by investigating the beginnings of bread, the beginnings of tomato sauce, and the beginnings of cheese-type foods, the origins of bread and tomatoes being particularly interesting as they never met until a comparatively short historical time ago, during the "discovery invasion" of the New World. So let us proceed with our research on both a holistic and a component approach, that is, pizza as a "construction" must have come from the fertile mind of one or more chefs who lived somewhere from which the idea spread across the world. Here, by the way, is your chance to teach about the Columbian Exchange in the 1500s and about culture contact of worldwide significance because the global repertory of foods was greatly expanded on both sides of the Atlantic and Pacific Oceans.

Mysterious Pizza

So, let us design a mystery, a detective search, for the origins and invention of pizza, a food made up of at least three key ingredients: dough, tomatoes, and cheese.

You could begin with a survey of your students to find out if they know where any or all of the three main ingredients originate, and how or who put them together into a "pizza." There could also be a subsidiary investigation of the origins of the word "pizza" and how pizza came to be associated with Italy—although Italians did not see a tomato until well into the sixteenth century, and did not at all like the looks of the red fruit on first contact.

Detective searches may be organized individually, encouraging self-directed research, or in groups, assigning each of the groups a different food or topic. We will develop this mystery mainly for group investigation, dividing the problem into three parts:

1 origin of bread;
2 origin of tomatoes;
3 origin of cheese.

The research does not have to be carried out in any particular order in our view, as long as the parts are added to the whole at the conclusion. We also suggest more power and people on the origins of bread as this seems to be a much larger and more complex quest than any of the others, with bread going very far back into history. Bread is also potentially controversial in the sense that its definition is very broad and many foods are called bread that may or may not qualify as fitting the criteria for pizza or pizza-like dough raised with yeast. Many ancient bread foods, such as the Hebrew Passover *matza*, or crackers, or pastes made of flour, raise issues of what bread is or should be and how pizza came into being.

A second warning must be issued in these days of "Googling" and web searches by students. Frequently, if not always, they pay little or no attention to who is presenting data or what its origins are in terms of publication, author, date, or place. We will, therefore, include some examples of our own Internet searches on the question of "who invented pizza," partly for fun, but also to illuminate the process of constructing a good sound historical inquiry. To be blunt, many published articles and opinions on the web about any topic are often vague or neglectful of citing sources in a serious and careful manner as would a good historian or social scientist. This presents problems as many claims are made for the invention of pizza but few, we found, can be documented with solid evidence or proof of creation. So, eaters, readers, and buyers, beware of your sources!

We present selected examples of food history as a "starter set" for you and your students to work on, as time and space cannot permit a complete panoply of materials. Thus, you should view our offerings as samples and suggestions for further, more in-depth inquiry into food history, a wonderful subject that has really come into its own in terms of solid historical research only in the last couple of decades. So take advantage of many of the excellent historical food thrillers that have been published and extend this mystery if you have the time and inclination.

Mystery Packet: The Origins of Bread

How long ago did people know how to make bread or something like bread? Let's take a quick look at some evidence to help us solve the mystery of bread as a component of pizza. Review Figures 6.1–6.7 and the document presented in this section, all quite old in terms of human history, and make a judgment: Is bread being made and by what methods? Do you find the activities portrayed familiar? Do you find the product being fashioned similar to or different from our own bread? What shapes are being made, what sizes, and what do you think is the basic plant or grain being used to make the product in each picture, or in the recorded document?

Figure 6.1 Authentic Neapolitan Pizza Marinara as Served by Pizzeria Di Matteo in Naples (image in public domain).

Figure 6.2 Homemade Focaccia with Olives, Rosemary and Sage. Photo: J. P. Lon.

Figure 6.3 Indian Na'an Bread. Photo: Leoboudv/Creative Commons.

Figure 6.4 Turkish Pizza, Also Called *Lahmacun* or *Lamajoon*. Photo: Kenneth Jorgensen.

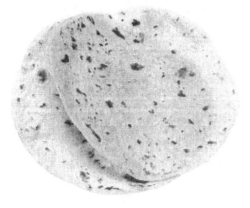

Figure 6.5 Two Flour Tortillas. Photo: Renee Comet for the National Cancer Institute.

Figure 6.6 Handmade *Shmura Matza* for the Jewish Holiday of Passover. Photo: Yoninah.

Figure 6.7 Bread from Pompeii (Preserved in the Volcanic Eruption of 79 c.e.). Photo: Beatrice/Creative Commons.

I then wash some sasku-flour and soak it in cold water and knead it with siqqu-brine.

I mix (missing) in a mortar, I sift it with a sieve, and I separate on the one hand the larger particles; on the other, the smaller ones. I combine in a mortar some (missing) with its ridu and egasliimmu . . . to grind the roasted seeds; I sift them with a sieve, and I separate, on the one side, the larger particles, and on the other, the smaller ones. I take some coarsely ground sasku-flour, with its ridu and egasilimu, which I sift and set aside.

(From the Yale Babylonian Tablets, ~ 3500 b.c.e.; Bottero, 2004, p. 33)

Questions

- How was bread made in Sumer when this tablet was written?

- Look up the time period and try to get an overall idea of the lifestyle in ancient Sumer, or Babylon, or Israel.

- Can you identify all of the ingredients? Do any of the techniques surprise you?

- Are the directions specific or general? Is the bread flavored or plain?

- Do you know how bread is made and could you make bread today?

Mystery Packet: The Origins of Tomatoes

The Tomato Had to Go Abroad to Make Good

One of the strangest things about the history of the tomato (*Lycopersicon esculentum*) is the fact that, although it is of American origin, it was unknown as food in this country until long after it was commonly eaten in Europe. Until hardly more than a hundred years ago it was generally thought to be poisonous in the United States. Long before it was considered here as fit to eat, it was grown only as an ornamental garden plant, sometimes called "love apple."

The mistaken idea that tomatoes were poisonous probably arose because the plant belongs to the Nightshade family, of which some species are truly poisonous. The strong, unpleasant odor of the leaves and stems also contributed to the idea that the fruits were unfit for food.

Our word *tomato* is a slight modification of *tomati*, the word used by the Indians of Mexico, who have grown the plant for food since prehistoric times. Other names reported by early European explorers were *tomatl*, *tumatle*, and *tomatas*, probably variants of Indian words.

In Their Native Andes, Tomatoes Grow Wild

Cultivated tomatoes apparently originated as wild forms in the Peru–Ecuador–Bolivia area of the Andes. Moderate altitudes in that mountainous land abound today in a wide range of forms of tomato, both wild and cultivated. The cultivated tomato is very tender to cold and also rather intolerant of extremely hot or dry weather, a characteristic reflecting the nature of the climate in which it originated.

Presumably the cultivated species of tomato was carried from the slopes of the Andes northward into Central America and Mexico in the same way as maize, by a prehistoric migration of Indians. Since few primitive forms of tomato are found in Central America and Mexico compared with the number in South America, this probably occurred in relatively recent times—perhaps in the last two thousand years.

Because of the highly perishable nature of the fruit, it seems likely that the tomato was among the last of the native American species to be adopted as a cultivated food plant by the Indians and that it remained of little importance until after the arrival of the white man. Lack of evidence of its use by North American Indians further suggests its rather late movement from South America.

For more than 200 years after 1554, when the first known record of the tomato was written, it was being gradually carried over the globe. European writers mentioned seeing it in far places, but not in what is now the United States.

Italians first grew the tomato about 1550 and apparently were the first Europeans to eat it. About 25 years later it was grown in English, Spanish, and mid-European gardens as a curiosity, with little or no interest in it then as food. The French gave it the name pomme d'amour; hence the English and early American term "love apple."

One early Italian writer called the tomato poma Peruviana, suggesting that it was introduced from Peru. Another called it poma d'oro, or "gold apple," indicating that the earliest introductions were yellow-fruited. By the middle of the 18th century the tomato was grown for food extensively in Italy and to some extent in many European countries.

Thomas Jefferson Grew Tomatoes

Not until after the Declaration of Independence do we find any record of the tomato as being grown by white men in this country. Thomas Jefferson, a remarkably progressive Virginia farmer as well as a statesman, grew it in 1781. It was supposedly introduced to Philadelphia by a French refugee from Santo Domingo in 1789 and to Salem, Massachusetts, in 1802 by an Italian painter.

Tomatoes were used as food in New Orleans as early as 1812, doubtless through French influence; but it was another 20 to 25 years before they were grown for food in the northeastern part of the country. Many persons now living recall being told that tomatoes were poisonous.

The various shapes and colors of tomatoes known today in the United States were found in America by the earliest explorers. Plant breeders have improved the size and smoothness of the fruit and the productivity of the plants, but have introduced nothing basically new in form or color.

As a food of worldwide importance, the tomato is about the newest. It has been cultivated and bred so assiduously in Europe that European varieties are now contributing important characters to the improvement of the crop in the United States. Italy has long been famous for its excellent tomato paste, made from small, oblong, rich, red tomatoes; and spaghetti is hardly spaghetti without tomato sauce.

After having made good abroad, the tomato has attained great importance in its native hemisphere. Today, in the United States alone, hundreds of thousands of acres yield millions of tons of tomatoes.

(PLANTanswers, n.d.)

Questions for Students

- Could you make a pizza *without* tomatoes or tomato sauce?
- Can you make a pizza without cheese?
- Can you make a pizza without bread?
- What is *most* essential to the definition of pizza?
- Can you think of a pizza that represents the Old World and the New World?

Mystery Packet: The Origins of Cheese

You would think that cheese would be easily traced back to its origins, but we really are not sure who invented the product, or what was its earliest form. Since the prehistoric domestication of animals, estimated at around eight to ten thousand years ago, there have been natural incentives to use the milk produced by the most common types of herds.

One theory holds that the Middle East was first in making cheese, but we are not sure which cultures started the process, as there are records from ancient Egypt and Mesopotamia showing milking of animals, and some sort of cheese-making. There are also Biblical references, for example in Genesis 18:8, Samuel 17:29, and Isaiah 7:22, and also in the story of Job: "Did you not pour me out like milk and curdle me like cheese?" (Job 10:10, Bible, New International Version).

The earliest domestications known were of sheep and goats, both milk producers, from which cheeses are still made, particularly in the Middle East. These are often hard cheeses, salty cheeses, and crumbly cheese made from curds, drained, and either artificially or naturally salted, mainly to aid preservation. The theory is that cheeses were first made by experimentation with pressing and salting curdled milk in animal stomachs or skin containers and draining them, followed by improvements in the size and quality of curds through the use of rennet (first noted by the ancient Egyptians by at least 2000 B.C.E.). Most of these cheeses were probably a good deal like our present-day "feta," a Greek cheese still made in the old-fashioned way, usually from sheep or goat's milk.

A second theory sees Central Asia as the origin of cheese-making because early nomadic peoples depended on their herds for almost every form of sustenance and developed many kinds of drinks, yogurts, and cheeses from the milk they collected. Milk came from many kinds of animals, including camels, goats, sheep, cattle, and horses. A favorite Mongol drink was and still is "kumiss," fermented mare's milk (mentioned by the Greek historian Herodotus in the fifth century B.C.E.), probably an acquired taste. Records from nomads tend to be a good deal less reliable than those from settled agricultural peoples, but let's be open-minded and allow for this possibility.

Theories abound about the age and origins of cheese production, but it was likely that many prehistoric peoples made different kinds of cheese. Many European cheeses made from cow's milk also date back a long way, and are usually smoother and more solid because cooler climes and nicer caves were available for storage. Middle Eastern cheeses had to be preserved because the weather was often hot and milk deteriorates quickly in hot sunny climates. Peoples of the Mediterranean basin (e.g., Greece, Italy, and France) are still among the world's biggest consumers of cheese on a per-person basis. Americans are not really that big on cheese, according to U.S. Department of Agriculture reports, but interestingly for our chapter the most popular cheese is mozzarella. Why? Well, because that is the preferred cheese placed on most pizzas, and pizza is a hot food in the United States.

Further evidence of cheeses in ancient history comes from a variety of texts and sources. First look at the quote from Homer and decide if you can figure out how Cyclops made cheese. Then check out his recipe against the quotes that follow from Soyer based on ancient texts. Search for areas of agreement and disagreement on cheese-making, and develop your own conclusions about styles and tastes. Develop a theory that explains how cheese was made and whether or not it was of great importance to the ancient Greco-Roman world. Did it help the Romans conquer so much territory?

Homer's *Odyssey* (reputedly written in the eighth century B.C.E.) describes the Cyclops (big guy with one eye) making and storing sheep and goat's milk cheeses:

> We soon reached his cave, but he (Cyclops) was out shepherding, so we went inside and took stock of all that we could see. His cheese-racks were loaded with cheeses, and he had more lambs and kids than his pens could hold . . .
>
> When he had so done he sat down and milked his ewes and goats, all in due course, and then let each of them have her own young. He curdled half the milk and set it aside in wicker strainers.
>
> (Homer, 1895)

Questions for Students

- If the *Odyssey* mentions cheese and the Bible mentions cheese, is this proof of its antiquity?

- Does the cheese-making in the *Odyssey* seem reasonable, or is it just milk?

- Is the Biblical reference in Job enough to tell us what the Hebrews' cheese was like?

- How would you define cheese? Is feta cheese? Is Brie cheese? Is pot cheese really a sort of cheese? Is yogurt cheese?

- Did/does cheese "go with" bread in ancient times and/or in modern times?

- Why might certain food groups evolve together in some areas of the world, whereas other places evolve in different directions?

- Are there any areas of the world that historically did not consume or produce dairy products, including cheese and milk? Why?

- Do you think there are any worldwide cheeses, or truly American cheeses? Give examples. What sort of cheeses do you like to eat if any? Why?

Cheese, from a Nineteenth-Century Source

Study these quotes to confirm or reject the ideas you developed in researching the quote from Homer about Cyclops making cheese. Then answer the questions at the end of the mystery packet, drawing you own conclusions about cheese and how it may relate to pizza.

A demi-god, Aristaeus, son of Apollo, and King of Arcadia, invented cheese, and the whole of Greece welcomed with gratitude this royal and almost divine present.

Sober individuals willingly ate some at their meals; gluttons perceived that it sharpened the appetite; and great drinkers that it provoked copious libations . . . The food was also known to the Hebrews, and the holy writings sometimes mention it.

Mare's milk, or that of the ass, makes an excellent cheese, but much inferior to that procured from the camel, for which an epicure could not pay too dearly. Cow-milk cheese, although more fat and unctuous, was only considered the third-rate.

The Phyrgians made exquisite cheese by artisanally mixing the milk of asses and mares. The Scythians only employed the former; the Greeks imitated them. The Sicilians also mixed the milk of goats and ewes.

The Romans smoked their cheeses to give them a sharp taste; they possessed public places expressly for this use, and subject to police regulations which no one could evade.

In the time of Pliny, little goat cheeses, which were much esteemed, were sent every morning to the market for the sale of the dainties, from the environs of Rome. With the addition of a little bread, they formed breakfast of sober and delicate persons. Asia Minor, Tuscany, the Alps, Gaul (France now), and Nimes especially, furnished very good ones for the table of the Romans, who sought in preference certain sweet and soft qualities. The barbarous nations esteemed only the strong cheese.

Columella informs us that sometimes the leaves and small branches of the fig tree were used to communicate an agreeable flavor. The same writer has transmitted to us a very simple process, much in use in his time, for preserving cheese. They first covered it with brine, and then dried it in a thick smoke obtained from straw or green wood.

[Roman] . . . dishes of which cheese served as the basis:

Salad of Cheese a la Bithyienne

Cut some slices of excellent bread; leave them for some time in vinegar and water; then make a mixture of this bread with pepper, mint, garlic, and green coriander; throw on it a good quantity of cow's cheese salted; add water, oil, and wine.

Dish of Tromelian Cheese

Take some fresh cheese; mix it well with pepper, alisander, dried mint, pine nuts, sun raisins, and dates; then add honey, vinegar, and afterwards garum, oil, wine, and cooked wine.

(Soyer, 1853/2004, pp. 173–5)

Questions for Students

- How long ago was cheese invented according to Alexis Soyer?

- To which peoples does the author attribute the use and production of cheese?

- Why did these ancient peoples make cheese? How did they use it? Was there one kind of cheese or many kinds of cheese? What kinds of animals were used for milk? Why?

- Does the author offer proof of the invention of cheese? Does he offer proof of the use of cheese in ancient times? Are historical documents cited?

- In this account, are any examples given of cheese being used on top of breads?

- Assuming the author's historical detective work was pretty good, and he is right about the use and perhaps origins of cheese in the Middle East, Anatolia, and Greece, would connections between bread and cheese culture be geographically close or far apart?

Pizza, Pizza-Like Breads and Flatbreads: A Sampler

Study each of the photos in Figures 6.1–6.7 and decide which qualify as pizza. Also think about each example as different from or similar to the others. Are all of these related? Do they spring from common geographical locations? Do any involve toppings? Do the toppings include cheeses, or tomatoes, or other ingredients? Are all made with a "riser" like yeast, or beer, or baking powder? Just what features separates pizza from bread, from other foods? Is pizza basically bread, or is it really a new invention? Decide precisely what the characteristics of pizza are and jot down your definition.

To Do

Research the origins of each of the bread-like, or pizza-like, foods pictured in Figures 6.1–6.7 and place these on a world map. Draw connecting lines between each example on the map. Do the foods seem to concentrate in one region, or are they spread across many regions and continents? Why? Can you draw any probable links between the different foods: Do they follow a pattern, a diffusion model? Are most or all copies of each other?

Mystery Packet: Who Invented Pizza?

We present four website accounts claiming that they know where and when pizza was invented, and by whom. In some ways these agree and in other ways they disagree about the origins of pizza as we know it and as it may have possibly evolved from the bread of ancient times. Some link pizza's origins with other foods, some don't, but all connect pizza with the invention of bread. Some make clear the connections between the New and the Old World through the combination of tomatoes or tomato sauce and cheeses or some sort of cheese. None in our opinion is particularly strong on historical scholarship, but that is exactly the problem faced with teaching and learning on the web. Nevertheless, using web sources makes for an interesting exercise in historical thinking and the use of sources, virtually (pun intended) an exercise in corroboration and reliability of reporting methods.

Read these accounts carefully and check the claims against historical evidence and a test of "reasonableness," comparing accounts to develop a "most common" story, or a concordant story, as historians might call it. (*Note*: A *concordant* story is one that many witnesses and researchers agree upon, both in general and in details.)

Claim No. One: Born in Shanghai?

Tujia *Pizza Proves that Chinese Invented Pizza*
Shanghaiist was taking a look at some of [a friend's] photos when we noticed a picture of a strange confection that's been nicknamed the "Chinese pizza." Some of you have probably already seen stores and street vendors selling these things for about 3 Yuan apiece. Apparently it's caught on big in Beijing and other big cities. The provenance of this "pizza" is supposedly from one of China's ethnic minorities, known as the *Tujia* . . . minority, who mostly hail from Hubei province. According to this [linked] article, in May of the last year the first *Tujia* pizza . . . franchise opened up in Hubei's provincial capital, Wuhan. In the next eight months franchises spread all over China—costs of franchising vary from 3,000 Yuan to 50,000 Yuan, though this article claimed that you could open one up in Shanghai for a 30,000 franchising fee. We won't tell you much

about the taste—we haven't had one yet—but evidently it's popular with people looking for a quick kebab type meal on the go, which means it might also be good for the [midnight] munchies, if they're open that late. It costs a mere 0.62 Yuan to make one of these, and yet they are sold to the unsuspecting public at a huge markup—3 Yuan!

How many can you sell a day? Some folks that set up shop in Beijing said that working from 8 am to 8 pm, they could easily break a thousand. In the first article (from Shanghai), an interviewee claimed they could sell 2,000 on a good day, and even 700 on a rainy day. According to that article, Wujiang Lu has some of the better pies around town, and that fits in quite nicely with the whole spirit of Wujiang Lu as one of the anti-corporate quasi-hipster foodie meccas of Shanghai. This random person's [linked] blog claims that they fell in love with these delicacies around People's Square, so there's another lead for you. That said, we think that if you stumble out of a bar at 3 in the morning with an empty wallet and some loose change jangling in your pockets, you will manage to find one of these places, if it's the last thing you do (that night).

(Chen, February 23, 2006)

Claim No. Two: Born in Italy?

History and Legends of Pizza (Excerpt)

In 1596, the tomato plant was exported to Naples by Spain where it was used as an ornamental plant. The first historical indication of the use of the tomato in the kitchen is found in the "Cuoco Galante (Naples—Ed. Raimondiane 1733) by Vincenzo Corrado Oritano," head chef of Prince Emanuel of Francavilla. The same Corrado in a successive tract on the foods most commonly used in Naples declares that the tomato was used to top both pizza and pasta, thus grouping together these two traditional products which helped to make Naples' culinary fortune and establish its place in the history of world cuisine. From this information, one can reconstruct the appearance of "pizza napoletana" as a disc of dough topped with tomato.

The first pizzerias, without doubt, were born in Naples and until the middle of the 20th century the product was exclusively a commodity of Naples and its pizzerias. From 1700 various *botteghe* were active in the city, called "pizzerie," whose fame arrived so far as the King of Naples, Ferdinando di Borbone, who in order to try this typical dish of the Neapolitan tradition, violated court etiquette by entering into one of the most renowned pizzerias. From that moment, the "pizzeria" was transformed into a fashionable locale, a place designated exclusively to the production of the pizza.

The most popular and famous pizzas in Naples were the "marinara" born in 1734 and the "margherita" from 1796–1810, which was offered to the Queen of Italy on a visit to Naples in 1889 precisely for the color of its condiments (tomato, mozzarella and basil) which brought to mind the flag of Italy. Over time, pizzerias were born throughout the cities of Italy and even abroad, but every one of these, if in a city diverse from Naples, always tied its very existence to the phrase "pizzeria Napoletano" or, alternatively, used a term which could evoke in some way its tie with Naples, where for almost 300 years this product has remained virtually unaltered.

(*Food History*, 2001)

Claim No. Three: Born in the USA?

American Pie: How a Neapolitan Street Food Became the Most Successful Immigrant of All (Excerpt)

Everybody likes pizza. Even those who claim to be immune to its charms must deign to have the occasional slice; a staggering 93 percent of Americans eat pizza at least once a month. According to one study, each man, woman, and child consumes an average of 23 pounds of pie every year.

But pizza wasn't always so popular. Food writers in the 1940s who were worldly enough to take note of the traditional Italian treat struggled to explain the dish to their readers, who persisted in imagining oversized apple-pie crusts stuffed with tomatoes and coated with cheese. "The pizza could be as popular a snack as the hamburger if Americans only knew about it," *The New York Times* lamented in 1947, illustrating its plaint with a photograph of a pie subdivided into dozens of canapé-sized slices.

Pizza had wedged its way into the nation's hearts and stomachs almost overnight, a phenomenon befitting a food that became synonymous with quick and easy. Americans seeking fun in the years after World War II found a good measure of it in pizza, a food that when eaten correctly (a matter of some debate among 1950s advice columnists) forced the diner's lips into a broad smile. Pizza, like teenagedom and rock 'n' roll, is a lasting relic of America's mid-century embrace of good times.

Modern pizza originated in Italy, although the style favored by Americans is more a friend than a relative of the traditional Neapolitan pie. Residents of Naples took the idea of using bread as a blank slate for relishes from the Greeks, whose bakers had been dressing their wares with oils, herbs, and cheese since the time of Plato. The Romans refined the recipe, developing a delicacy known as placenta, a sheet of fine flour topped with cheese and honey and flavored with bay leaves. Neapolitans earned the right to claim pizza as their own by inserting a tomato into the equation. Europeans had long shied away from the New World fruit, fearing it was plump with poison. But the intrepid citizens of

Naples discovered the tomato was not only harmless but delicious, particularly when paired with pizza.

Cheese, the crowning ingredient, was not added until 1889, when the Royal Palace commissioned the Neapolitan pizzaiolo Raffaele Esposito to create a pizza in honor of the visiting Queen Margherita. Of the three contenders he created, the Queen strongly preferred a pie swathed in the colors of the Italian flag: red (tomato), green (basil), and white (mozzarella).

Pizza crossed the Atlantic with the four million Italians who by the 1920s had sought a better life on American shores. Most Italians weren't familiar with the many regional variations their fragmented homeland had produced, but a longing for pan-Italian unity inspired a widespread embrace of a simplified pizza as their "national" dish. Fraternal "pizza and sausage" clubs, formed to foster Italian pride, sprouted in cities across the Northeast. Women got in on it too, participating in communal pizza exchanges in which entrants competed with unique pies, some molded into unusual shapes, some with the family name baked into the dough.

Although non-Italians could partake of pizza as early as 1905, when the venerable Lombardi's—the nation's first licensed pizzeria—opened its doors in Lower Manhattan, most middle-class Americans stuck to boiled fish and toast. The pungent combination of garlic and oregano signaled pizza as "foreign food," sure to upset native digestions. If pizza hoped to gain an American following beyond New York City and New Haven, it would have to become less like pizza. By the 1940s a few entrepreneurs had initiated the transformation, starting a craze that forever changed the American culinary landscape.

The modern pizza industry was born in the Midwest, not coincidentally a place of sparse Italian settlement. Although pizza had pushed into the suburbs as second-generation Italians relocated, most of the heartland was pizza-free. Its inhabitants had neither allegiance nor aversion to the traditional pie. The region also boasted an enviable supply of cheese.

Despite such advantages, Ike Sewell still wasn't thinking pies when he partnered with Ric Riccardo to open a Chicago restaurant. Sewell, a native of Texas, planned on offering a menu of Mexican specialties. Riccardo willingly agreed, having never tried Mexican food. His first meal changed his mind so completely that, he liked to say later, he fled to Italy to recover from it. While there, he sampled classic Neapolitan pizza and found it much better than Sewell's Mexican offerings. Sewell eventually agreed to forgo enchiladas for pizza, but not until he'd inflated the thin-crusted Neapolitan recipe to make it more palatable to Americans. "Ike tasted it and said nobody would eat it, it's not enough," Evelyne Slomon, author of *The Pizza Book*, said. "So he put gobs and gobs of stuff on it."

Sewell's lightly seasoned deep-dish pie, introduced in 1943, the signature item at Pizzeria Uno, was the first true American pizza. The pie was a uniquely Chicago institution, like a perennially losing major-league baseball team, that other cities showed no interest in adopting. Until Uno's opened its first location outside Chicago in 1979, people had to go to East Ohio Street to sample anything like Sewell's idea of a pie. But its success liberated pizzeria owners nationwide to tinker with their product, ultimately paving the way for the megafranchises.

Sewell was followed in the next two decades by scores of independent operators who deleted the traditional herbs and went easy on the garlic in hopes of gaining a bigger clientele. Pizza was no longer the province of first- and second-generation Italians. Americans of every ancestry wanted a slice of this pie. "I make any kinda pizza you want," the New York pizzeria owner Patsy D'Amore told *The Saturday Evening Post* in 1957. "One day a man order a lox pizza with cream cheese. It turn my stomach, but I make it for him." Professional pizza chefs like the unnamed Japanese-American woman who stumped the panel of the TV show "What's My Line?" in 1956, and the Mexican-Americans who helped make pizza the second-best seller at the 1952 Texas State Fair (edged out only by the irresistible corn dog), and fledgling franchises like Pizza Hut, gradually shed all Italian imagery from their advertising campaigns.

But despite the best entrepreneurial efforts, most Americans remained unfamiliar with pizza well into the 1940s. "We had to give it away at first," Eugenia DiCarlo told a McNeese State University interviewer of her husband's attempt to establish a pizzeria in Lake Charles, Louisiana, in 1947. "They had never, never heard of it down here. And, boy, every time they'd take a piece of it, they liked it. And more and more liked it, told other people, and then got to the place where that was the biggest part of our business."

(Miller, 2006, April/May)

Claim No. Four: Born We Know Not Where?

Who Invented Pizza?

Pizza is one of those foods for which we will never know a specific origin. For one thing, the definitions of pizza are many and varied. Putting stuff on flat bread as a meal certainly goes back as far as ancient Rome. The word "pizza" itself appears just before 1000 A.D., in the area between Naples and Rome, meaning "pie."

There are traditional pizza-like dishes in Provence where bread (or sometimes a pastry) is topped with onion, tomato, anchovies, and olives. In the Middle East, *lahma bi ajeen* is a pizza base with minced onions, meat, and flavorings.

So we need to start with some definitions. Shall we confine our attention to American pizza, now found throughout the world? If so, no problem—it was invented in America in the 1950s. That's probably not the answer you were looking for, although the New World did make possible pizza as we know it today.

Instead let's define modern pizza as the tasty conjunction of flat bread, tomato sauce, and cheese. Most food historians point to Naples as the area of origin, and to *Napoletana*, the pizza of Naples, as the archetype of this type of pizza.

The word "pizza" itself is probably related to *pitta* (bread) so let's start with the crust. In ancient times, all bread was basically flat, and treated as a food in and of itself. The idea of bread as a carrier or holder of other food pretty much started in the Middle Ages, what we today might call an open face sandwich. It wasn't originally a new way of eating—the bread was a sort of place mat, to help keep the table clean during meals. Only the rich could afford plates, so a flat piece of (say) hard barley bread on the table was used to hold the meal, mostly meat and drippings. Bread was specially baked for that purpose. After the meal, sometimes the bread was consumed, and sometimes given to the dogs.

The closed sandwich has its origins in the 18th century, but that's a different story.

Next ingredient: cheese. Cheese itself dates back to prehistoric times and was probably discovered by accidental fermentation. Mozzarella, a soft, fresh cheese traditionally made from the milk of water buffalo, originated in 15th century Naples. Mozzarella nowadays is made from cow's milk. You can still find buffalo-cheese (or a blend of buffalo and cow cheese) in Salerno, but it's too expensive and delicate for pizza topping, we're told.

That brings us to tomato sauce—the New World's contribution to pizza, since the tomato was a New World plant. Initially Europeans regarded the tomato with suspicion and fear. It had a strange texture, was too acidic to eat green, and looked spoiled when ripe. It disintegrated when cooked, and was even suspected of being poisonous.

But eventually it caught on. New plants from America arrived in Iberia and spread throughout the Mediterranean. Italy probably got the tomato shortly after Spain—its soil and climate, similar to that of Central Mexico, helped the import thrive. The first written mention of the tomato in Italy is 1544; it was fried and eaten with salt and pepper.

By 1692, we have the first recipe for Italian tomato sauce, with chili peppers, so the modern pizza was just around the corner.

Alas, we shall never know the genius who first put together the bread, tomato sauce, and cheese. But that's how pizza (as I've defined it) came to be.

There are a many types of pizza, of course. Even in Naples, there is no consensus on what exactly constitutes a Neapolitan pizza. Burton Anderson writes that the most basic pizza is *marinara*—flat bread with oil, tomato, garlic, and oregano. It was stored on voyages so that sailors (*marinai*) could make pizza away from home. The pizza *Margherita* is just over a century old, named after the first queen of the united Italy, using toppings of tomato, mozzarella cheese, and fresh basil—the red, white, and green of the Italian flag. We also have *calzone* (pizza with an enclosed filling), *pizza maniata* (kneaded), *pizzette* (miniature) and *pizza bianca* (no toppings).

Italian immigrants brought pizza to the United States, in the early 1900s. However, it was the 1950s when pizza caught on outside the Italian-American community, and quickly spread throughout the U.S. and became an international food, now found in every country.

(*The Straight Dope*, April 11, 2001)

Questions for Students

- Which account goes back into past history to trace pizza's evolution?

- How far back does the account look for origins?

- Do other accounts corroborate this story or contradict it?

- Where do the accounts place the origins of bread?

- Why do many accounts locate the invention of pizza in Italy? Is it likely that the Chinese invented pizza? Is it likely that Americans invented pizza? What theory is most likely?

- Do the accounts explain how pizza made its way to the United States or other countries in the world?

- Could pizza, as we know it (a tomato sauce, cheese, and bread combination), have been invented before Columbus "discovered" America, or not? Why?

- Which account do you think proves its points best—offers pictures, facts and figures, references to historical sources—and which the least?

- Which account presents a "reasonable judgment" about the origins of pizza? For example, which history provides details about the evolution of bread, tomatoes, and cheese, or at least two of these?

- Which account admits uncertainty in its investigation, in history?

- Which seems most sure of its claims?

- How do you decide on trustworthiness? How do you decide on evaluating claims, especially when they are competing?

- What is most important in building trust in historical accounts: facts, reasons, sources, one or more research findings? Explain.

- Do accounts in newspapers or on the web count for more than accounts researched by historians and social scientists? Who is more likely to "get it right" and why?

- Collect at least a half-dozen pizza recipes and compare ingredients, mixing methods, and baking directions. Do they all pretty much agree on what a pizza is and how it is made?

- Do they agree on a shape—round, square, rectangle, flat, high, low—or is there no particular shape or size? Why? Is there a reason given or none at all?

- Are variations big or small in the recipes? Are most of the variations in toppings or in basic ingredients?

- Try out one of the recipes at home and then taste it. Are there any ingredients you would like to add?

- Design a traditional pizza, and a modern one, and decide how you would define the pizza pie.

Summary and Conclusions

Food history has recently seen a wonderful upsurge in attention from both popular journalists and professional historians and social scientists. Given the complexities and fragmentation of the so-called "postmodern" condition, students and teachers often are unaware of the origins or evolution or invention of those features of daily life we all take for granted such as food, clothing, and shelter. Food is, in our view, a particularly terrific mystery because we all like to eat, and students are often fascinated by questions about how foods came about, their health value, and the way they are harvested and produced for final consumption. Most students know little about cooking, or foods, and are dependent on supermarket harvesting many times removed from farm life or the natural world. In addition, there are now whole food industries claiming to be "natural" or "organic" or "biotic" and such, charging higher prices for what is perhaps quality food untouched by chemicals, preservatives, or genetic engineering.

Investigating food origins, recipes, and cultural diffusion of products and crops is very easy to do as there are a great many web avenues open to investigation, as well as new and old scholarship, and a plethora of cooking magazines. We prefer to center mysteries around big ideas such as diffusion of materials and products, evolution of crops, exchanges of ideas and farming methods, and culture contact and adaptation. One of these big ideas will serve as a focal point for further investigations, although we recognize and applaud ambitious projects that try to encompass many ideas.

Some easy examples for teachers to develop are:

1 The uses and abuses of corn (maize) from ancient to modern times (extra credit for the linguistic analysis of word origins and confusions: where did the term "corn" come from—not Native American for sure?).
2 The evolution and consumption of noodles, dumplings, and noodle-like foods across the world (with extra credit for crossing cultures and trying a whole range of noodles made of rice, wheat, corn, and tofu, as well as other materials).
3 The origin and hybridization of citrus fruits from early times to the present: for instance oranges, lemons, grapefruit, citron, and limes (with extra credit for answering questions such as: Did they always look like that and were they so big at birth?).
4 The domestication of familiar farm animals, for example cows, horses, goats, and sheep—what did the first animals kept by people look like and do these still exist? (with extra credit for investigating llamas, alpacas, and vicunas, or chickens and turkeys).
5 The invention and evolution (if any occurs) of our favorite sauces and snacks, such as Bolognese sauce, or marinara, or marsala (with extra credit for looking into cream sauces, wine sauces, soy sauces, and sweet and sour sauces, and don't forget peanuts and peanut sauces and butters).
6 The origin of potatoes, a worldwide favorite that actually comes in many forms, not just white and red, that has influenced vast numbers of people's eating habits, and is usually associated with Ireland but is not historically from Ireland at all! (with extra credit for finding out all the varieties of the spud, all its names, and at least ten different kinds of favorite potato products eaten in many nations, e.g., chips, samosas, French fries, cakes, latkes, etc.)

Feel free to add your own favorites to amuse and educate your students but be sure to check your sources first so that you can be certain of having some controversy about origins and exchanges, forms, and functions of a particular food. And don't forget to add discussions about the healthy or not so healthy methods of preparation of different foods and where the ideas of baking, frying, mashing, marinating, and squashing foods originate from to influence our current highly sophisticated international palates and multi-cultural menus.

A last question: If it is such a big wide sophisticated globalizing multi-ethnic world of food out there, how come we don't seem to know much about historical origins, or migrations, or health values? Most foods we take for granted now came from very different ecological settings across the continents and have been diffused and disseminated, cross-bred and genetically manipulated from early times to take the form and shape and color we are used to in our everyday lives. Breads, grains, fruits, and vegetables, as well as many members of the domesticated animal world, have been traded, adapted, and bred to suit a wide range of environments and now represent the world food basket. But do you know the origins?

References and Further Reading

Acquaah, G. (2002) *Horticulture: Principles and Practices*, Upper Saddle River, NJ: Prentice-Hall.

Balinska, M. (2008) *The Bagel: The Surprising History of a Modest Bread*, New Haven, CT: Yale University Press.

Belasco, W. and Scranton, P. (eds.) (2002) *Food Nations: Selling Taste in Consumer Societies*, New York: Routledge.

Bottero, J. (2004) *The Oldest Cuisine in the World: Cooking in Mesopotamia*, Chicago: University of Chicago Press.

Buonassisi, R. (2003) *Pizza from Its Italian Origins to the Modern Table*, New York: Firefly.

Buzby, J. (February 2005) "Cheese consumption continues to rise," *Amber Waves: The Economics of Food, Farming, Natural Resources, and Rural America*, USDA Economic Research Service. Online. Available at http://www.ers.usda.gov/AmberWaves/February05/Findings/CheeseConsumption.htm (accessed January 20, 2010).

Chen, P. (February 23, 2006) "*Tujia* pizza proves that chinese invented pizza," *The Shanghaiist*. Online. Available at http://shanghaiist.com/2006/02/23/tujia_pizza_pro_1.php (accessed February 6, 2010).

Curwen, E. C. and Hatt, G. (1953) "Plow and pasture: The early history of farming," *The Scientific Monthly* 78 (1): 49.

DuPaigne, B. (1999) *The History of Bread*, New York: Harry Abrams.

Flandrin, J.-L. and Montanari, M. (2000) *Food: A Culinary History* (English edn by A. Sonnenfeld), New York: Penguin Books.

Food History. (2001) "History of pizza." Online. Available at http://www.world-foodhistory.com/2007/02/history-of-pizza.html (accessed December 1, 2009).

Halter, M. (2000) *Shopping for Identity: The Marketing of Ethnicity*, New York: Schoken.

Helstosky, C. F. (2008) *Pizza: A Global History*, London: Reaktion Books.

Homer (1895) *The Odyssey* (trans. Samuel Butler), London: A. C. Fifield.

Kemp, B. J. (1989) *Ancient Egypt: Anatomy of a Civilization*, London: Routledge.

Laffal, F. (1975) *Breads of Many Lands*, Essex, CN: Gallery Press.

Mair, V. (ed.) (2006) *Contact and Exchange in the Ancient World*, Honolulu: University of Hawaii Press.

Menzel, P. and D'Aluisio, F. (2004) *Hungry Planet: What the World Eats*, Napa, CA: Material World Press and Ten Speed Books.

Miller, H. (2006) "American pie: How a Neapolitan street food became the most successful immigrant of all," *American Heritage Magazine* 57 (2). Online. Available at http://www.americanheritage.com/articles/magazine/ah/2006/2/2006_2_30.shtml (accessed December 1, 2009).

Nicholson, P. T. and Shaw, I. (eds.) (2000) *Ancient Egyptian Materials and Technology*, Cambridge, UK: Cambridge University Press.

PLANTanswers (n.d.) "The tomato had to go abroad to make good," *PLANTanswers: An Archive of Gardening Information Assembled by Dr. Jerry Parsons*. Online. Available at http://aggie-horticulture.tamu.edu/plantanswers/publications/vegetabletravelers/tomato.html (accessed December 1, 2009).

Pollan, M. (2006) *The Omnivore's Dilemma: A Natural History of Four Meals*, New York: Penguin Books.

Reinhart, P. (2004) *American Pie: The Search for the Perfect Pizza*, New York: Ten Speed Press.

Ridgwell, J. and Ridgway, J. (1986) *Food around the World*, Oxford: Oxford University Press.

Riley, G. (2007) *The Oxford Companion to Italian Food*, New York and London: Oxford University Press.

Schenone, L. (2003) *A Thousand Years over a Hot Stove: A History of American Women Told through Food, Recipes, and Remembrances*, New York: W. W. Norton.

Smith, A. F. (1994a) *The Tomato in America: Early History, Culture and Cookery*, Columbia: University of South Carolina Press.

Smith, A. F. (1994b) *The Tomato in America*, Champaign-Urbana: University of Illinois Press.

Sokolov, R. (1993) *Why We Eat What We Eat*, New York: Simon & Schuster.

Soyer, A. (1853, unabridged replication 2004) "Cheese," in *Food, Cookery, and Dining in Ancient Times*, Mineola, NY: Dover Publications.

Staller, J. (June 1997) "As American as pizza pie," *Smithsonian Magazine* 28 (3): 138.

Tannahill, R. (1988) *Food in History*, 2nd edn, New York: Three Rivers Press.

Teubner, C., Ehlert, F.-W., and Mair-Waldburg, H. (1998) *The Cheese Bible*, New York: Penguin.

The Straight Dope (April 11, 2001) "Who invented pizza?," The Straight Dope Science Advisory Board. Online. Available at http://www.straightdope.com/columns/read/1695/who-invented-pizza (February 9, 2010).

Websites

Food History. A resource featuring articles on various foods and recipes. Articles draw on multiple disciplines—economics, sociology, etc.—for understanding food in history and culture. Available at http://www.world-foodhistory.com.

Food History News. A guide to resources on food history, by the editors of what started as the *Food History News* newsletter. Available at http://foodhistorynews.com.

The Food Timeline. A chronological database on the history of food and cooking. Available at http://www.foodtimeline.org.

seven
Incas and Spaniards

Though nothing can bring back the hour
Of splendour in the grass, of glory in the flower;
We will not grieve, rather find
Strength in what remains behind.
(William Wordsworth, 1770–1850, "Ode: Intimations of Immortality")

Let's start with an appetizer to Incas and Spaniards, two images (Figures 7.1 and 7.2), the second a recent photo of a Peruvian couple celebrating their Indian history by dressing up for a fiesta as Inca and queen. We place on view two examples for you to examine to raise questions about historical authenticity, what is true to history.

Each of these images communicates a good deal about views of the Incas, but the styles are different, and perhaps the "feeling." Based on examining each of the pictures, can you learn anything about dress, technology, and lifestyle; character, attitudes, and social status; artistic styles and goals? Can you learn about how people saw the Inca rulers in later time periods? As time flows on, can we remember accurately or does the culture we live in influence and change our visions of the past?

How do the two images compare with those of the Incas in the calendar pictures, February and December (see Figure 7.3)? Is the eighteenth-century drawing more life-like, equally strange, and more or less European? Why? Is the photo of the Peruvian couple more lifelike, true to ancient times, or largely invented? How can you tell?

Choose any number of upper-class or noble women in the Guaman Poma de Ayala calendar pictures, and compare them with Figure 7.1. Ask your own questions about

Figure 7.1 Inca King and Queen, Eighteenth-Century Drawing by Mestizo Artist, Cuzco, Peru. Source: Anon, Corbis.com.

Figure 7.2 Annual Celebration of Inca Culture at Tihuanaco. Native Participants. Photo: June, 2002, Corbis.com.

their dress, the artifacts displayed, and the differences between men and women, at least upper class, in the Inca Empire? Then compare the Guaman Poma de Ayala calendar pictures to the couple in Figure 7.2. Same results or different?

Would the Inca nobles have probably understood the status and symbols of the Spanish invaders? Why or why not? Were they from societies that had sharply divided social classes, or from societies of equals? How would culture and social class influence the presentation of images?

You Decide: Two Sets of Inca Representations

Is each of the two sets of Incas depicted authentically, as they really were in the sixteenth century? Do all show the same dress and symbols of power, or are they different? Is each set shown as noble and powerful? How, according to the eighteenth-century artist, did noble women and men dress and present themselves? How does the photo of the Peruvian couple dressed as Inca (king) and Coya (queen) compare with the eighteenth-century drawing? How do they compare with Guaman Poma de Ayala's woodcuts, Figures 7.3–7.6, from the period of the conquest in the late sixteenth/early seventeenth centuries?

Do you think one or both representations are authentic, true to life? What do you think art may have looked like before the Spanish arrived, untouched by outsider influence? Were the artists' styles likely to have been influenced by European drawing, and art, or do you see the art itself as "Indian"? Does the Peruvian couple seem to dress authentically in commemorating the Incas? Can they? Why or why not? Which artist, eighteenth-century or Guaman Poma de Ayala, do you think has more Spanish/European style and which more "Indian" or Incan style? How can you decide? In historical images, how can you tell what is authentic, true to the time, and what is not?

How Do you Decide on Authenticity in History?

You, the teacher, try your skills on each picture before offering the set to students. Note that there were few or no paintings or carvings of Inca men and women left by the Spanish when they destroyed valuable records, art, and religious objects. Thus, historians and archeologists had very little to go on concerning what the noble class really looked like until the work of Spanish-born or mestizo Peruvian artists toward the end or after the period of the Conquest of Peru was found. How can we trust these as true records? But these works are reprinted in almost every book and article about Incas and Spaniards because that is all we have, and many historians feel that we are lucky to have these because so much was destroyed, either through war or by purposeful destruction. So when interpreting the pictures, do you think these show weak, moderate, or strong European styles, such as drawing faces, or drawing in the round in three dimensions, or adding signs and symbols of power that were common in Europe, but unusual or absent

Figure 7.3 The Inca Yearly Calendar Cycle According to Guaman Poma de Ayala.

Mystery Packet: Yearly Calendar Cycles

We have heard a lot about the Incas, but rarely are we invited to take a look inside their culture through the eyes of an Inca artist. Figure 7.3 shows twelve woodcut drawings describing the rituals and holidays celebrated every year throughout the Inca Empire in Peru. For extra credit, can you read the writing on the drawings? What language is it? How could you figure out the message and the meaning by yourself? How do you explain the writing and spelling as the Incas did not keep records this way? Why is the sun shining brightly in December?

What facts can you gather from these pictures? Is it easy to get acquainted with pictures from the past, especially in another language? Why or why not? How would you interpret their meaning? Could you create a set of rules that might help you focus on the pictures? (For instance, how can you tell Incas from Spaniards?)

Figure 7.3 Continued.

Why were they drawn? Is the artist (same person for all) sending a message? Is the pictorial evidence reliable or biased in favor of one side or the other? How can you tell? If you place the pictures in historical context, what sort of history would you write about contact between Incas and Spaniards? Do the pictures suggest a mystery to you, one or more, and how would you describe the mystery in your own words?

Pick out one picture to examine under a magnifying glass for details. Overall, do you see anything surprising? Is the artist taking a stand with his pictures, in other words, is he critical or disapproving of one side, the other, or both? How can you decide about point of view?

Write your own story of Inca civilization based on these twelve images. Write a set of rules or questions that might help you understand historical images like these.

in Peru? Does the native couple get it right in dressing up for carnival as Incas or do they, too, show "outsider" influence? Depending on your answer, how much more or less would you trust the pictures? What other materials and evidence would you like to have to make sure your interpretations are probably solid?

A Real Mystery in Pictures and Passages

The Incas and the Spaniards is a popular history topic that is often hurried over in many world history courses by accepting the rather astounding victory of the Spaniards over the Inca Empire as pretty much quite understandable and determined by the superiority of European technology and military accomplishments. Most of the materials usually provided to students are drawn from largely European or Spanish sources, made all the more likely because Inca record keeping was carried out using a system of knotted strings called *quipu*, or *kipu*, a "writing system" (Figure 7.4), most of which were destroyed along with the knowledge of the record keepers. Thus, we are left with pretty much one-sided views of what happened and why, and research is very much alive and ongoing right now to learn more about what happened before, during, and after the conquest using better archeology and underappreciated and less well-known sources. We will use two of these less appreciated sources in this chapter as our primary evidence packet.

Figure 7.4 Quipu: The Inca System of Writing. Drawing by Guaman Poma de Ayala.

Peru itself still shows the divisions between European and Indian cultures, both alive and well at the time of this writing. It is amazing that such divisions and issues still exist after five hundred years of socialization and control by people of largely European origin. We will present a mystery treat for our finale that provides a modern-day interpretation of Incas and Spaniards in the form of a chess set you will want to look at and discuss with your classes. Meanwhile, back to our main event: interpreting primary and secondary sources on the fall of Peru.

There are many mysteries surrounding the events of the early sixteenth century when Spanish conquistadors first came into contact with the major peoples of Mesoamerica and South America. We are missing huge quantities of evidence because of direct and willful destruction by the Spanish and others, mostly in the interests of obliterating native religious structures, texts, and symbols. We have largely one-sided accounts of events from the conquerors, not a very trustworthy situation, and very little from the Incas. Accompanying the one-sided accounts is the still general and pervasive atmosphere of viewing Indian civilizations as savage, barbaric, less successful than Western civilizations (proven by their defeat and destruction, if nothing else), as well as exotic and strange, engaged in human sacrifice and other unspeakable rites. Finally, there is a moral dimension, a sense of approval and/or disapproval of one side or the other, or both, as culpable for crimes against humanity, religious prejudice, and social structures we are both familiar and unfamiliar with in our own culture.

Texts often portray Spaniards in the New World as cruel and ruthless, while picturing the Incas and others as totalitarian and bloodthirsty, or noble and simple-minded, or all of the above at the same time. Thus, we have an ideal situation for classroom discussion and the development of mysteries, a lovely combination of bias, unknowns, prejudice, fragmentation, and sweeping moral judgment by both eyewitnesses and present-day historians. Possibilities for discussion are nearly endless, and play into the traditional questions about how so few European explorers and soldiers (about 175 or so) could upset so large an empire as the Incas (millions).

For the purposes of this mystery, most of the evidence will be drawn from two unusual sources. The first is Garcilaso de la Vega, the son of an early intermarriage between a Spanish father and an Inca noble mother, who left us one of the earliest accounts of the conquest, dating to the late sixteenth and early seventeenth centuries. He presents an interesting figure in that he knows a great deal about both cultures and offers his account in a way that is sometimes quite different from those of conquistadors or priests, or from that of an Inca noble. Thus, his writing needs interpretation and investigation as a special case in which perhaps both perspectives may be found, or one or the other, or some amalgam of the two, and that is for us to think about as historical detectives.

The other source, not as well known until quite recently, is a chronicle of Peruvian history in the form of hundreds of woodcuts with text in old Spanish and Quechua or other Indian languages that miraculously survived the conquest complete and in good condition. These are the work of Guaman Poma de Ayala, also the product of an intermarriage but whose exact origins and upbringing are truly mysterious, although he claims to be born of Inca nobility and both of his parents spoke Quechua, the language of the Incas. His is one of the earliest full-scale accounts of the Inca Empire from its origins to its downfall, and includes depictions of contact with the Spanish. *The First New Chronicle and Good Government* (Guaman Poma de Ayala/Frye, 2006) contains 398 line drawings and runs to more than eight hundred pages of text. Guaman also presents himself in his book (Figure 7.5), rather in a Spanish way, don't you think . . . or what *do* you think?

Scholars discovered a full version of the text in the Royal Library of Denmark in 1908 that has slowly become more available with efforts at preservation and copying, as well as translation, and parts have by now been checked, edited, and reproduced in portions for public consumption. This text and the pictures, probably first published in 1613–14, will be one of our major primary sources for this mystery because of the wealth of information held within, and because of their often unusual, forceful, dramatic, and moral nature. Much like the written history by de la Vega, Guaman Poma de Ayala's work raises the same questions of perspective and feeling, so the investigator must approach interpretation asking if the artist has an agenda, and just who that agenda favors: Spanish, Incas, both, or neither. Not a great deal is known about the author/artist or his life, but

Figure 7.5 A Self-Portrait of the Author and Artist Guaman Poma de Ayala.

he seems to have become educated in Spanish as well as understanding native languages. Guaman Poma de Ayala's book combines global views of history, detailed accounts of the Andes peoples, particularly the Incas, and chronicles of conquest along with eyewitness accounts of current events. He sometimes offers Catholic morality copied from catechisms, satires, recommendations for reform, and personal reflections. From a Spanish point of view this vast heavy-bound book must have seemed confusing and upsetting because it often presents graphic exhibits of the treatment of natives by the conquerors. However, it provides an unusual and structurally meaningful account of Peruvian life that is perhaps without peer. That is why we are using it, but we are also using it not only for information but as a mystery in itself, learning how to interpret a primary source that has a lot of quirks. For example, the drawings are often muddy, letters reversed, with writing appearing at the top, bottom, or in the picture itself in two or more languages, usually Spanish and a Peruvian tongue such as Quechua or Aymara.

From a more intensive study of the chronicle, it seems that the author sought to influence the King of Spain, to whom it is dedicated, to allow more autonomy to native peoples rather than local government, and to permit as much retention of native culture as possible within a population he portrays as loyal to the Catholic faith (Guaman Poma de Ayala/Frye, 2006, pp. xxi–xxvi). The author sees himself not as an "Indian" or commoner, but as a leader, an "*apo capac*," Andean noble who bears a significant name, that is, *Waman*, king of birds, and *Puma*, king of beasts. Guaman Poma de Ayala addressed the King of Spain, setting out his goals, as follows:

> Many times I have doubted, Your Royal Sacred Catholic Majesty, whether to accept this enterprise, and many more times after taking it up I have wished to go back, judging my intentions to be reckless and finding my capacities insufficient to the task of finishing it, in accordance with its reliance on histories written in no script whatsoever, but solely on quipus (knotted cords used as records) and on the accounts and reports of the oldest Indian men and women, elders and eyewitnesses, that they may swear to it, and that any sentence that may be passed be thereby valid.
>
> And thus I spent countless days and years amidst discourses that go back to the beginning of this kingdom, until, overcome by my advanced years, I accomplished this age old desire, which was always to investigate, despite the crudeness of my wit, my blind eyes, little sight, little learning, and lack of a graduate degree, a doctorate, a master's or even Latin. Yet, as the first in this kingdom with the occasion and ability to serve your Majesty, I resolved to write about the history, descendant, and famous deeds of the first kings, lords, and captains, our grandfathers; and about the nobles and the lives of the Indians, their generations, and their descent from the first Indians—the Wari Wirachocha Runa, and the Wari Runa (descendants of Noah of the Flood), the Purun Runa, and the Acu Runa.
>
> I would also write about the twelve Incas, their idolatries and errors, about their

wives, the queens (Coyas); about the princesses . . . noblewomen, and captains . . . And about the contest between the legitimate Inca, Topa Cusiwalpa Wascar Inca, and his bastard brother, Atawalpa Inca; . . . and about Quiso Yupanqui Inca and Manco Inca, who defended himself from the damage inflicted by the Spaniards in the days of the Emperor . . .

May Your Majesty benignly receive this humble small service, together with my great hope; for me, this will be a blessed and restful reward for my toil.

In the province of Lucanos, on the first of January of 1613,
Your humble subject,

Don Felipe de Ayala

(Guaman Poma de Ayala/Frye, 2006, pp. 4–7)

The author helps us out, or at least the King of Spain, by explaining his purposes, complaints, and humble apologies, as well as thanks. How would you characterize Guaman Poma de Ayala? What kind of person was he and who is he "actually" writing about? And who is he defending, Incas or Spaniards?

To conclude this section, let's look at an example of one of the artist/author's woodcuts joining a Spaniard and an Inca (Figure 7.6). Think about how you and your students might interpret this picture, in which a well-dressed Spaniard, a gentleman, sits across from an Inca noble who is serving him what seems to be food and drink. Words are coming from their mouths, representing their speech to each other.

Figure 7.6 The Inca Asks, "What Would you Like to Eat?" and the Spaniard Replies, "Gold and Silver." Drawing by Guaman Poma de Ayala.

The Inca asks, "What would you like to eat?" and the Spaniard replies, "Gold and silver." This exchange can be interpreted in many ways; however, a strong underlying agenda is implied as the Inca is acting as host and asking a normal question of his guest, while the reply can be interpreted as unusual, perhaps hostile, perhaps demanding, perhaps truthful.

How would you judge de Poma's intentions in adding these words to the picture? Would you argue that the artist is friendly to Indian or Spanish causes, both, or neither? What can we learn about relationships from this picture? Does it agree with Guaman Poma de Ayala's overall views as expressed in the letter to the King of Spain? Write your own conclusions about the "temper of the times" of the conquest based on the evidence you have so far.

Do the art and documentation accurately reflect the time? As a major source of knowledge, how has Guaman Poma de Ayala influenced your thinking about contact between a European and a Native American society? If you feel brave and bold, predict a future for Spaniards and Incas up to the present day.

Plan of Action

This mystery invites detective work on the perspectives of witnesses and historians, both contemporary and current, in the way in which they formulate explanations about events that on the surface seem puzzling. Why indeed were a pitiful few Spanish soldiers able to bring down a mighty empire? Why did the Incas not resist more forcibly right away? Why did the Indians submit after the loss of their leader, or did they? Were Inca and Spanish cultures very different or very similar in many ways, and does this make a difference in developing an adequate explanation? Our chronicler of history, Guaman Poma de Ayala, will suggest many causes and factors to you if you but examine the evidence carefully and put the clues together to form a theory. We will help you out by organizing and selecting pictures that build a base for interpretation and then offer multiple suggestions for tentatively solving the mysteries. There are many more you can research on your own and add to the richness of your investigation, if you so desire.

First, even before the chapter opens, we invite you and your students to play detectives on the twelve plates that offer an account of the monthly rituals common to the Inca Empire as depicted by Guaman Poma de Ayala (Figure 7.3). You are free to make lists of details that you think are important and to develop an interpretation of Inca life, religion, statecraft, celebrations, fears and joys, perhaps forming work groups (one group for each two pictures) and then combining perceptions and conclusions into a whole interpretation of their technology, beliefs, and lifestyle. Ask students to draw a "mental map" of the Incas and Spaniards. They can do this as a list or in pictures or as a "web" of ideas. Then gather them into small groups to compare and collate results. You may also engage students with the present through examining a chess set of Incas and Spaniards made for sale and bought by one of the authors in a native market near Cuzco, Peru, in 2008.

Mystery Packet: Drawing Inferences from a Peruvian Chess Set

Examine the three photographs of an Incas and Spaniards chess set from modern Peru (Figures 7.7–7.9). How has the craftsperson portrayed the Spanish? The Incas? Are their facial expressions the same or different? Who is shown as more noble, fierce, angry, or courageous? Why would the native artist choose the two sides for a chess game, and how did the artist construct the people and animals on each side? Why, five hundred years after the conquest, are native artists still portraying the two sides in conflict? What do you think the modern politics of Peru is like and how do Peruvians view their history? What does chess represent as a game? Could other events in history also be turned into a chess game? Why or why not?

Figure 7.7 Two Views of a Chess Set from Peru: Inca Side of the Set.

Figure 7.8 Two Views of a Chess Set from Peru: Spanish Conquistadors Side of the Set. Photos: J. Zevin.

Figure 7.9 Entire Chess Board (Purchased in Cuzco Highlands by J. Zevin). Photo: J. Zevin.

Students should keep notes on their decisions and interpretations for later on in the mystery, adding factors as they go, both pictorial and written. We will help you to dig into many of the details, but, true to our faith in the process of investigation and big messy mysteries, you must remember that we are offering our own fallible insights, along with those of other scholars and teachers.

Factors added to the base will include:

- examples of conflicts between and among Spanish and Incas;
- examples of conflicts between Incas and Incas;
- examples of conflicts between Incas and former Indian allies;
- examples of authority by Inca and Spanish rulers;
- examples of religious practices and customs, Spanish and Inca;
- examples of violence in executing or assassinating leaders;
- examples of persecution and repression;
- examples of disease and disorientation among Indian peoples;
- examples of explicit or implicit moral judgments;
- examples of possible cultural amalgamation between Indian and Spanish ideas.

We invite you to participate in our "plan of action," which is in effect our unit plan for this mystery—a many-layered, complex affair, often poorly understood—before digging into the data from the time period, the sixteenth and early seventeenth centuries in Peru. We hope you will be surprised, interested, and engaged by what is presented.

The case of the Incas and Spaniards can be approached on several mystery levels: minor, middling, and major. First, there is what we would call the popular mystery of the collapse of the Inca Empire. This is perhaps a minor mystery if accepted at face value, but certainly a middling one if you review and re-examine the sources. The factors involved in this are far more complex than the common view of superior Spanish conquistadors invading and defeating, tricking and deceiving Inca rulers and their subjects. You will learn that there was a great deal of trouble shortly before the Spanish entered the area between members of the Inca ruling family, two brothers competing for the throne, Huascar and Atahualpa. There were also indications of rumblings among subject peoples in the Inca Empire, many of whom had separate identities and languages from their overlords. In addition, Inca views of the Spanish were subject to cultural customs and norms that probably worked in favor of the newcomers, the Incas holding customs and beliefs that may be viewed as analogous to those of, or at least quite understandable by, the conquerors.

Second, there is the less well-known mystery of explaining the decline and fall of empires, a middling to major mystery that demands definition and philosophy, as well as a knowledge of at least several empires that have risen and fallen in history. This is a topic discussed and investigated by many noted scholars past and present. Even the word and image of empire evokes strength and power, domination and conquest, but, as we know, even the strongest imperial states tend to decline and "fall" for a variety of reasons. Perhaps we need to raise the question of just what an empire is and how we may define it. We may forget that the Spanish were themselves building an empire at the very time of the invasion, led by the Hapsburg emperor in Europe, Charles V, and that the Incan Empire collapsed and was replaced by a European power, bringing Peru into the modern world system of trade and capital. Why empires decline and collapse is a mystery as many seem very strong on the surface but show fractures under certain conditions such as invasion, rebellion, economic decline, and political weakness. Empires, some would argue, have certain inherent problems, one of which is authority, which may be changed from the top down with relative ease, particularly under conditions of internal rivalry or external threat.

Third, the evidence itself presents mysteries of authentication, concordance, and conflict. Here we have a big and critically important major mystery that recurs over and over in examining evidence and drawing defensible conclusions. Evidence, for example notably in cases of conquests, can be markedly one-sided, corrupt with reporting errors, both purposeful and inadvertent. The conquerors like to write their own histories unimpeded by contentious foes and counterarguments. In the case of the Spanish, their leaders and spiritual guides purposely destroyed countless documents and records across the Americas, melting art objects into lumps of gold, and killing high-ranking keepers of recording systems, so that relatively little is left from the conquered to compare with the records of the new overlords. Most of the records we have are architectural, or from diaries and histories kept by Catholic priests, with a few very rare codexes, or woodcuts, or art objects made by the hands of Incas or Aztecs or Mayans or their immediate descendants who were part of or familiar with both Spanish and Indian cultures.

Even here, most of these records are a bit after the fact, dating to a generation or two past the conquest, and most of the authors or artists are themselves of "mixed" blood—mulattoes, criollos, and mestizos, who are the children of (usually) upper-echelon Spanish fathers and Indian princesses, but other intermarriages as well.

Thus, we have a rather strange and varied but interesting set of sources to look at, and we must reserve judgment on their accuracy and their emotional state. We are focusing on the work of Guaman Poma de Ayala, half-native, half-European, because we think he has a rather distinctive interpretation of events that doesn't quite square with anyone else's completely, offering judgments and caricatures of events as well as factual depictions of local customs, cultures, and leaders. Thus, one mystery involves deciding how much to trust, how to make sense of, our evidence, to develop our own interpretation of contact and conflict between two seemingly very different cultures. Garcilaso, the historian, also had mixed heritage, and both are controversial in that we are never quite sure of their loyalties and perceptions, perhaps tending toward empathy with the Indians sometimes, and with the Spanish at other times.

What we would really love to have is a diary by the last Inca rebel who fled to the interior mountains of Peru, or perhaps the notes of Pizzaro's Indian maids, or a master interpreter of the record-keeping system of knotted strings called *quipu*. You and your students might like to think about what they would like to uncover as "dream" evidence that would give us a balanced view of the dramatic events taking place in Peru in the sixteenth and seventeenth centuries, a drama that is still being played out in a modern country, still deeply divided in geography and population between the descendants of Spanish, Indian, and mixed citizens.

To Do: A Family Account

How is your family governed? Who are the major players? If someone wrote a family history or account of your family, noting who is boss and who is submissive, or not, which member would you trust the most to tell the tale? Would you like to have the story told by an outsider, relative, foreigner? Which of those would you trust, if any? Write an account of a family event, and see if other members of your family agree with it or want to change it. If they want to change the story, let them, and then compare their ideas with your own.

Given these three areas of mystery, we propose a sequence of evidence that will provide an initial set of woodcuts for students to interpret, followed by a series of supplements consisting of primary source pictorial and written evidence, mostly from Guaman Poma de Ayala and Garcilaso de la Vega. These will be presented in a way that is designed to help you and your students add or subtract factors in the historical equation that seeks to explain the mystery of the Inca collapse, Spanish success, raising questions along the way about the sources themselves.

Primary sources will be followed by secondary sources, excerpts from historians and social scientists seeking to explain the Inca collapse in particular, and the collapse of empires in general, with a view to developing theories about the rise and fall of imperial civilizations. You are invited to compare historians' and social scientists' views with your own, with the evidence, and with each other, working to decide on the best interpretation or perhaps working out a satisfying amalgam of ideas and theories.

We have chosen historians not so much for their contrast as for their viewpoints, and ability to complement each other from very different times and perspectives. Garcilaso represents an historian of the time, a Peruvian, while Prescott represents a later American re-teller of the tale for the interested public of the nineteenth century when travel abroad became popular. Davies gives us a rather dramatic but recent professional history of Peru and the Incas, while Ferguson and Wallerstein provide theoretical definitions and explanations for the rise and fall of imperial states that can be applied to Peru or to almost any examples in ancient, modern, or future history.

Finally, we will review and critique the quality of our evidence, its trustworthiness, quantity, viewpoint, and moral center, asking ourselves why an artist or writer or historian might take the position expressed in a story, image, or text. We will take a deep view of culture, bias, and feeling imbedded in what might at first glance seem like "objective" history, of which there is probably none. The postmodern questions that arise should call into question (though not necessarily reject) the evidence—not only its content but also how it is "framed" and presented, how symbols and language are used to influence the viewer and reader, and whether the authors/artists/historians have agendas for influencing our views of the Incas and Spaniards, clashing civilizations, the rise and fall of empires, and our sense of empathy and sympathy for the participants of a long past event that is still of interest and of influence to us today.

Throughout, ideas and suggestions will be offered for classroom conversations, detective work, independent study, and group work, along with lists of additional resources and materials for the highly motivated interested in pursuing this topic more fully.

Let's think about the suggestions we can draw from Guaman Poma de Ayala's drawings. For example:

- What do Guaman's drawings suggest about Inca rituals before the Spanish arrived?
- What do Guaman's drawings suggest about Inca authority before the Spanish arrived?
- What do Guaman's drawings suggest about the Inca lifecycle before the Spanish arrived?
- What similarities or differences do you notice between Spanish and Inca overlords?
- What differences or similarities do you notice between Spanish and Inca religion?
- Overall, would you say the Inca peoples, subjects of the empire, were used to freedom or authority, religious ritual or diversity, direction or initiative?
- What features of the new lifestyle after the Spanish took control might be seen as different: health and disease, economic enterprise, more freedom, or a class system?

Explain how you have arrived at your conclusions using pictures and quotes.

To Do: Developing an Interpretation

Choose one woodcut that interests you and examine every single little detail in it, including words. Make a list of everything you find. Next, develop your own interpretation of that picture, asking if the artist had a purpose, hidden or explicit, or both, in creating the image you have selected for intensive detective investigation.

Historians' Views

Now that you have developed your own view of the contact and clash between Incas and Incas, as well as between Incas and Spanish, based on visual primary sources of a sort, take a look at several noted historians' views on Peru in particular, and empires in general.

The historians have undoubtedly looked at many of the sources you have, and a good deal more, but we want you to boldly go where historians have gone before in assessing their use of the evidence and the theories they offer to explain the course of events. Keep in mind that historians face many of the same problems you do: partial evidence, fragmentation of sources, destruction of records, bias and prejudice, lack of concordance, etc. They are professionals, but subject to most if not all of the pressures that a teacher experiences in presenting lessons on the past, so forge forward with your own verdict on the works presented.

Garcilaso de la Vega on the Fall of the Incas

- How does Garcilaso explain the fall of the Inca Empire?
- How would you describe his style of writing?
- Where do his sympathies lie: with the Incas, the Spanish, impartial?
- What good luck did the Spanish find in Peru?
- Why were the two brothers, Huascar and Atahualpa, enemies?
- What happens when an empire is divided into factions, competing royal families?
- Why did the Spanish argue about killing the emperor Atahualpa?
- What did they finally do and for what reasons?
- Who would you agree with: those for or those against putting the Emperor to death? Why?
- Which factors does Garcilaso view as key to the downfall of the Incas?
- Does our historian make any moral judgments on the Incas, the Spanish, others?
- What judgments, if any, would you make on empire destruction or empire building?

We have read that the daughter of the former king of Quito bore Huaina Capac a son named Atahualpa. As he grew older, this prince became a pleasant gentleman, well built and with an attractive face, as were all the Incas and their sisters, the pallas. He was brave, bold, and courageous and had no fear of combat. His mind was extremely active, his judgment clear, and he was of a shrewd, clever, even wily disposition, with the result that his father loved him very tenderly and liked to have him constantly near him. He would have gladly left him the Empire, if the law of succession had not forbade him to deprive his legitimate, first-born son, Huascar Inca, of the throne. But his love for Atahualpa was such that he resolved to leave him the kingdom of Quito, despite all traditions according to which no one could prejudice the unity of the Empire.

Huaina Capac therefore summoned Huascar Inca, who was living in Cuzco, and having gathered together, with his two princes, all his other sons and numerous head captains and curacas, he addressed the legitimate heir as follows:

"It is well known, Prince, that according to the desires of our ancestor the Inca Manco Capac this kingdom of Quito should fall to you. It has always been thus, and all the land that we have conquered has been annexed to the Empire and subjected to the jurisdiction and power of our imperial city of Cuzco. However, since I love your brother Atahualpa very dearly, and since, too, it pains me to see him poor, it would give me infinite pleasure if you would kindly agree to let me withdraw the kingdom of Quito, which I should like to leave to him, from my conquests to be inherited by yourself. You know, moreover, that this kingdom comes from his maternal ancestors and that, today, it could belong to his mother. In this case, your brother would live there as king, as his virtues merit he should do, and, like the good brother that he is, he would help and serve you much better than if he remained poor. In compensation for this little that I ask of you, many other provinces and vast kingdoms will, with time, be added to all those that you are already certain to receive by inheritance, and your brother will not fail to help you conquer them, as a loyal soldier and captain; then I shall be able to leave you with a contented heart, when our father the Sun calls me to come and rest beside him."

Prince Huascar Inca replied that it was a pleasure as well as an honor for him to satisfy the desire of his lord and father, and that if the latter wanted to give Atahualpa other provinces as well, he should not hesitate to do so.

Huaina Capac was very pleased with this reply. Huascar returned to Cuzco and Atahualpa took possession of the kingdom of Quito, to which his father added other provinces. He surrounded him with experienced captains, and also made him a present of a part of his army, that he might be served, aided, and advised in all matters. In other words, Huaina Capac acted with this prince like a passionately devoted father, who aims at nothing more than the happiness of his beloved son. He decided to spend the rest of his days in Quito, as much in order not to leave Atahualpa, as to supervise and appease the maritime provinces bordering on this kingdom, and which had remained warlike, barbarous, and constantly on the verge of revolt; finally, in order to entirely appease them, he was obliged to move a large part of their population, and replace them by calm, peace-loving peoples, chosen from distant places. This, as we have already told, was the remedy commonly resorted to by the Inca kings to avoid disorder and rebellion.

(de la Vega, 1961, pp. 289–90)

Four or five years passed calmly after Huaina Capac's death. Atahualpa reigned in peace in Quito, without appearing to have any other concern than the welfare of his subjects, and Huascar did the same in Cuzco. Nevertheless, when Huascar considered the limits of his Empire and sought by what means he might enlarge it, following the example set by his ancestors, he was seized with doubt, then with fear. With Chile to the south, the ocean to the west, and the cordillera of the Andes to the east, further conquests seemed out of the question; and the road to the north, which was the only one available, was now closed to him by the kingdom of Quito. With the result that, little by little, he began to regret having yielded to his father's desire in giving this kingdom to Atahualpa. Who knew, after all, whether one day this prince, taking advantage of the situation, might not make a campaign of his own and, increasing his power, which was already great, become his rival and threaten to rob him of the Empire?

This fear began to grow in Huascar's mind, to such an extent, in fact, that unable to stand it any longer, he resolved to send one of his intimates with the following message to Atahualpa:

"You are certainly aware of the fact that, according to the laws of the first Inca, Manco Capac, the kingdom of Quito and all of your provinces belong to the crown and to the Empire of Cuzco. By rights, therefore, I was in no way obliged to relinquish the government of this kingdom to you, and if I did so, it was not because I was forced or compelled, but merely not to oppose your father's wishes. Now that he is no longer with us, I am willing, out of respect for his memory, not to go back on this decision, but on two conditions. These are: first, that you will make no attempt to add so much as a particle of land to the extent of your kingdom, since any newly acquired land belongs by rights to our Empire; the other is that, leaving everything else aside, you will swear allegiance to me and acknowledge that you are my vassal."

Atahualpa listened to this message with all the appearances of the most complete humility and submission. He then took three days to reflect upon it and replied, with shy shrewdness, in a very cautious tone that, in his heart of hearts, he had always considered himself to be vassal of his only lord the Capac Inca; that not only would he not increase the kingdom of Quito, however slightly, but that if his majesty wished to take it back, he would return it immediately, and, like any other of his relatives, would come and live at his court and offer to serve him in peace as in war, according to what it might please his prince and lord to command.

The messenger remained at Atahualpa's court, as he had been ordered to do, to await fresh instructions from the Inca, to whom this declaration was transmitted with the greatest possible celerity by the imperial post. Huascar's reply was not long in coming; being now relieved of his fears, he took pleasure in confirming his brother's titles and prerogatives as king of Quito, and asked him to come to the Cuzco court, at a given date, to pay his homage and take the oath of faithful, loyal allegiance. To which Atahualpa replied that nothing would give him greater pleasure than to carry out His Majesty's wishes; and that in order to give greater solemnity to the taking of the oath he would make to him, he begged Huascar to kindly authorize all the provinces of the kingdom of Quito to come with him in order to celebrate together, in Cuzco, funeral ceremonies for his father Huaina Capac, according to their own traditions and customs; after which they would all take the oath with him.

Huascar agreed to all his brother's requests. He gave him a free hand to organize as he saw fit the funeral ceremonies for Huaina Capac, adding that he would be very happy to see them celebrated in the imperial city according to the customs of the provinces of Quito; and that, in fact, Atahualpa could himself choose the date of this journey.

Thus the two brothers were both equally satisfied; one without imagining that a plot was afoot to rob him of the Empire and even of his life; the other, so taken up with his schemings that, in the end, instead of profiting from them, he became their last victim.

(de la Vega, 1961, pp. 295–7)

Atahualpa's generals had a clear understanding of the situation; their fortunes depended on speed. So they immediately sought out Huascar, in order to engage him in battle before he should have received more numerous reinforcements. The encounter took place on a broad plateau, some two or three leagues south of Cuzco. No peace offers preceded the fighting, and it immediately became a terrible melee that lasted all day. But Huascar's recruits were able to resist very long the attacks of an enemy who was superior to them both in numbers and in experience. They became disbanded and the king himself was obliged to flee with what was left of his guard, reduced now to one thousand men, at the most. Atahualpa's army soon overtook and captured him: and thus it was that Huascar, having been made a prisoner by his brother's generals, saw the last of his faithful troops meet death before his very eyes; most of them fell under the blows of the enemy, or took their own lives in order not to witness any longer their sovereign's downfall. Others preferred to surrender, in order to share their Inca's fate and show the sincerity of their loyalty to his cause.

One can imagine the satisfaction of Atahualpa's generals, whose relatively easy victory had permitted such a rich capture as the royal person of the Inca Huascar! They set up a guard composed of four captains and experienced soldiers who never left him, keeping permanent watch over him night and day. The news of the defeat and imprisonment had been immediately proclaimed throughout the Empire, in order to discourage any possible attempts to resist on the part of his followers, and a special courier had carried the announcement of his victory to Atahualpa.

As a matter of fact, the entire history of the war that set these two brothers, Peru's last kings, one against the other, may be summarized in the events of this day. The other battles mentioned by certain Spanish chroniclers were but skirmishes, during which all frontier garrisons clashed with one another; and the story of Atahualpa's imprisonment and miraculous escape is nothing but a romance that this king invented himself to further his cause. Those who have read the chroniclers know that he had pretended he had been taken prisoner by Huascar and that the Sun had come to his assistance, and had allowed him to escape in a crack in the wall, after having transformed him into a snake. This fable, which took advantage of the Indians' natural credulity, had no other aim than to excuse Atahualpa's own tyranny and cruelty, by presenting him as the preferred son of the Sun-god, and therefore the natural heir of the Incas.

Atahualpa's cruelty, for which he was to become so balefully famous, was not long in manifesting itself in the worst possible manner. With his usual deceit, while feigning a desire to return Huascar to the throne, he summoned to Cuzco all the Incas who were scattered about in the different provinces of the Empire as governors and in other official positions, or as camp commanders, captains, and soldiers. The pretext for this gathering was a grand council that he wanted to hold, so he said, with all those of royal blood, in order to promulgate new laws that would determine the future relationship between the two kingdoms, and permit all their subjects to live in lasting peace and fraternity.

This invitation had the effect desired by its author: all the Incas who were not prevented, by age or illness, from traveling, hastened to Cuzco at the date mentioned, except for those—and they were few—who continued to mistrust this prince. And when they were all gathered together, Atahualpa gave orders that every last one of them should be put to death; for, in reality, it was in this way that he intended to make sure that the future would be his.

. . . [T]hey were not afraid to condemn to death so great and powerful a king as Atahualpa, and he was notified of his sentence . . . Many of the Spaniards protested vehemently when they heard the sentence, not only among Pizarro's companions, but among those of Almagro, because these latter were men with generous hearts, capable of feeling pity.

"How can one dare to put to death a monarch who has never done us the slightest wrong, but, on the contrary, has always shown us perfect courtesy! If we have something to reproach him with, the only thing we can do is to send him to Spain; for we are not competent to judge a king, the decision belonging only to the Emperor. We must consider the question of Spain's national honor. What will the world say when it is learned that we executed a king who has been taken prisoner, after giving him our word that we would liberate him for a ransom, a substantial part of which has already been collected [?] . . .

It is not permissible to kill a man without having heard his story and allowed him to present his defense."

. . . And they concluded by saying that they would appeal his sentence before Charles V . . . Indeed, they did not only protest by word of mouth, but also in writing, and they notified the judge of their dissent. In reply, they were told that they had conducted themselves as traitors to the royal crown of Castile and to their sovereign, the emperor, since they were trying to keep the number of his territories and kingdoms from increasing; that the death of this tyrant would ensure all of them their lives and the Empire, whereas if he were allowed to live it would endanger both. They were told that reports would be sent to His Majesty concerning the mutinies and disorders their attitude had occasioned . . .

In fact, things came to such a pass that they would have hurled themselves at one another and been killed, if God had not stopped it by making others, who were less impassioned than they, intervene between the two groups, and thus succeed in appeasing the Inca's defenders, by telling them that their own lives and the king's service rendered imperative; that is was not right to quarrel over infidels to divide Christians; and that, lastly, there were only fifty persons sharing their point of view, whereas more than three hundred upheld the point of view of the court; and that if they should come to blows, they would only destroy themselves as well as such a rich kingdom as this one, which was theirs for all time, if they put its king to death.

These threats—or these good reasons—finally calmed Atahualpa's protectors, and they consented to his execution, which others carried out.

Once the two kings, Huascar Inca and Atahualpa, who were brothers as well as enemies, were dead, the Spaniards remained supreme masters of both Peruvian kingdoms, there being no one left to oppose or even contradict them, because all the Indians, whether they belonged to Quito or to Cuzco, had remained, after their kings were gone, like sheep without a shepherd.

The war between Huascara and Atahualpa was therefore indirectly the cause of the total downfall of the Inca Empire, from which the Spaniards benefited, as the great Huaina Capac had predicted on his deathbed. But if our Lord God permitted discord between the two brothers, it was because, in His infinite mercy, He wanted in this way to allow the preachers of His gospel and of His Catholic faith, to more easily bring their enlightenment to the gentiles of Peru.

(de la Vega, 1961, pp. 363–5)

Davies on the Fall of the Incas

- How does Davies tell the story of the fall of the Incas?
- What reasons does he point out as key causes for their downfall?
- According to Davies, was either Inca leader a hero?
- Why were the two brothers fighting with each other, over what?
- How did the Spanish manage to defeat and capture the Inca Atahualpa?
- Would you consider the Spanish leaders lucky, insightful, brutal, better equipped than the natives, all of the above, something else? Why?
- Does Davies see Atahualpa as a great leader, Pizzaro?
- How did the Inca emperor die, and what effects did his death have on the empire?
- Were the Spanish fighting alone, or did other Indians help them? Why?
- What helped the Spanish win victories over the Indians?
- Would you say that Davies echoes Garcilaso de la Vega's account, or are there significant differences?
- Does Davies make any judgments on the decline and fall of the Incas?
- Which historian would you trust more: the one writing just after the fall of the Incas or the one writing today?

[T]he Inca realm at the time of the Spanish conquest remained a divided king-dom, in which no final reconciliation had been achieved between the main factions. Surviving accounts . . . stress the gruesome ferocity of the civil war.

The Chronicler Juan de Betanzos is unsparing in his criticism of Huascar, whom he portrays as licentious and cruel. But he is scarcely more flattering when writing of Atahualpa, his own father-in-law, whose atrocities he also describes in detail.

. . .

The victor's (Atahualpa) vengeance was pitiless. Due to certain special ties that linked Huascar and his grandfather, Tupac Inca, not only were the men and women of their ruler's panaca slaughtered, but Tupac's own mummy was burned to cinders, an act of sacrilege so horrific as to be unthinkable in more settled times. The forces of Atahualpa even pillaged the shrines of the holy city of Cuzco.

Huascar's rival, Atahualpa, was confirmed favourite of the armies of the north, previously led by Huayna Capac. Steeled by the rigors of endless campaigning against savage opponents, this force proved to be the strongest in the empire. However, after its decisive triumph, little attempt was made to seek reconcilia-tion with the defeated supporters of Huascar, who had certainly enjoyed wide support not only in Cuzco but in many parts of the empire.

. . .

At the very moment when he (Atahualpa) was celebrating the capture of his rival, Huascar, he received ominous tidings of the approach of a small band of beings so strange that they may have come from outer space. Francisco Pizarro had landed at the head of a contingent . . . of 62 horsemen and 106 foot soldiers . . .

On 24 September 1532, this minute but intrepid force set forth into the inte-rior; though they were still in territory not fully incorporated into the Inca empire, the civil war had left its mark upon its inhabitants; towns were in ruins and from the trees hung many bodies of defiant Indians, loyal to Huascar.

By the most extraordinary coincidence, Atahualpa and his forces were camped near Cajamarca, which happened to lie directly on Pizarro's line of march . . . The Spaniards were by now becoming conscious of the power and sophistication of the empire that they had encountered. Isolated from the sea by a long march, they were now in the midst of a force which de Soto and Pizarro estimated at 40,000!

Notwithstanding their own military experience and skill, and the superiority of their weapons, the invaders had marched into an impasse. They were no doubt mindful of the tactic that had succeeded so well in Mexico, the kidnapping of the ruler, though confronted with such odds it would have been easier for the Inca to capture Pizarro!

. . .

Eighty lords carried (the Inca) on their shoulders, all wearing a rich blue livery. His own person was elaborately adorned with his crown on his head and a collar of large emeralds on his neck. He was seated on the litter, on a small stool with a rich saddle cushion. He stopped when he reached the square . . . When he reached Cajamarca, Atahualpa was most surprised to find not a single Spaniard . . . Pizzaro launched his ambush, and his cavalry charged into the mass of the emperor's lightly armed followers. Some resisted, but the mounted Spaniards managed to seize and overturn the royal litter, whose occupant was thus captured. The Spanish cavalry then charged out into the plain and carnage followed, in the course of which several thousand Indians perished . . .

Pizarro duly drew up a document that guaranteed Atahualpa's freedom if (a roomful) of gold was provided within a specified time . . . Atahualpa appears to have suffered from a naïve illusion that the Spaniards would honor their promise to release him in return for the gold, even to the point of assuming that they would set him free, they would simply pack up their spoils and depart for ever.

. . .

The end was pitiless. As night was falling on 26 July 1533, Atahualpa was led into the middle of the square and tied to a stake. Pressed by Friar Valverde, he requested baptism; as a consequence, instead of being burned alive, he was garroted by a piece of rope . . .

By killing Atahualpa, in Indian eyes the Spaniards had cast themselves in the role of champions of Huascar and as such enjoyed a degree of support among certain elements of the population. However, not only Ecuador, but also much of central Peru was controlled by Atahualpa's northern armies, commanded by his general, Quizquiz. Huascar himself had been killed by his own guards, on order of Atahualpa, when the latter was already a Spanish captive . . . Their southward march was facilitated by the splendid highway built by the Incas.

The Spaniards fought no fewer than four battles against these armies; after the final conclusive encounter in the mountains above Cuzco, the forces of Quito simply lost heart and vanished. The occupation of the outer marches of the empire presented fewer problems. In July, 1535, Diego de Almagro left Cuzco for Chile at the head of a well-equipped force, supported by great trains of porters, together with 12,000 Indians under the command of Paullu, a son of Huayna Capac (Father of the Inca Princes).

(Davies, 2004, pp. 188–9)

Prescott on the Conquest of Peru

- Why does Prescott describe Peru as "mild" despotism?
- What kind of power did an Inca have over his subjects? Why?

- Who controlled Peruvian society according to Prescott?
- What other empires does Prescott think the Incas were like? Why? Do you agree?

The government of Peru was a despotism, mild in its character, but in its form a pure and unmitigated despotism. The sovereign was placed at an immeasurable distance above his subjects. Even the proudest of the Inca nobility, claiming a descent from the same divine original as himself, could not venture into the royal presence unless barefoot . . . As a representative of the Sun, he stood at the head of the priesthood, and presided at the most important religious festivals. He raised armies, and usually commanded them in person. He imposed taxes, made laws, and provided for their execution by the appointment of judges, whom he removed at pleasure. He was the source of everything that flowed—all dignity, all power, all emolument. He was, in short, in the well known phrase of the European despot, "himself the state."

. . .

It was the Inca nobility, indeed, who constituted the real strength of the Peruvian monarchy. Attached to their Prince by ties of consanguinity, they had common sympathies and, to a considerable extent, common interests with him. After the lapse of centuries, they still retained their individuality as a peculiar people. They were to the conquered races of the country what the Romans were to the barbarous hordes of the Empire, or the Normans to the ancient inhabitants of the British Isles.

(Prescott, 1847, pp. 14, 22–3)

Wallerstein on the Fall of the Incas and the Fall of Spain's Empire

- How does Wallerstein explain Spain's discovery of America?
- Why was Spain able to launch fleets of ships to explore and conquer distant lands?
- Why did the Spanish want gold and silver? What were they doing with the wealth?
- How did they use Inca metals to profit, and did it help them build their empire?
- What role does trade play in forming empires according to Wallerstein?
- Why does Wallerstein think that the Spanish were unable to take advantage of the Conquest of Peru?
- Did the Spanish improve their own economy, Peru's economy, neither, or both?
- Does the world economy of the sixteenth century seem simple or complicated? Explain.
- What really matters to Wallerstein in forming empires or in wrecking them?
- Does Wallerstein's story compare with Davies'? Garcilaso's? Why or why not?
- What factors does Wallerstein talk about: mostly economic, political, or social? Why?

[I]t was not luck that accounts for Spain's discovery of America. She was the country best endowed in the context of the times "not only to seize the opportunities that were offered, but to create them for herself." . . . Spain succeeded . . . in the sixteenth century in creating a vast empire in the Americas, one as large as the cost of maritime transport would permit. It meant the lightning growth of transatlantic trade, the volume increasing eightfold between 1510 and 1550, and threefold again between 1550 and 1610. The central focus of this trade was a monopoly in Seville, which in many ways became the key bureaucratic structure of Spain. The central item was bullion. At first, Spaniards simply picked up the gold already mined by the Incas and used for ritual. It was a bonanza. Just as this was running out, the Spaniards succeeded in discovering the method of silver amalgam which enabled them to profitably mine the silver which existed in such abundance, and which represented the truly significant inflow of bullion to Europe.

The "lightning growth of trade" was accompanied by a spectacular political expansion in Europe as well . . . The nascent world economy seemed as though it might become another imperium. Charles V (of Spain) was not alone in the attempt to absorb the European world economy into his imperium. Francis I of France was trying to do the same thing, and France had the advantages of size and centrality.

(Wallerstein, 1974, pp. 169–71)

[O]ne crucial bottleneck became the growing financial demands of imperial state machineries and the consequent inflation of public credit which led to imperial bankruptcies of mid-century. Charles V had run through states and their merchants as sources of finance . . . The consequences for the extended Hapsburg Empire were great. It led directly to the beginning of Spain's decline.

. . . [B]ureaucratically, she (Spain) was already spread too thin to exploit her empire properly. To maintain her empire in America, she had to invest in a growing bureaucracy to keep the Spanish colonists and their allies among the Indian nobility under control.

(Wallerstein, 1974, p. 180)

Nor did Spain have the energy to control entirely its own settlers. To keep their political loyalty, it made many economic concessions. One of these was to forbid Indians independent bases of economic power . . . The settlers were nonetheless dependent on continued Spanish support, not so much against Indian and African slave rebellions, as against English and other intrusions into their trade and hence their profit margins.

. . .

[Moving to the Americas] provided a job outlet for Spaniards who needed it and an immediate source of income for the Spanish state, since positions in the American colonial bureaucracy were sold. On the other hand, the growing population of Spaniards living off the land in America in the face of economic contraction (in Europe), along with the disastrous demographic decline of the Indians under early Spanish rule, combined to create a "century of depression" in Spanish America.

(Wallerstein, 1974, pp. 186–9)

Ferguson on Imperial Power

- Does Ferguson present a general theory of empire?
- What does he see as the advantages of empire, if any?
- What does he see as possible disadvantages of empire, if any?
- Does he help your understanding of the fall of the Incas? Why or why not?
- Overall, would you say Ferguson favors empires or disapproves of their formation?

[I]mperial power can be acquired by more than one type of political system. The self-interested objectives of imperial expansion range from the fundamental need to ensure the security of the metropolis by imposing order on enemies at its (initial) borders to the collection of rents and taxation from subject peoples, to say nothing of the perhaps more obvious prizes of new land for settlement, raw materials, treasure and manpower, all of which, it should be emphasized, would need to be available at lower prices than they would have cost in free exchange with independent peoples if the cost of conquest and colonization were to be justified. At the same time, an empire may provide "public goods" — that is, intended or unintended benefits of imperial rule flowing not to the rulers but the ruled and indeed beyond to third parties; less conflict, increased trade or investment, improved justice and governance, better education . . . or improved material conditions.

. . . [I]mperial rule can be implemented by more than one kind of functionary; soldiers, civil servants, settlers, voluntary associations, firms and local elites all can in different ways impose the will of the center on the periphery. There are almost as many varieties of imperial economic system, ranging from slavery to laissez-faire, from one form of serfdom to another.

. . .

The precise combination of all these variables determines, among other things, the geographical extent, and of course the duration, of an empire.

(Ferguson, 2005, pp. 11–12)

Evaluating Historians' Views

- Which accounts of the Incas and Spaniards did you enjoy most? Why?
- Does it matter when historians write about the past? Does it matter if they are from that time, or if they write later on? Does it matter who and what they are and for whom they wrote? How might an audience and culture shape a history, even someone like de la Vega? After all, did de la Vega write for a mostly Indian or Spanish audience?
- What makes for a trustworthy and believable account?
- Does detail impress you and raise the evaluation score?
- Does a good story impress you and raise the score?
- Are you most impressed with theory about empires, with big, broad general interpretations that apply to many cases, or do you like to stick to particular examples? Why?
- Is it easy or difficult or impossible to write history without making generalizations or judgments?
- Can empires work for the better? Can empires cause pain and suffering?
- Do you have any final verdicts to pronounce on the Spanish in Peru? On the Incas and their empire?
- How would you judge an empire's success or failure, including our own American Empire?
- Who helped you the most in understanding the Conquest of Peru: de la Vega, Prescott, Davies, Wallerstein, or Ferguson, or a combination of all or most? Explain.

To Do: A Final Project

Write your own three-hundred-word history of the Incas and the Spaniards for younger children, say ages eight to ten years. How would you tell the story? What would you put in as most important and what might you leave out? Who would you feel most sorry for, if anyone? Would you make value judgments or avoid them? Why? What do you think would be the point of your history of the Incas and the Spaniards?

Summary and Conclusions

Thus, we have come to the end of our Incas and Spaniards mystery, focusing on both visual interpretation and written records, each of which has added, we hope, to our understanding of a complex event, the meeting of two worlds, new and old. We hope that working out this mystery has deepened your appreciation of the clash of civilizations, and has offered insights to the state of world affairs in the sixteenth and seventeenth centuries, demonstrating how European politics and policies impacted upon the native peoples of South America.

The Incas themselves are a subject of mystery because the Spanish destroyed most of the original materials and *quipu*, leaving us with rather sparse and often biased sources to work with; thus our decision to show you the striking woodcuts of Guaman Poma de Ayala as historical evidence that is a melding of both Spanish and Inca viewpoints. Civil war in Peru gave the Spanish a great opportunity for conquest at precisely the right time, and they shrewdly exploited local conflicts to their advantage. In addition, we suggest that the drawings offer insights into an Inca psychology that was largely authoritarian, imperial, and tightly controlled, with reverence for multiple gods and goddesses expressed as idol worship. *Huacas* (spiritual figurines) are shown in a number of Guaman Poma de Ayala's drawings, and they are revered in much the same way as saints are later, a practice that could easily be converted by Catholic missionaries to their faith. Even though comparatively few Spanish conquistadors destroyed the Inca Empire, they too represented an empire, with many similarities as well as differences, but most playing into their hands at the time they invaded Peru. Historians, new and old, provide us with dramatic interpretations of events from political and economic perspectives that make the Incas and Spaniards much more than a local dispute, but a world event, strongly influenced by the development of imperial conflict and capitalism in early modern Europe. In effect, Peru became a colonial outpost of Spain settled on the base of a once mighty, already organized and tamed empire constructed by native Inca overlords. There is, of course, much more to know and be said about this complex topic, and we leave that to your initiative for further study.

Contact between Europeans and native peoples, such as between Spaniards and Incas, is part of what is often called the Columbian Exchange, which produced massive changes in global eating habits and food supplies, dramatically altering the lives of local peoples in the Americas. Spaniards—descendants of Celts and Romans, speaking a Latin language—conquered much of South America, but also produced resistance by many native peoples attempting to save the integrity of their own cultures. Overall, we might argue that contact over the last five hundred years or so has produced a *monde du metisse* or mixed (mestizo) world, but with persisting remnants of two different traditions, native and European.

References and Further Reading

Bauer, B. (1992) *The Development of the Inca State*, Austin: University of Texas Press.

Cabello de Balboa, M. (1951) *Miscelanea Antartica*, Lima: Universidad de San Marcos.

Canizares-Esguerra, J. (2001) *How to Write the History of the New World*, Palo Alto, CA: Stanford University Press.

Davies, N. (1995) *The Incas*, Boulder: University of Colorado Press.

Davies, N. (2004) *The Ancient Kingdoms of Peru*, London, UK: Andean World.

de Betanzos, J. (1987) *Suma y Narracion de los Incas*, Madrid: Atlas Press.

de la Vega, G. (1961) *The Incas: Royal Commentaries of the Inca* (trans. Maria Jolas from the critical edition of Alain Gheerbrandt), New York: Orion Press.

de la Vega, G. (1970) *El Inca. Prima Parte de Lost Commentaries Reales de los Incas*, Buenos Aires: Angel Rosenblatt Press.

Ferguson, N. (2005) *Colossus: Rise and Fall of the American Empire*, New York: Penguin Books.

Guaman Poma de Ayala (2004) *Historia de los Incas, Relacion de su Gobierno*, Cuzco: Royal Copenhagen Museum.

Guaman Poma de Ayala (2006) *The First New Chronicle and Good Government*, abridged (trans. and ed. David Frye), Indianapolis: Hackett Publishing.

Guaman Poma de Ayala (2009) *The First New Chronicle and Good Government* (trans. Roland Hamilton), Austin: University of Texas Press.

Hemming, J. (1970) *The Conquest of the Incas*, London, UK: Macmillan.

Hyslop, J. (1984) *The Inca Road System*, New York: Academic Press.

MacQuarrie, K. (2006) *The Last Days of the Incas*, New York: Simon & Schuster.

Malpass, M. A. (1996) *Daily Life in the Inca Empire*, Indianapolis: Hackett Publishing.

Marrin, A. (1989) *Inca and Spaniard: Pizarro and the Conquest of Peru*, Springfield, IL: Atheneum Press.

Meltraux, A. (1970) *History of the Incas*, New York: Schoken Books.

Moseley, M. E. (1992) *The Incas and Their Ancestors*, London, UK: Thames & Hudson.

Prescott, W. H. (1847) *History and Conquest of Peru*, New York: Lippincott.

Santillan, H. (1968) "Relacion de Origen, Descendencia, Politica y Gobierno de los Incas," in F. E. Barba (ed.), *Cronicas Peruanas de interes Indigena*, Madrid: Atlas.

Sarmiento de Gamboa, P. (1988) *Historia de los Incas*, Buenos Aires: Editores Emcee.

Wallerstein, I. (1974) *The Modern World System I: Capitalist Agriculture and the Origins of the European World-Economy in the Sixteenth Century*, New York: Academic Press.

Zuidema, R. T. (1990) *Inca Civilization in Cuzco*, Austin: University of Texas Press.

eight
Secrets of Secret Societies

A dozen wise men can be more easily caught than a hundred fools!

(Russian proverb)

In this chapter, we invite you and your students to investigate some famous and some not-so-famous secret societies formed in the course of history (e.g., Figure 8.1). Secret societies, in our view, are a special form of human behavior that provides multiple, overlaying mysteries—both real mysteries and those that can be "manufactured" for the classroom. Here, we introduce each secret society so that you will feel on solid ground when it comes to teaching, but we will also provide you with manufactured mysteries for students in the form of authentic documents. The manufacturing takes the form of eliminating proper names, dates, and places from the documents so that students must engage in a search for context by reading cues, finding clues, and conducting their own (Internet) research.

Thus, the mysteriousness of documents will be increased as a way to engage students in historical inquiry. In other chapters, the mystery may reside in comparing sources, contrasting historians, examining multiple interpretations, or arguing theory. But in this chapter, the documentary evidence will first be presented as a kind of simulation that mimics the often fragmentary and eroded sources historians have to reconstruct on the way to developing an explanation or theory. Thus, our investigation of secret societies in history will proceed largely inductively: sources first, interpretation second, and comprehensive explanation or theory last.

Figure 8.1 Skull and Crossbones Secret Society at Yale University, c.1947, G. H. W. Bush Left of Clock. This secret society is based at Yale University, in New Haven, Connecticut. The society's alumni organization, which owns the society's real property and oversees the organization's activity, is the Russell Trust Association, and is named after General William Huntington Russell, founding member of the Bones' organization along with fellow classmate Alphonso Taft. In conversation, the group is known as "Bones," and members have been known as "Bonesmen." Photo: George Bush Presidential Library and Museum, Yale Years, Archive # HS306.

Rationale

Each of the secret societies we have chosen plays an important role in history, and each produced a rather striking statement of principles often in the form of an "oath" or "constitution" or "declaration" meant to be spoken aloud at meetings behind closed doors, not for general consumption by the public. What makes secret societies so fascinating is not only their secretiveness but also the elaborate metaphors and allegorical language used to describe their goals and operating methods.

Secret societies usually develop in historical contexts in which there are deep-rooted conflicts between local populations and rulers. The rulers can vary considerably: some local and native, others dominating by means of conquests, armed might, and imperial hegemony. The societies often begin by fighting for good causes, at least in *their* eyes, but may turn into closed communities that wreak violence on those who don't agree with them or who support the governmental authorities. Many also have more than one element of gore and mayhem (usually appealing to middle and senior high students), calling for sacrifice, bloodshed, and passion, usually directed against some set of authorities.

In today's world there are actually quite a few secret revolutionary societies operating around the globe, although we usually refer to these as *terrorist groups*. Examples include Al-Qaeda, the Tamil Tigers, Shining Path, Euzkadi (Basque separatists), and Zapatistas, and perhaps the rather peaceful and persecuted Falun Gong. Many students may be surprised to discover that many secret societies begin with nationalist or religious freedom fighters who represent noble ideals in a repressive political atmosphere, but who later take on the characteristics of their enemies and slowly grow into radicals, revolutionaries, or terrorists. This has happened many times in world history, leaving us present-day folks with a very negative view of current realities. Perhaps the best example of this is the Mafia, which began as a nationalistic movement opposing foreign rule in Italy and morphed into a secret criminal organization, often exploiting and controlling the very people it once sought to liberate.

One of the mysteries we would like you to think about is why people are willing to join rebellious, angry, violent groups, even to the point of their own death and destruction, often taking their secrets with them to the grave. So although this is a rather gruesome subject to deal with, it is a topic we believe needs serious discussion and has wide application throughout great swaths of history. Despite (or because of) the nasty aspects of many secret societies, student interest should be attracted by the first-hand documentation, which in many cases rivals television violence and movie mayhem.

It is often easier to study groups that operated in the past rather than those working now because we have historical perspective. Where a group once seemed heroic, or darkly violent and menacing, we can see why it changed over time to act destructively within its nations, or even across continents. Distance helps us to view groups and actions more objectively, we hope, although once we get into the subject we may very well become upset all over again or maybe for the first time.

Defining a Secret Society

A big question to open with concerning secret societies is definition. Is any group of two or more people who join together and keep secrets a society? What size does a society have to attain to be considered? How many secrets have to be kept? Does the group need revolutionary goals or can goals be conservative as well? Does the group have to have political goals, or are social or economic goals sufficient?

Are street gangs secret societies? What about clubs, or sorority and fraternal organizations, like the Masons, the Elks, or Knights of Columbus? Can the group be local, or does membership have to be cross-national or international? In short, where do we draw the line on what we consider qualified secret societies.

For the purposes of this chapter, the definition will be opened and re-opened any number of times, drawing students into discussion as they construct their own working definitions. Along with questions of definition, we also need to consider the causes and conditions that give rise to secret societies.

Secret societies may arise for many causes, with varying social conditions and historical events contributing to their development. However, there seem to be clear, strong patterns exhibited by local, national, and international groups, past and present, that we may loosely characterize as secret societies. A test case may be Al-Qaeda, or Falun Gong: do these groups qualify as secret societies?

First of all, secret societies are most often found in what the organizers view as an oppressive and undemocratic political situation. Members of secret societies usually dislike or intensely hate the government in power, and join together to oppose it by means fair and foul. Because the situation is undemocratic, members of secret societies have little means to express their grievances or work for change. They are out of power, or never had any power. As conditions become worse and worse, and there is increasing persecution (particularly in the eyes of the members), these groups resort to violence, bombings, murder, warfare, and the kinds of skullduggery that are found in a potboiler mystery story.

But in history, there are examples of violent political conflict and persecution to fill many books. In the case of secret societies, many of the leaders and members were literate and did us the favor of leaving behind wonderful documents that were designed to induct people into membership, justify goals and methods (however scary), and outline organizational duties and responsibilities. In some ways, secret societies mimic clubs, exclusive groups, and military hierarchies.

Defining what we mean by secret societies should be the subject of an opening discussion with students, because it is not always clear how secret they are, or what their true goals may be. We suggest that you open with a tentative definition (or several) and keep revising them as you proceed through the examples we provide—and include others you might like to add as well.

Using the Mystery Packet

First, you and your students should read, describe, identify, and interpret each document, keeping in mind that the relevant dates, names, and places have been removed to enhance the mystery. Thus, you will have to supply context—through clues, cues, language, signs, and symbols—as a step toward placing each document into some "guessed" historical time and place. Part of the mystery of this reading activity will be to gather clues that will reveal time, place, people, and historical context.

Second, you and your students should compare and contrast each document, each group, each society, according to several criteria, for example:

1 goals and purposes;
2 plan of action;
3 literary and graphic styles;
4 loves and hates;
5 rituals and ceremonies;
6 politics and social status;
7 organization and leadership;

 8   support or rejection of violence;
 9   historical context;
10   any other criterion you would like to add!

Third, after students have compared societies—identifying patterns, noting likenesses and differences—they should form hypotheses about the probable *causes* of particular secret societies, short and long term, based on their own statements in their oaths, constitutions, etc. You and your students will engage in historical interpretation from unreliable (i.e., one-sided) sources. This is a great activity in and of itself in that it leads to questions about how historical perceptions are formed and whether they emerge from one-sided or many-sided sources of information. You and your students will also address a potentially terrifying problem, because it raises questions about viewpoint and value judgment. This is the issue of which of our secret societies had legitimate causes and which were more like terrorists, which were seeking constructive outcomes and which destructive. (The quip is that "one person's freedom fighter is another person's terrorist.")

The Secret Societies (For your Eyes Only!)

We will examine a set of documents drawn from a variety of secret or semi-secret groups that have arisen in the course of world history. Each was chosen because it has special historical significance (and there are many other worthy groups to study) and because each is from a different culture and continent: Europe, America, Asia, and Africa. Thus, we get to look at a broad swath of groups, and compare their principles and characters, as well as look for potential connections and lines of influence from one to another.

We ask a special favor of you in this chapter: go along with reading each document, as is, with parts missing, acting in your role as detective rather than classroom leader for now. In effect, we are asking that you play a student approaching rather mysterious and unfamiliar territory, making educated guesses about meaning, signs, and symbols, language, probable context, time and place, and historical significance.

Each document is faithful to its original (as far as we can check) but proper names, dates, and places have been deleted to make the detective work more about investigative interpretation and close reading than about identification of historical settings. We ask you to play student and pinpoint details of interest, note any words, signs, symbols, or clues that you think will help you understand the document and its authors.

Once your interpretation has been formulated, you can start making predictions or inferences about the time and place of each document and work to set them in the context of world history. You can pose questions to stimulate thinking about causes and consequences of secret societies, such as:

1   What are common goals for secret societies?
2   Who or what organizations do secret societies usually oppose and hate?
3   Do the documents generally support peaceful or violent political action? Why?

4   Do the documents seem legal, polemical, open, democratic, and/or angry? Why?

5   How would you describe the emotional charge in each document and as a group?

6   When might people decide to join a secret society? Would membership change their lives?

7   Would you be willing to join any of those groups whose documents you have read? Why or why not? What would membership mean?

8   As a group, do the documents from secret societies remind you of any current events, recent news, or groups today? How or how not?

9   If you compared one of the documents to the Declaration of Independence, or U.S. Constitution, would there be more similarities or more differences?

10 How might secret societies be brought into the open? Would a nation or group of nations be better off or worse off if secret societies developed within them? Why?

Mystery Packet: Causes and Consequences of Secret Societies

Constitution of the Black Hand (Union or Death) (Serbia)

I. Purpose and Name

Article 1. For the purpose of realizing the national ideals—the Unification of Serbdom—an organization is hereby created, whose members may be any Serbian irrespective of sex, religion, place or birth, as well as anybody else who will sincerely serve this idea.

Article 2. The organization gives priority to the revolutionary struggle rather than relies on cultural striving, therefore its institution is an absolutely secret one for wider circles.

Article 3. The organization bears the name: "Ujedinjenje ili Smrt."

Article 4. In order to carry into effect its task the organization will do the following things:

Following the character of its *raison d'etre* it will exercise its influence over all the official factors in Serbia—which is the Piemont of Serbdom—as also over all the strata of the State and over the entire social life in it;

It will carry out a revolutionary organization in all the territories where Serbians are living;

Beyond the frontiers, it will fight with all means against all enemies of this idea;

It will maintain friendly relations with all the States, nations, organisations, and individual persons who sympathise with Serbia and the Serbian race;

It will give every assistance to those nations and organisations who are fighting for their own national liberation and unification.

II. Official Departments of the Organization

Article 5. The supreme authority is vested in the Supreme Central Directorate with its headquarters at Belgrade. Its duty will be to see that the resolutions are carried into effect.

Article 6. The number of members of the Supreme Central Directorate is unlimited—but in principle it should be kept as low as possible.

Article 7. The Supreme Central Directorate shall include, in addition to the members from the Kingdom of Serbia, one accredited delegate from each of the organisations of all the Serbian regions: (1) Bosnia and Herzegovina, (2) Montenegro, (3) Old Serbia and Macedonia, (4) Croatia, Slovenia, and Symria (Srem), (5) Voyvodina, (6) Sea-coasts.

Article 8. It will be the task of the Supreme Central Directorate to carry out the principles of the organization within the territory of the Kingdom of Serbia.

Article 9. The duty of each individual Provincial Directorate will be to carry out the principles of the organization within the respective territories of each Serbian region outside the frontiers of the Kingdom of Serbia. The Provincial Directorate will be the supreme authority of the organization within its own territory.

Article 10. The subdivisions of the organization into District Directorates and other units of authority shall be established by the By-Laws of the organization which shall be laid down, and if need be, from time to time amended and amplified by the Supreme Central Directorate.

Article 11. Each Directorate shall elect, from amongst its own members, its President, Secretary and Treasurer.

Article 12. By virtue of the nature of his work, the Secretary may act as a Deputy President. In order that he may devote himself entirely to the work of the organization, the Secretary's salary and expenses shall be provided by the Supreme Central Directorate.

Article 13. The positions of President and Treasurers shall be un-salaried.

Article 14. All official business questions of the organization shall be decided in the sessions of the Supreme Central Directorate by a majority of votes.

Article 15. For the execution of such decisions of the organization, the absolute executive power shall be vested in the President and the Secretary.

Article 16. In exceptional and less important cases the President and the Secretary shall make the decisions and secure their execution, but they shall report accordingly at the next following session of the Supreme Central Directorate.

Article 17. For the purpose of ensuring a more efficient discharge of business, the Supreme Central Directorate shall be divided into sections, according to the nature of the work.

Article 18. The Supreme Central Directorate shall maintain its relations with the Provincial Directorates through the accredited delegates of the said provincial organisations, it being understood that such delegates shall be at the same time members of the Supreme Central Directorate; in exceptional cases, however, these relations shall be maintained through special delegates.

Article 19. Provincial Directorates shall have freedom of action. Only in cases of the execution of broader revolutionary movements will they depend upon the approval of the Supreme Central Directorate.

Article 20. The Supreme Central Directorate shall regulate all the signs and watchwords, necessary for the maintenance of secrecy in the organization.

Article 21. It shall be the Supreme Central Directorate's duty punctually and officially to keep all the members of the organization well posted about all the more important questions relative to the organization.

Article 22. The Supreme Central Directorate shall from time to time control and inspect the work of its own departments. Analogically, the other Directorates shall do likewise with their own departments.

III. The Members of the Organization

Article 23. The following rule, as a principle, shall govern all the detailed transactions of the organization: All communications and conversations to be conducted only through specially appointed and authorized persons.

Article 24. It shall be the duty of every member to recruit new members, but it shall be understood that every introducing member shall vouch with his own life for all those whom he introduces into the organization.

Article 25. The members of the organization as amongst themselves shall not be known to one another. Only the members of Directorates shall be known personally to one another.

Article 26. In the organization the members shall be registered and known by their respective numbers. But the Supreme Central Directorate must know them also by their respective names.

Article 27. The members of the organization must unconditionally obey all the commands given by their respective Directorates, as also all the Directorates must obey unconditionally the commands which they receive direct from their superior Directorate.

Article 28. Every member shall be obliged to impart officially to the organization whatever comes to his knowledge, either in his private life or in the discharge of his official duties, in as far as it may be of interest to the organization.

Article 29. The interest of the organization shall stand above all other interests.

Article 30. On entering into the organization, every member must know that by joining the organization he loses his own personality; he must not expect any glory for himself, nor any personal benefit, material or moral. Consequently the member who should dare to try to exploit the organization for his personal, or class, or party interests shall be punished by death.

Article 31. Whosoever has once entered into the organization can never by any means leave it, nor shall anybody have the authority to accept the resignation of a member.

Article 32. Every member shall support the organization by his weekly contributions. The organisations, however, shall have the authority to procure money, if need be, by coercion. The permission to resort to these means may be given only by Supreme Central Directorate within the country, or by the regional Directorates within their respective region.

Article 33. In administering capital punishment the sole responsibility of the Supreme Central Directorate shall be to see that such punishment is safely and unfailingly carried into effect without any regard for the ways and means to be employed in the execution.

IV. The Seal and the Oath of Allegiance

Article 34. The Organization's official seal is thus composed: In the center of the seal there is a powerful arm holding in its hand an unfurled flag on which—as a coat of arms—there is a skull with crossed bones; by the side of the flag, a knife, a bomb and a phial of poison. Around, in a circle, there is the following inscription, reading from left to right: "Unification or Death", and in the base: "The Supreme Central Directorate".

Article 35. On entering into the organization the joining member must pronounce the following oath of allegiance:

"I (the Christian name and surname of the joining member), by entering into the organization "Unification or Death", do hereby swear by the Sun which shineth upon me, by the Earth which feedeth me, by God, by the blood of my forefathers, by my honor and by my life, that from this moment onward and until my death, I shall faithfully serve the task of this organization and that I shall at all times be prepared to bear for it any sacrifice. I further swear by God, by my honor and by my life, that I shall unconditionally carry into effect all its orders and commands. I further swear by my God, by my honor and by my life, that I shall keep within myself all the secrets of this organization and carry them with me into my grave. May God and my comrades in this organization be my judges if at any time I should wittingly fail or break this oath!"

V. Supplementary Orders

Article 36. The present Constitution shall come into force immediately.

Article 37. The present Constitution must not be altered.

Done at Belgrade this 9th day of May, 1911 A.D.

Signed:

Major Ilija Radivojevitch
Vice-Consul Bogdan Radenkovitch
Colonel Cedimilj A. Popovitch
Lt.-Col. Velimir Vemitch
Journalist Ljubomir S. Jovanovitch
Col. Dragutin T. Dimitrijevitch
Major Vojin P. Tanksoitch
Major Milan Vasitch
Col. Milovan Gr. Milovanovitch

(Pozzi, 1935)

Questions: The Rules of the Union or Death Society

- Why does the constitution call for union or death?

- What are the jobs of the organization? Will the organization pay attention only to its own business or link itself to outside groups as well?

- What is the Supreme Central Directorate and why should its members be kept low?

- Is the Directorate a kind of government? How can you decide?

- What duties are assigned to members? Why does the membership drive include the rule that "every . . . member shall vouch with his own life for all those whom he introduces"?

- Why must commands be obeyed "unconditionally": what does that mean exactly?

- Why are contributions necessary, even by coercion?

- What is the seal or symbol of the organization (see Figure 8.3)? Do you like it?

- Read the oath aloud. Why does the oath call for swearing "by the blood of my forefathers" and "by my God"?

- What are the consequences for breaking the oath or giving up secrets?

- Would you have liked to join if you had been there?

- When and where and by whom do you think this statement was written?

Teacher's Contextual Background: Union or Death Society

On October 6, 1908, Austria annexed Serbia and Herzegovina, taking control directly. A few days later, a number of men, some public officials and army officers, held a meeting in City Hall in the capital, Belgrade, and formed a secret society called *Narodna Odbrana*, which might be translated as People's Defense or Nation's Defense. Thus began the effort to develop an organization to work against Austria and its empire. Extensions of this group were formed in almost all of the Slavic provinces and states in the Balkans. At first, they trained members for a possible war between Austria and Serbia, but Austria's pressure on the Serbian government forced them to redirect their efforts toward education and propaganda.

As a result, many dissatisfied members formed a new secret organization to continue terrorism against Austria, with ten leaders meeting on May 9, 1911, to form the "Union or Death" society, also known popularly as the Black Hand (Figure 8.2). They developed a constitution, seal (Figure 8.3), oath, and set of offices to fill, gathering several hundred to several thousand (accounts and estimates vary greatly) members by the beginning of WWI. Many were Serbian army officers who swore

Figure 8.2 Leaders of the Serbian Union or Death Society (image in public domain).

Figure 8.3 Union or Death Society Official Seal, Appeared in *The Origins of the First World War* by Sidney Bradshaw Fay (1921) (image in public domain).

absolute allegiance to the organization and trained as guerillas and saboteurs. Small cells were formed locally with only a few (the top ten leaders) having knowledge of the total capacity and placement of the members. Colonel Dragutin Dimitrijevic was considered the leader of the executive committee. They were known to the Serbian government, and supported by high-ranking people, while also opposing some of what they saw as weak government policies.

By the start of WWI, the Black Hand both influenced and intimidated members of the government, and refusing their demands could result in assassination. Dimitrijevic, the leader, decided that Archduke Ferdinand, soon to visit Sarajevo, should be assassinated. And so he trained three young men in bombing and sharpshooter techniques.

One was Pincip, who would eventually kill the Archduke as he paraded through the streets of the Bosnian capital, setting off WWI. They were hoping that Russia would aid them, although Russia had previously shown timidity in interfering with Austria on behalf of its Slavic brethren, the Serbs. Princip and six colleagues, all highly trained in terror techniques, were sneaked across the border into Bosnia, where they hung out in Sarajevo for at least a month. Rumors circulated that an attempt was in the making, but the evidence seems to indicate that neither the Serbian government nor the Black Hand nor the National Defense organization did anything to stop them.

Pincip and many others, all local, were arrested and placed on trial on October 12, 1914. As far as anyone knew, the ringleaders of the organization were free and enjoying their liberty in Belgrade. When the prosecutor asked Princip if he admitted guilt, he is reported to have replied, "I am not a criminal, for I have removed an evildoer. I meant to do a good deed."

And, as they say, the rest is history.

Tai Pings (China)

The Ten Heavenly Commandments
1   Honor and worship the Lord God

2   Do not worship false gods

3   Do not take the name of the Lord God in vain

4   On the seventh day, worship and praise the Lord God for his grace

5   Be filial and obedient to thy Father and Mother

6   Do not kill or injure men

7   Do not indulge in wickedness and lewdness
      In the world there are many men, all brothers; in the world there are many women, all sisters. For the sons and daughters of Heaven, the

men have men's quarters and the women have women's quarters; they are not allowed to intermix. Men or women who commit adultery or who are licentious are considered monsters; this is the greatest possible transgression of the Heavenly Commandments. The casting of amorous glances, the harboring of lustful imaginings about others, the smoking of opium, and the singing of libidinous songs are all offenses against the Heavenly Commandment.

8   Do not steal or rob

Poverty and riches are granted by the Lord God, and whosoever steals or plunders the property of others transgresses the Heavenly Commandment.

9   Do not think tell (or spread) falsehoods

All those who speak wildly, falsely, or treacherously, and those who use coarse or vile language transgress against the Heavenly Commandment.

10   Do not think covetous thoughts

When a man looks upon the beauty of another's wife or daughter and then covets that man's wife or daughter; when a man looks upon the richness of another man's possessions and then covets that man's possessions; or when a man engages in gambling and buys lottery tickets and bets on names, all of these are transgressions against the Heavenly Commandment.

(de Bary and Lufrano, 2001, pp. 220–1; from Xiao Yishan, *Taiping Tianguo congshu*)

You Decide: Interpreting the Tai Ping Commandments

- Are these commandments like or unlike the Ten Commandments of the Bible?
- What rewards are offered to those who have rendered meritorious service in the second part? Why might the people who read this be asked to engage in agriculture in peacetime and fight the enemy and bandits in wartime?
- Why is land distributed based on numbers, not sex? Would this be popular or unpopular?
- Why is land for all to till, all to eat, all to share? Whose blessings are given for sharing land and produce?
- What sorts of products are people asked to grow? Why are some products saved by the state? Who is the Supreme Ruler? The Heavenly Father? The Lord God on High, the True Ruler of Great Peace?

- Does this document represent a well-organized group or a poorly organized group?
- Why are there festivals and ceremonies ordered?
- Why is there so much emphasis on sharing, cooperating, and compassion?
- What kind of language is used throughout the selections: formal or informal, practical or flowery, individual or communal? Why?
- What clues can be gathered from these documents about the character, origins, and time periods of the people who wrote this material?
- What was probably the overall purpose of the direction and exhortations given to people?
- Why the mix of religion and military ideas and practices? Was this written during a peaceful or warlike period? How can you tell?

Teacher's Contextual Background: Tai Pings

China was a heavily populated country in ancient times, and by the early part of the nineteenth century contained a very large number of people. China was also a distinctive nation with its own languages and cultures, usually led by rulers who were of Chinese origin. Monarchs ruled through large administrations across a vast territory and most people from peasants to nobles recognized and supported their governments.

At the start of the nineteenth century, Western powers—England, Germany, Portugal, and later the United States—began to interfere in Chinese affairs. In 1842, China lost the "Opium War" with Britain because the English wanted to profit from the sale of opium to the Chinese, a big market. Many other takeovers and influences from the Western powers created anger among Chinese people, who resented foreigners making decisions for them. In addition, China was ruled in the nineteenth and twentieth centuries by a dynasty, the Manchus, who many considered foreign themselves.

Merchants were angry about the loss of trade to the West. Peasants were burdened by high taxes. Many were hungry or starving in parts of China. There was a recession during the 1840s and a feeling that the Chinese government was not coping with the problems that had arisen. Bandit armies roamed parts of the countryside.

A young man, Hung Hsiu-Ch'uan (born 1813, died 1864), of peasant origin came into contact with Christian missionaries on a visit to the large city of Guangdong in southern China (Figure 8.4). He absorbed and studied the religious pamphlets they gave out. After a rough period in which Hung failed his civil service examination, a very important event in China, he was dejected and depressed. Perhaps he felt he had failed his family and village, who had paid for his studies. In any case, Hung began to have visions. He believed in visions. Confucius visited him in one vision,

Figure 8.4 Contemporary Portrait of Hung Hsiu-Ch'uan, Leader of the Taiping Rebellion, Approximately 1860 (image in public domain).

and Christ in another. Hung thought Christ, his elder brother, had chosen him as the younger brother to bring help to the local people. A very charismatic person, Hung gathered followers from local communities. He also went to study with an American Southern Baptist missionary, Rev. Issachar Roberts, who taught him the basics of Christianity. Hung taught school for a while, leading a movement to destroy idols. The local authorities tried to stop him, so he and his disciples moved west into an area of China with minority groups who liked his message and became known as "God Worshippers." Again the authorities saw him as a troublemaker and pressured him to cease his activities.

Slowly Hung's movement grew as China declined economically and politically. Parts of the country became nearly lawless, and many areas built their own defenses. The movement became known as Tai Ping, or "Great Peace," harking back to a mythical era of order and harmony in ancient times. Hung and his leaders developed a full-scale revolt and prepared for war. Their attitudes were anti-foreign and anti-government.

The community took its own taxes and created a treasury. A code of conduct and laws were declared for all to follow. Equal protection was accorded to women and men, rich and poor, most unusual in this time. Many more peasants and townspeople joined the movement.

A skillful military chief, Yang Hsiu-ch'ing, who became known as the Eastern King, joined the Tai Pings. Peasants were molded into a powerful and well-trained force. All were asked to worship the one True God, as well as give reverence to old Chinese traditions. Thus the Tai Pings may represent a fusion of East and West. The Tai Ping army fought off an attack by government forces in 1850, and went on to expand their rule to a large section of south central China, eventually choosing the important city of Nanjing as their capital. Tai Ping armies held off the imperial armies for at least ten years.

However, the Manchu Emperor and his generals organized a very strong army to destroy the Tai Pings and their movement. Meanwhile, the movement itself ran into problems with rural communities and refused the support of foreigners or Mandarins.

In 1864, Nanjing was breached by government troops, and the Tai Ping leaders were killed in a massacre of their supporters. Some historians consider the Tai Pings a "warm-up" for later rebellions such as the Boxers and the Communists.

The Ku Klux Klan, 1868

Organization and Principles of the Ku Klux Klan, 1868

Appellation

This organization shall be styled and denominated the Order of the —

We, the Order of the —, reverentially acknowledge the majesty and supremacy of the Divine Being and recognize the goodness and providence of the same. And we recognize our relation to the United States government, the supremacy of the Constitution, the constitutional laws thereof, and the Union of states thereunder.

Character and Objects of the Order

This is an institution of chivalry, humanity, mercy, and patriotism; embodying in its genius and its principles all that is chivalric in conduct, noble in sentiment, generous in manhood, and patriotic in purpose; its peculiar objects being:

First, to protect the weak, the innocent, and the defenseless from the indignities, wrongs, and outrages of the lawless, the violent, and the brutal; to relieve the injured and oppressed; to succor the suffering and unfortunate, and especially the widows and orphans of Confederate soldiers.

Second, to protect and defend the Constitution of the United States, and all laws passed in conformity thereto, and to protect the states and the people thereof from all invasion from any source whatever.

Third, to aid and assist in the execution of all constitutional laws, and to protect the people from unlawful seizure and from trial, except by their peers in conformity to the laws of the land.

Titles

Section 1. The officers of this Order shall consist of a Grand Wizard of the Empire and his ten Genii; a Grand Dragon of the Realm and his eight Hydras; a Grand Titan of the Dominion and his six Furies; a Grand Giant of the Province and his four Goblins; a Grand Cyclops of the Den and his two Night Hawks; a Grand Magi, a Grand Monk, a Grand Scribe, a Grand Exchequer, a Grand Turk, and a Grand Sentinel.

Section 2. The body politic of this Order shall be known and designated as "Ghouls."

Territory and its Divisions

Section 1. The territory embraced within the jurisdiction of this Order shall be coterminous with the states of Maryland, Virginia, North Carolina, South Carolina, Georgia, Florida, Alabama, Mississippi, Louisiana, Texas, Arkansas, Missouri, Kentucky, and Tennessee; all combined constituting the Empire.

Section 2. The Empire shall be divided into four departments, the first to be styled the Realm and coterminous with the boundaries of the several states; the second to be styled the Dominion and to be coterminous with such counties as the Grand Dragons of the several Realms may assign to the charge of the Grand Titan. The third to be styled the Province and to be coterminous with the several counties; provided, the Grand Titan may, when he deems it necessary, assign two Grand Giants to one Province, prescribing, at the same time, the jurisdiction of each. The fourth department to be styled the Den, and shall embrace such part of a Province as the Grand Giant shall assign to the charge of a Grand Cyclops.

Questions to Be Asked of Candidates

1   Have you ever been rejected, upon application for membership in the—, or have you ever been expelled from the same?

2   Are you now, or have you ever been a member of the Radical Republican Party, or either of the organizations known as the "Loyal League" and the "Grand Army of the Republic"?

3   Are you opposed to the principles and policy of the Radical Party, and to the Loyal League, and the Grand Army of the Republic, so far as you are informed of the character and purposes of those organizations?

4   Did you belong to the Federal Army during the late war, and fight against the South during the existence of the same?

5   Are you opposed to Negro equality both social and political?

6   Are you in favor of a white man's government in this country?

7   Are you in favor of constitutional liberty, and a government of equitable laws instead of a government of violence and oppression?

8   Are you in favor of maintaining the constitutional rights of the South?

9   Are you in favor of the re-enfranchisement and emancipation of the white men of the South, and the restitution of the Southern people to all their rights, alike proprietary, civil, and political?

10   Do you believe in the inalienable right of self-preservation of the people against the exercise of arbitrary and unlicensed power.

(Available online at http://www.albany.edu/faculty/gz580/
his101/kkk.html)

Questions: Understanding KKK Titles and Rules

- Why does the organization look to the Divine Being for goodness and guidance?

- And why do they recognize the supremacy of the Constitution and laws? What kind of group is this as far as you can tell?

- What are the major values of the group: what is meant by chivalry, mercy, patriotism, etc.? Why do they want to protect the weak, the innocent and defenseless? Who is attacking them? Why are they so strong in expressing belief in law and order?

- What are the titles of the leaders? Do you like these titles? Who is the boss? Who are the next most important and so on? Why such fanciful titles? And why are the rest, the body politic, called "Ghouls"? What is a ghoul?

- How is the organization developed, and why does it have territories and departments?

- Are we probably living in a large or a small nation? How can you tell?

- What sorts of questions are asked of candidates for office or membership in this group?

- Why do they ask if you've ever been part of the Radical Republicans, or Grand Army, or Loyal League? Are these important clues to the character and purposes of this organization?

- Why do they want to know which side you served on during the war? Why do they want to know if you are opposed to Negro equality and in favor of a white man's government?

- Yet they also want to know if you are in favor of constitutional liberty and equitable laws? Do these questions go together? Can you make sense of them and the organization?

- Why are the authors speaking in the language of freedom and inalienable rights, yet also asking about the "re-enfranchisement" and "emancipation" of "white men"?

- If you put all the clues together, can you infer the likely purpose and intention of this group? What are they really for or against or can't you tell?

- Is it usually easy or difficult to understand the purpose of an organization, especially a secret or underground type of group, from their stated oath, aims, or constitution?

- When and where and by whom do you think this statement was written?

Teacher's Contextual Background: Ku Klux Klan

The Ku Klux Klan, a rather mysterious organization, had its birth shortly after the U.S. Civil War, along with other anti-Northern groups. The KKK was secret. All members were inducted as though into a prestigious secret club, participating in an elaborate ritual of membership. Secrecy was strongly demanded by the leaders. Members expressed loyalty and obedience by taking oaths to uphold the organization. Oaths had a legal and religious sense we don't always perceive now, but for Klan members this had an emotional appeal. Most oaths were directed at members or attacked the new privileges and freedoms granted to African Americans who were no longer slaves.

Most Klans were set up by Confederate veterans who wanted to set the clock back to the "good old days" when white folk, especially the elite, controlled the rest of the population. They wanted power returned to the former slave owners. According to historical records, a large group of Klan members gathered in Nashville, Tennessee, in 1867 to declare themselves a national organization, elect officers, administer oaths, and lay down rituals for all to follow. Secrecy was important because the South was occupied by Union forces and because the freed slaves knew their former owners and members of the community.

Thus, the organization created dramatic rituals and took to wearing sinister costumes designed to intimidate outsiders and freed black people (Figure 8.5). White cloaks with peaked conical hats were adopted, oddly reminiscent of the Catholic Spanish Inquisition. Titles were given out like Grand Dragon or Grand Wizard, and the whole Klan had a sort of military organization—all the better to scare people and remain underground, even though many white and black people knew who were the powers directing the KKK and related groups such as the Southern Cross or Knights of the White Camelia.

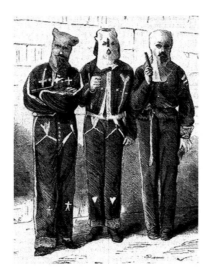

Figure 8.5 Disguised Klan Members Captured in Mississippi. Source: Drawing, from photograph, published in *Harper's Weekly*, January 27, 1872.

Some local Klans retained their own identity and made their own rules; others followed the "national" organization. According to Union army officers stationed in the South and government administrators sent from Washington, D.C. to keep order, many Klan members were engaged in illegal activities. These actions included bootlegging whisky, "moonshine," and vigilante attacks, burning out strangers and black people attempting to assert their rights. Leadership, however, was largely drawn from the upper classes, in some cases former Democratic office holders who opposed Reconstruction.

Thousands of people were killed, wounded, or burned, some lynched, by Klan groups throughout the South during the Reconstruction period and beyond. Klans worked to repress black freedoms, and to drive off Northern supporters, whom they termed "scalawags" and "carpetbaggers." Because those serving in the Confederacy had been disenfranchised, they also worked to restore the vote to former soldiers and officers. Although President U. S. Grant and Congress passed a civil rights act in 1871 guaranteeing equal rights before the law, the KKK expanded across the South in a campaign of terror directed against Republican leaders and all people, black or white, supporting the Loyal Leagues.

The document presented above is a KKK oath from the Reconstruction period (1865–77) and a fine example of the kinds of questions posed to potential members and recruits. The KKK still exists in many places in the South and "border" States to this day. KKK groups were and still are strongly anti-black and anti-immigrant, anti-Catholic, and anti-Jewish. The KKK from time to time has resurfaced in U.S. history, particularly in periods of social change, such as the 1920s or 1960s when minorities, African Americans, immigrants, or others were to be granted more rights before the law, or greater degrees of equality.

Al-Qaeda

Excerpts from Osama bin Laden's Fatwa of 1996

A fatwa is a legalistic opinion based on holy Muslim texts, written by a religious leader, meant to clarify parts of Islamic *shariah*, or law. Below is an excerpt from a fatwa issued by Osama bin Laden in 1996, first published in the London-based newspaper *Al Quds Al Arabi*.

Praise be to Allah, we seek His help and ask for his pardon. We take refuge in Allah from our wrongs and bad deeds. Who ever been guided by Allah will not be misled, and who ever has been misled, he will never be guided. I bear witness that there is no God except Allah—no associates with Him—and I bear witness that Muhammad is His slave and messenger . . .

It should not be hidden from you that the people of Islam had suffered from aggression, iniquity and injustice imposed on them by the Zionist–Crusaders alliance and their collaborators; to the extent that the Muslims blood became the cheapest and their wealth as loot in the hands of the enemies. Their blood was spilled in Palestine and Iraq. The horrifying pictures of the massacre of Qana, in Lebanon are still fresh in our memory. Massacres in Tajakestan, Burma, Cashmere, Assam, Philippine, Fatani, Ogadin, Somalia, Erithria, Chechnia and in Bosnia-Herzegovina took place, massacres that send shivers in the body and shake the conscience. All of this and the world watch and hear, and not only didn't respond to these atrocities, but also with a clear conspiracy between the USA and its allies and under the cover of the iniquitous United Nations, the dispossessed people were even prevented from obtaining arms to defend themselves.

The people of Islam awakened and realized that they are the main target for the aggression of the Zionist–Crusaders alliance. All false claims and propaganda about "Human Rights" were hammered down and exposed by the massacres that took place against the Muslims in every part of the world . . .

The latest and the greatest of these aggressions, incurred by the Muslims since the death of the Prophet (*Allah's blessing and salutations on him*) is the occupation of the land of the two Holy Places—the foundation of the house of Islam, the place of the revelation, the source of the message and the place of the noble Ka'ba, the Qiblah of all Muslims—by the armies of the American Crusaders and their allies. (We bemoan this and can only say: "No power and power acquiring except through Allah.")

Under the present circumstances, and under the banner of the blessed awakening which is sweeping the world in general and the Islamic world in particular, I meet with you today. And after a long absence, imposed on the scholars (Ulama) and callers (Da'ees) of Islam by the iniquitous crusaders movement under the leadership of the USA; who fears that they, the scholars and callers of Islam, will instigate the Ummah of Islam against its enemies as their ancestor scholars—may Allah be pleased with them—like Ibn Taymiyyah and Al'iz Ibn Abdes-Salaam did. And therefore the Zionist–Crusader alliance resorted to killing and arresting the truthful Ulama and the working Da'ees (we are not praising or sanctifying them; Allah sanctify whom He pleased). They killed the Mujahid Sheikh Abdullah Azzaam, and they arrested the Mujahid Sheikh Ahmad Yaseen and the Mujahid Sheikh Omar Abdur Rahman (in America) . . .

Under such circumstances, to push the enemy—the greatest Kufr—out of the country is a prime duty. No other duty after Belief is more important than the duty of had. Utmost effort should be made to prepare and instigate the Ummah against the enemy, the American–Israeli alliance—occupying the country of the two Holy Places and the route of the Apostle (Allah's Blessings and Salutations may be on him) to the Furthest Mosque (Al-Aqsa Mosque). Also to remind the Muslims not to be engaged in an internal war among themselves, as that will have grave consequences namely:

1   Consumption of the Muslims human resources as most casualties and fatalities will be among the Muslims people.

2   Exhaustion of the economic and financial resources.

3   Destruction of the country infrastructures

4   Dissociation of the society

5   Destruction of the oil industries. The presence of the USA Crusader military forces on land, sea and air of the states of the Islamic Gulf is the greatest danger threatening the largest oil reserve in the world. The existence of these forces in the area will provoke the people of the country and induces aggression on their religion, feelings and prides and push them to take up armed struggle against the invaders occupying the land; therefore spread of the fighting in the region will expose the oil wealth to the danger of being burned up. The economic interests of the States of the Gulf and the land of the two Holy Places will be damaged and even a greater damage will be caused to the economy of the world. I would like here to alert my brothers, the Mujahideen, the sons of the nation, to protect this (oil) wealth and not to include it in the battle as it is a great Islamic wealth and a large economical power essential for the soon to be established Islamic state, by Allah's Permission and Grace. We also warn the aggressors, the USA, against burning this Islamic wealth (a crime

which they may commit in order to prevent it, at the end of the war, from falling in the hands of its legitimate owners and to cause economic damages to the competitors of the USA in Europe or the Far East, particularly Japan which is the major consumer of the oil of the region).

6 Division of the land of the two Holy Places, and annexing of the northerly part of it by Israel. Dividing the land of the two Holy Places is an essential demand of the Zionist–Crusader alliance. The existence of such a large country with its huge resources under the leadership of the forthcoming Islamic State, by Allah's Grace, represents a serious danger to the very existence of the Zionist state in Palestine. The Nobel Ka'ba—the Qiblah of all Muslims—makes the land of the two Holy Places a symbol for the unity of the Islamic world. Moreover, the presence of the world largest oil reserve makes the land of the two Holy Places an important economical power in the Islamic world. The sons of the two Holy Places are directly related to the life style (Seerah) of their forefathers, the companions, may Allah be pleased with them. They consider the Seerah of their forefathers as a source and an example for re-establishing the greatness of this Ummah and to raise the word of Allah again. Furthermore the presence of a population of fighters in the south of Yemen, fighting in the cause of Allah, is a strategic threat to the Zionist–Crusader alliance in the area. The Prophet (*Allah's blessing and salutations on him*) said: (around twelve thousands will emerge from Aden/Abian helping—the cause of—Allah and His messenger, they are the best, in the time, between me and them) narrated by Ahmad with a correct trustworthy reference.

7 An internal war is a great mistake, no matter what reasons are there for it. The presence of the occupier—the USA—forces will control the outcome of the battle for the benefit of the international Kufr.

. . .

[Y]ou horses (soldiers) of Allah ride and march on. This is the time of hardship so be tough. And know that your gathering and co-operation in order to liberate the sanctities of Islam is the right step toward unifying the word of the Ummah under the banner of "No God but Allah."

From our place we raise our palms humbly to Allah asking Him to bestow on us His guide in every aspects of this issue.

Our Lord, we ask you to secure the release of the truthful scholars, Ulama, of Islam and pious youths of the Ummah from their imprisonment. O Allah, strengthen them and help their families.

Our Lord, the people of the cross had come with their horses (soldiers) and occupied the land of the two Holy places. And the Zionist Jews fiddling as they wish with the Al-Aqsa Mosque, the route of the ascendance of the messenger of Allah (*Allah's blessing and salutations on him*). Our Lord, shatter their gathering, divide them among themselves, shaken the earth under their feet and give us control over them; Our Lord, we take refuge in you from their deeds and take you as a shield between us and them.

Our Lord, show us a black day in them!

Our Lord, show us the wonderment of your ability in them!

Our Lord, You are the Revealer of the book, Director of the clouds, You defeated the allies (Ahzab); defeat them and make us victorious over them.

Our Lord, You are the one who help us and You are the one who assist us, with Your Power we move and by Your Power we fight. On You we rely and You are our cause.

Our Lord, those youths got together to make Your religion victorious and raise Your banner. Our Lord, send them Your help and strengthen their hearts.

Our Lord, make the youths of Islam steadfast and descend patience on them and guide their shots!

Our Lord, unify the Muslims and bestow love among their hearts!

O Lord pour down upon us patience, and make our steps firm and assist us against the unbelieving people!

Our Lord, do not lay on us a burden as Thou didst lay on those before us; Our Lord, do not impose upon us that which we have no strength to bear; and pardon us and grant us protection and have mercy on us, Thou art our patron, so help us against the unbelieving people.

Our Lord, guide this Ummah, and make the right conditions (by which) the people of your obedience will be in dignity and the people of disobedience in humiliation, and by which the good deeds are enjoined and the bad deeds are forebode.

(bin Laden, 1996)

Teacher's Contextual Background: Al-Qaeda

Osama bin Laden was born in 1957 and grew up in Riyadh, Saudi Arabia. He was the son of a well-off Yemeni immigrant who moved to Mecca, the holy city of Islam, in the 1930s looking for a better business environment. At that time, Saudi Arabia was just beginning to industrialize by investing in oil production, agreeing to financial and technical help from the Western nations, especially the United States.

Saudi Arabia contains some of the holiest places known to Islam. Millions make pilgrimage every year (the "*haj*") to Mecca, and there are other shrines as well as the birthplace of Mohammed, founder of Islam. Although most of the Saudis were once largely tribal and nomadic, they were united under the present royal family into a modern nation. However, most of the population was also highly religious, belonging to a conservative form of Islam called Wahabism. This could be described as a fundamentalist view of the faith, with strict observance of rituals, holidays, and social values.

Osama's father was a great success, making millions in the construction industry trading on ties to the royal family. Osama was a seventeenth son as his father followed local custom and faith, and had several wives. As a young man he grew up in an increasingly wealthy and privileged class, most of whom were given high levels of education, at least the males. Wahabism was taught along with typical school subjects taught in the West.

Osama and others developed a strong interest in religion and began to oppose westernization that was bringing great wealth to Arab society. It was also bringing foreigners, particularly Americans, to the country, including armed forces. Saudis and Americans were in the oil business together. Although the wealth was appreciated, the intrusions of Western values were not by many Saudis, among them Osama. Many joined anti-Western religious groups, opposed democratic values, and tried to stop the diffusion of new ideas and innovations. They preferred tradition.

As a young man, Osama worked with and supported the Muslim Brotherhood in Syria, helping them try to overthrow the president of the country. When the Russians invaded Afghanistan, Osama became the family representative in the Afghan *jihad* against the Soviets. He worked with a leader of the Muslim Brotherhood to defeat the Russians, and he met Egyptians led by Al-Zawahiri, who set up an anti-Western organization, Qaeda al Ma'lumat. Raising money for the Afghan warrior groups, Osama became well known in the Middle East by 1990 or so.

The Al-Qaeda group evolved into a refuge for born-again militants and men who had been part of the religious Muslim Brotherhood, mostly Sunnis. This group drew from many Middle Eastern nations, and attracted those looking for active rebel groups to join. Many people tolerated these groups because they were angry about the decline of their own culture and religion. Bin Laden became increasingly outspoken on many topics, advocating that his own country was occupied by foreign non-Muslim armies and workers, and they should all be expelled. The presence of Westerners was seen as "polluting" the purity of Islam. When Osama began publishing manifestos condemning the Saudi government, the leaders took away his nationality and froze all bank accounts. After this, the Al-Qaeda organization went underground and began a campaign of terrorism, speaking out through media, and supporting conservative militant groups throughout the Middle East.

Although small, the group planned and carried out the attack on the World Trade Center Twin Towers in New York on September 11, 2001. At the time, not much was known about their values and beliefs, but you will now have the opportunity to learn more about them, and to compare them to other secret societies in this chapter.

The Mau Mau (Kenya)

Oath of the _____ _____

The man is roused by a knock on the door of his hut late at night. He is taken by a roundabout route to . . . a hut in a clearing, blindfolded.

He (or She) would be ordered to eat a piece of roasted sacrificial flesh thrust against his (her) lips. This would be done seven times and after each time he or she would have to repeat the oath. Then the lips would be touched with blood seven times, the oath being repeated after each. Next a gourd of blood would be passed round his or her head seven times; he or she would be ordered to stick seven thorns into a Sodom apple and pierce the eye of a sheep or goat (usually removed while it was alive) seven times with a thorn. (Then they would be ordered to speak 3 oaths, as follows:)

First Oath

1   If I ever reveal the secrets of this organization, may this oath kill me.

2   If I ever sell or dispose of any _____ land to a foreigner, may this oath kill me.

3   If I ever fail to follow our great leader, _____ _____, may this oath kill me.

4   If I ever inform against any member of this organization or against any member who steals from Europeans, may this oath kill me.

5   If I ever fail to pay the fees of this organization, may this oath kill me.

Second Oath

6   If I am sent to bring in the head of any enemy, and I fail to do so, may this oath kill me.

7   If I fail to steal anything I can from the European, may this oath kill me.

8   If I know of any enemy to our organization and I fail to report him to my leader, may this oath kill me.

9   If I am ever sent by a leader to do something big for the _____ _____, and I refuse, may this oath kill me.

10   If I refuse to help in driving Europeans from this country, may this oath kill me.

11   If I worship any leader but _____ _____, may this oath kill me.

Third Oath

12   If I am called upon do to so, with four others, I will kill a European.

13   If I am called upon to do so, I will kill one of our own people who is against us, even if it be my mother or my father or brother or sister or wife or child.

14   If called upon to do so, I will help to dispose of the body of a murdered person so that it may not be found.

15   I will never disobey the orders of the leaders of this society.

(From the *Times* of Nairobi, November 8, 1952, p. 1)

Questions

- Why was someone roused at night and taken blindfolded to speak the three oaths?

- What kind of ritual was performed beforehand and why is there an emphasis on blood and animals? Where in the world are we?

- What does "may this oath kill me" mean?

- Does the first oath think well or badly of Europeans? Of "the leader"? Who is the leader?

- Should each member pay dues to the organization, and is it OK if dues are stolen?

- What does the second oath say a member should do? Is this oath like the first one or different?

- What is the big goal of the second oath. Who is to be driven from the country? Why?

- What do you think is going on in this time and place? Why would those against Europeans have to operate in secret, take oaths, and steal or kill or both?

- Why does the third oath ask for killing? Who can be killed according to the third oath?

- Is killing or death restricted to outsiders or may insiders be put to death as well? Why? Can the leaders be disobeyed? What are the consequences for informing or disobeying or hiding from the leaders?

- What would you say is the overall intent and purpose of the organization?

- Is it usually easy or difficult to understand the purpose of an organization, especially a secret or underground type of group, from its state oath, aims, or constitution?

- When and where and by whom do you think this statement was written?

Teacher's Contextual Background: The Mau Mau

The historical context for the Mau Mau oath was colonial rule by Britain that exerted control over almost all of Kenya by 1890. The British brought in English and other European settlers, about thirty thousand by 1930, who ruled over more than a million Kikuyu "tribal people," and many other smaller groups as well. After WWII, about three thousand European settlers owned large farms, usually the richest land, while the African population of about five million occupied the poorest land, but were not allowed to own it themselves. The Kikuyu people in particular had strong leadership, the major leader being Jomo Kenyatta, and a political organization (the KAU or Kenyan African Union). The Kikuyu also possessed a distinctive culture and language of their own. At one point during the rebellion period, Jomo Kenyatta, who liked to wear a leopard skin and carry a spear at public appearances, was arrested and sentenced to seven years in prison. Oppression, lack of rights, exclusion from land ownership, political exclusion, and many other issues brought about the emergence of an independence movement in the 1950s, with considerable political activism and organization. Some scholars believe that the Mau Mau (Figure 8.6) were a splinter group that broke off from the Kenyan African Union on the issue of using violence to ensure that native peoples rejected European rule; others believe the Mau Mau were led by the Kenyan leader, Jomo Kenyatta.

Thus, Kenya as a whole, and the Kikuyu in particular, were growing more and more uncomfortable with and opposed to colonial rule, forming independence groups that were lobbying for freedom and sovereignty over their own affairs. Because Great Britain pretty much refused to withdraw and often brutally repressed even peaceful protests much less peasants' revolts, and frequently jailed political leaders, the Mau

Figure 8.6 Mau Mau Members Gather in the Jungle. Source unknown.

Mau were designed to frighten the rulers, and intimidate and encourage the locals, while working to draw worldwide attention to their campaign for freedom from colonial rule. As Great Britain's problems multiplied worldwide, Kenyan leaders stepped up their efforts to change their situation.

The Mau Mau organization called itself the Land Freedom Army, or Freedom Struggle Association, and never the Mau Mau, which is not a word in the Kikuyu language. The origins of the term are unknown, but it may have been invented by the English to make the rebels sound more African and savage, thereby making them seem less human. Much of the struggle between Africans and British over the issue of independence was a propaganda war of support and rejection, loyalty and intimidation, aimed mainly at the native peoples of Kenya. Kenyatta, Mboya, Odinga, and other African leaders were imprisoned numerous times for many excuses. The vast majority of people killed during the rebellion from approximately 1951 or 1952 until 1959 were Africans, mostly those who refused to take the underground "oath" or oaths of allegiance to the freedom struggle association, which became commonly known as Mau Mau. The "oaths," as they were called, were more than just a promise, and in the eyes of many native peoples had both moral and magical properties. Swearing an oath was accompanied by rituals and ceremonies, with strong psychological undertones that frightened many, including Europeans. The English rulers of Kenya went so far as to invent a counter-oath for Kikuyu to swear as an antidote to the secret society oath, but this usually did not work or if it did result in withdrawal and silence then it invited assassination and political murder.

Only a handful of white settlers and British military personnel were verifiably murdered by the rebels, but far more rebels and civilian Kikuyu people were destroyed by British forces and by the so-called Mau Mau terrorists. As talks began to establish an African government in Kenya in 1959–60, the terror abated rapidly, and all but disappeared by independence in 1963. The frequently jailed Jomo Kenyatta then became the father of his country, just as his adopted name implied.

The Bolshevik Party (Russia)

Advice for the Formation of an Organization of Secret Revolutionaries

This wonderful truth (which the hundred fools will applaud) appears obvious only because in the very midst of the argument you have skipped from one question to another. You began by talking, and continued to talk, of catching a "committee", of catching an "organization", and now you skip to the question of getting hold of the "roots" of the movement in the "depth." The fact is, of course, that our movement cannot be caught precisely because it has thousands and thousands of roots deep down among the masses, but that is not the point we are discussing. As far as "the roots in the depths" are concerned, we cannot be "caught" even now, in spite of all our primitiveness; but, we all complain, and cannot but complain, of the case with which the organizations can be caught, with the result that it is impossible to maintain continuity in the movement. If you agree to discuss the question of catching the organizations, and stick to that question, then I assert it is far more difficult to catch ten wise men than it is to catch a hundred fools. And this premise I shall defend no matter how much you instigate the crowd against me for my "anti-democratic" views, etc.

As I have already said, by "wise men" in connection with the organization, I mean professional revolutionists, irrespective of whether they are students or workingmen. I assert:

1 That no movement can last without a stable organization of leaders to maintain continuity;

2 That the more widely the masses are drawn into the struggle and form the basis of the movement, the more necessary it is to have such an organization and the more stable it must be (for it is much easier then for demagogues to sidetrack the more backward sections of the masses);

3 That the organization must consist chiefly of persons engaged in revolution as a profession;

4 That in a country with a despotic government, the more we restrict the membership of this organization to persons who are engaged in revolution as a profession and who have been professionally trained in the art of combating political police, the more difficult it will be to catch the organization; and

5 The wider will be the circle of men and women of the working class or of other classes of society able to join the movement and perform active work in it.

The question as to whether it is easier to catch "a dozen wise men or a hundred fools," in the last analysis, amounts to the question considered above, namely, whether it is possible to have a mass organization when the maintenance of strict secrecy is essential to success. We never give a mass organization the degree of secrecy that is essential for the persistent and continuous struggle against the government. But to concentrate all secret functions in the hands of as small a number of professional revolutionists as possible, does not mean the latter will "do the thinking for all" and that the crowd will advance from its ranks increasing numbers of professional revolutionists, for it will know that it is not enough for a few students and workingmen waging economic war to gather together and form a "committee" but that professional revolutionists must be trained for years; the crowd will think not of primitive ways but of training professional revolutionists.

(Lenin, 1902)

Questions

- As leaders of the Bolsheviks, how does each dress (Figure 8.7)? As workers, statesmen, soldiers, middle class people? What does their style communicate to you? Do they seem friendly or frightening, as far as you can tell? If you met them on the street, would you think they were leaders of a secret society and political party? Why or why not?

- Why does the author defend his views that it is easier to catch a hundred fools than ten wise men? Who are the wise men? Would you agree if you were sitting across the table from the author? Why does he defend himself against charges of being "anti-democratic"?

- Who is he probably writing to in this piece, insiders or outsiders?

- What are the author's rules for a movement or organization?

- How important are leaders?

Figure 8.7 Three Bolsheviks at a Meeting: Trotsky, Lenin, and Kamenev (image in public domain).

Teacher's Contextual Background

The original Bolsheviks were part of a larger party, the Marxist Russian Social Democratic Party, but broke away in 1903 to form their own organization. Bol'shoi means big or large in Russian and the Bolsheviks were given that name after being the majority in a major vote. There were actually fewer Bolsheviks than Mensheviks at the 1903 Second Party Congress, and they continued to be a minority party within Russia until the days of the Revolution in 1917. Because Czarist Russia was a police state in many ways, opposition political groups went underground at times to keep safe from the state's secret police. The overall political atmosphere was moderately oppressive but rather ineffective. Therefore Lenin advocated keeping the party small and secret, organizing through cells or small groups kept separate from each other, their locations and membership known only to party leaders.

In 1905, Bolsheviks and Mensheviks each formed their own separate parties. Before the revolution there was a lot of jockeying between and among parties that opposed the monarchy, but it was not at all clear which group would come out on top. As the October Revolution took shape, the larger parties tended to try to deal with the government of the Czar while the Bolsheviks organized a 'vanguard party' of communists that spread propaganda among workers and peasants, and especially the army, with a slogan of "Peace and Bread." The Czar was toppled because the government's policies, e.g., war, lack of free speech, economic disaster, etc. were deeply disliked. A provisional government was formed under Kerensky but didn't last long, leading to massive strikes about unpopular policies. Czarist General Kornilov attempted a takeover, but this was defeated, with the Bolsheviks playing a key role. This greatly increased their popularity and led to a series of election victories in local soviets, leading to Bolshevik control of most of the nation by the end of 1917. Lenin, Trotsky, and Stalin became the heads of state, and the Czar and his family were executed.

Summary and Conclusions

Secret societies, some well documented and others obscure, have been born throughout recorded history, usually for religious and political purposes. In this chapter we have examined and discussed a sample from different continents and cultures: the Serbian Black Hand, Tai Pings, Mau Mau, KKK, and Al-Qaeda.

You have had the opportunity to interpret the "oaths" or statements of each organization from its own point of view rather than that of its opponents or enemies. In historical investigations, we think it is very important, even crucial, to read and understand the ideas and goals of those who many consider quite nasty and evil. People in world history act for reasons they consider important, and even when we disagree strongly with the goals of an organization or group, it is still in our interests to grasp their views. Otherwise, we will fall into the three problems outlined early in this book: ethnocentrism, egocentrism, and econ-centrism.

We have provided a framework for teaching about secret societies, choosing the less benign ones for dramatic effect. You are welcome to include others such as the Freemasons or Skull and Bones, who are oriented more toward community building and charity than violent overthrow of governments.

Hopefully, you have enjoyed reading the documents from secret societies and will be able to employ these in the classroom to bring mystery alive in teaching history. And perhaps you will be motivated to expand our small set into a major study of rebellion, sabotage, and terrorism, particularly long-term causes rather than only effects upon us. As we have suggested in this chapter, offer the documents as mysteries in and of themselves before providing context and background.

Dissatisfaction with conquests and hatred of overlords, particularly imperial cultures, have engendered many social movements, both peaceful and violent, working against rule by people seen as conquerors and controlling "outsiders." This has caused both local and worldwide revolutionary, terrorist, and social movements with connections and roots in the thinking of leaders from other times and places, for example the transfer of Marxist ideas to Lenin, and the borrowing of Gandhi's ideas by Martin Luther King, Jr. We still have much to learn about the effects of imperialism and intervention in the affairs of other peoples, particularly those with cultures quite different from our own, and we pray we do not repeat the mistakes of the past.

References and Further Reading

Axelrod, A. (1997) *The International Encyclopedia of Secret Societies and Fraternal Orders*, New York: Facts on File.

bin Laden, O. (1996) "Declaration of war against the Americans occupying the land of the two holy places," originally published in *Al Quds Al Arabi*, London. Full-text English translation available online. Available at http://www.pbs.org/newshour/terrorism/international/fatwa_1996.html (accessed March 10, 2009).

Booth, M. (1999) *The Dragon Syndicates: The Global Phenomenon of the Triads*, London: Doubleday Britain.

Carr, C. (2003) *The Lessons of Terror*, New York: Random House.

Carruthers, S. L. (1995) *Winning Hearts and Minds: British Government, the Media and Colonial Counterinsurgency, 1944–1960*, London: Leicester Press.

Clough, M. S. (1955) *Mau Mau Memoirs*, London: Lynne Rienner.

de Bary, W. T. and Lufrano, R. (compilers and eds.) (2001) *Sources of Chinese Tradition*, vol. 2, 2nd edn, New York: Columbia University Press.

Dewar, M. (1989) *The Art of Deception in Warfare*, London: David and Charles.

Elkins, C. (2005) *Imperial Reckoning*, New York: Henry Holt.

Foner, E. (1989) *Reconstruction: America's Unfinished Revolution, 1863–1877*, New York: Perennial Classics, pp. 432–6.

Glenny, M. (2008) *McMafia: A Journey Through the Global Criminal Underworld*, New York: A. A. Knopf.

Gurr, T. R. (1970) *Why Men Rebel*, Princeton, NJ: Princeton University Press.

Heckethorn, C. W. (1997) *The Secret Societies of all Ages and Countries*, Whitefish, MT: Kessinger.

Kepel, G. and Milelli, J-P. (eds.) (2008) *Al Qaeda in its Own Words*, Cambridge, MA: Belknap Press of Harvard University

Lenin, V. I. (1902) *What is to be Done?*, Moscow: Progress Publishers.

Michael, F. (1973) *The Taiping Rebellion: History and Documents*, Seattle: University of Washington Press.

Moore, B. (1978) *Injustice: The Social Bases of Obedience and Revolt*, White Plains, NY: M. E. Sharpe.

Parker, N. (1999) *Revolutions and History*, Cambridge, UK: Polity Press.

Pozzi, H. (1935) *Black Hand over Europe, Consisting of War is Coming Again* (trans. Francis J. Mott), London: The Francis Mott Company. Online. Available at the WWI Document Archive maintained by Brigham Young University, http://wwi.lib.byu.edu.

Remak, J. (1967) *Origins of World War I: 1871–1914*, Lafayette, LA: Peter Smith Publications.

Roberts, G. (1955) *The Mau Mau in Kenya*, London: Hutchinson Press.

Roberts, J. M. (1972) *The Mythology of Secret Societies*, New York: Scribner's.

Robbins, A. (2004) *Pledged: The Secret Life of Sororities*, New York: Hyperion Press.

Smyth, J. (1992) *The Men of No Property: Irish Radicals and Popular Politics in the Late 18th Century*, New York: Palgrave, Macmillan.

Spence, J. D. (1996) *God's Chinese Son*, New York: W. W. Norton.

Thompson, J. (1982) *My Life in the Klan*, New York: Putnam.

Trelease, A. W. (1995) *White Terror: The Ku Klux Klan Conspiracy and Southern Reconstruction*, Baton Rouge: Louisiana State University Press.

Wade, W. C. (1987) *The Fiery Cross: The Klu Klux Klan in America*, New York: Simon & Schuster.

Wallerstein, I. (1984) *The Politics of the World Economy: The States, the Movements, and the Civilisations*, Cambridge, UK: Cambridge University Press.

Whalen, W. J. (1966) *Handbook of Secret Organizations*, Milwaukee, WI: Bruce Publishing.

Wolff, E. R. (1970) *Peasant Wars of the Twentieth Century*, New York: Harper & Row.

nine
Where are the Women in World History?

WITCH (Women's Independent Taxpayers, Consumers, and Homemakers)
Double, bubble, war and rubble,
When you mess with women, you'll be in trouble.
We're convicted of murder if abortion is planned,
Convicted of shame if we don't have a man,
Convicted of conspiracy if we fight for our rights,
And burned at the stake if stand up to fight.
Double, bubble, war and rubble,
When you mess with a woman you'll be in trouble.
We curse your empire to make it fall—
When you take on one of us, you take on all.

(Morgan, 1970, p. 618)

Not even girls want to be girls so long as our feminine archetype lacks force, strength, and power. Not wanting to be girls, they don't want to be tender, submissive, peace-loving as good women are. Women's strong qualities have become despised because of their weakness. The obvious remedy is to create a feminine character with all the strength of Superman plus all the allure of a good and beautiful woman.

(William M. Marsten, creator of Wonder Woman, 1943)

Women are fairly scarce in textbooks. Throughout the entire history of the world, although women have been the majority of the human population for most of its evolution, they are fairly rare, and, if investigated with students and teachers of history, given far less detail and attention than men in terms of both image and text, and quantity and quality of presentation. Women are rare even in their archetypical roles as mothers and wives and goddesses, and almost never seen as children at all. In short, we have a major mystery on our hands, and may again ask, "where are the women in world history, and why are they treated so poorly?" This chapter is an inquiry into the scarcity of women in world history.

In 2004, a team of investigators writing in *Social Education* undertook a study of six best-selling American history textbooks and found that in them the ratio of women to men had slowly risen from about 3 in 100 in the 1960s, to about 6 in 100 in the 1980s, to 10.6 in 100 in the 1990s, with the last book analyzed dating to 1999 (Clark, Allard, and Mahoney). Thus, over three decades of American history textbook writing, the amount of space devoted to women has improved from 3 to 6 to a little less than 11 in 100. In a similar study, the authors found a slightly lower ratio of 8 women for every 100 men in *world* history textbooks (Clark, Ayton, Frechette, and Keller, 2005).

Once in a while, when the arts and sciences are discussed in history, women pop up as culture heroines, celebrities, performers, researchers, and discoverers. Here and there, stray women appear in historical situations because they were prominent parts of a largely male story, or because researchers and feminist historians (both male and female) have rehabilitated female contributors who had been lying on a shelf and needed dusting off. As the noted historian Gerda Lerner points out:

> If we teach a US survey following a traditional textbook, the text will barely mention women. If we then simply "add" women, we have improved on this outline but not by much. The women we have added will either be women much like the men we talk about or they will look inferior by comparison with the men. To make women central to our conceptual framework we must assume that what they do and think is equally important with what the men do and think. If we make such an assumption, we will ask about every unit we teach: what were the women doing while the men were doing what we are teaching? and, going an analytical step further, how did the women interpret what they were doing?
>
> (Gerda Lerner keynote address, Lowell Conference on Women's History, 1988, reprinted in *Why History Matters*, 1997, p. 143)

In historical texts, the problem with female representation is not only because of gender bias, but also because of historical bias in favor of political and economic history over cultural, social, and ecological history. Thus, as most of our texts describe male figures who (one could argue if one were mean-spirited) engineered governments, wars, and imperialistic schemes, and caused the loss of enormous amounts of lives and capital, these texts have pushed women's roles in history aside to make room for the drama of bloodlust and sweeping warfare.

We believe that the role of women in world history is a many-layered onion that can be peeled back to offer an array of problems—historical blindness, bias, memory failure, and unequal treatment. Their roles are communicated in narratives that are subtle and obvious, charmingly cloying and amazingly brutal. Deeply imbedded in how we write about, picture, and portray women in world history are questions of gender bias, social structure, biological differences, and cultural values. These are the questions we hope to investigate in this chapter, by providing you with a framework for detective work into a number of famous and ordinary women. Each case study is one piece of an overall puzzle through which we seek to illuminate and test different theories about the role of women in world history.

Questions: Heads of State

- Did you know that, as of spring 2008, there were twenty-five female heads of state in the world? (*State* refers to country or nation.)

- How many can you name? How many can you visualize?

- If you were given photos of each, how many would you recognize? Would you recognize more male or more female heads of state?

- In general in history, would you be able to name, visualize, and recognize more male leaders or more female leaders? Why?

- How might you explain your ability to recognize world leaders, male and/or female? Is it personal knowledge and study, schooling, media reporting, social values, or a combination of all of the above? (If you choose *combination*, please explain how you would sort out the ratios, or percentages, for each factor?)

Mysteries in the History of Women

How do we study women in world history? How careful should we be of the evidence presented? Does it matter who the author is and where she or he originates? How do we detect bias, one way or the other? Can history be neutral? If not, how do we handle values and beliefs imbedded in writing, music, and pictures of women? What place do you think women should receive in history? What conclusions may we draw about the kinds of evidence that are most revealing of women's roles in world history, and what kinds of evidence are untrustworthy?

Mysteries abound: Did high-ranking women achieve their status by merit or by inheritance? Did they bring about significant social change or go down the middle of the road? Who worked most for social change—middle-class or working-class women—and did they achieve results? Did most women make it on their own merit, or did they have male and/or female support? Who tended to provide support in society and who opposed change? Were women themselves on the cutting edge of gender, or were they subservient to the interests of men, the nation, their class? How were prominent women treated in history—with great affection and respect, or with derision and criticism?

We propose a walk across world history through women's lives, lives that symbolize the values and beliefs accorded women across many times and places. A variety of biographies and autobiographies, images and visuals, will be presented to stimulate thinking about where women are in world history, and why texts and authors tend to favor certain categories of women over others.

We present a few categories or roles that seem to recur in history—goddesses and mothers, leaders and warriors, rebels and career women—to help us understand who has been admitted into the halls of fame and who might need to be re-evaluated for a better or more complete treatment. We invite our mystery readers to analyze examples in terms of criteria for personal success, social change, and leadership. We invite analysis of the role and place of women in the world in which we live, and from which we have evolved, dragging with us all the baggage of attitudes and values, ethics and feelings, given to us by the past.

Plan of Action for Women in World History

This chapter is designed to challenge a lot of ideas about women in world history—who they are, what roles they play, and whether any have appeared on the world stage. Male historical figures are generally accepted as making a difference, or even serve as the objects of worship or condemnation (particularly as government leaders or war heroes), but we challenge you to ask students to name twenty prominent women in world history in any walk of life, leader to peasant, and we predict that most will not even be able to come up with a dozen examples. Try this poll as a classroom project, and save and post the results. (Later in this chapter, we invite you and your students to study women as they appear on coins all over the world through an independent research project. We provide two samples to start with, one ancient and one modern: Queen Zenobia of Palmyra and Susan B. Anthony. Students then move on to their own research, and perhaps even design their own coin for a woman of their choice.)

To return to our main point, we have structured this major mystery around the key ideas (reviewed at the chapter's end) that women are viewed as limited by their gender, by family and child rearing, and by physical "weakness" and emotionality. You are welcome to debate any and all stereotypes about women and girls, but to this we want to add a few key elements not often discussed in world history: roles, social mores or values, historical context, and degrees of male dominance, as well as economic rules and systems.

Steps and Strategies

Each step of the way, you and your students will have to decide if and how each example fits the elements above. All of the women presented in this chapter suggest that there is a lot more at work than merely their gender in subordinating, diminishing, or distorting the presence of women in world history. For example, as you read the materials, many clearly had more opportunity to "come out" during a revolution than during a nice settled period of social status quo under the monarchy. Even royal women had to be careful of the predominantly male view of leadership, and play the game successfully by partially disguising or downplaying their initiative even in a society that was fairly open to female participation in economic and political life.

Overall, this is designed to have you and your students think about women in world history as significant players, or missing persons, or perhaps something in between. Our teaching plan concludes with a series of theories that serve as final assessments of thinking about women in world history.

To Do: Can a Woman Become U.S. President?

- Research the campaign for president waged by Hillary Clinton (Figure 9.1), and test out the theories about the role of women in this chapter. Was Clinton a viable candidate? Was she criticized for policy or personal issues, or complimented? Why? Was she attacked on the basis of her gender? How and why, or why not? Did her being a woman make a difference in her bid to be president against a man from the same political party?

- Do Americans generally elect many female leaders? Are women prominent more as workers, entertainers, leaders, rebels? Overall, do you think the evidence of popular behavior in the United States views women as equal to men in every way? Explain.

Figure 9.1 Official Portrait of Hillary Rodham Clinton, Current U.S. Secretary of State. Source: U.S. State Department.

Choosing Examples

We have selected examples of women that will stimulate questions about female roles in world history and (we hope) will disturb settled notions of who is important, interesting, and meaningful. We present three groups of women: mothers and goddesses, leaders and warriors, careerists and rebels. Another way of looking at them would be as examples of gender roles (goddesses, wives, and mothers), workers (scientists, activists, media stars), and leaders (queens, politicians, revolutionaries, soldiers).

Each case can be viewed from multiple perspectives, for example a goddess can be a mother, a mother can be a heroine, a heroine can be a career woman. Might a woman break out of role boundaries and become a warrior equal to or more impressive than a man? Might a worker be a leader, a rebel for a cause, or an outright revolutionary? Might a community activist, a media star, a nurse, also change views of gender and alter the way society views the proper and accepted role of women? Just what kinds of actions or achievements change social definitions of women? You and your classes are encouraged to look up your own examples to compare with the few we include in this chapter as a way of testing this hypothesis.

Of Goddesses and Mothers

We hope to juxtapose examples in such a way that they resonate with and against each other. Is the goddess Athena setting an example for rebellion or for adjustment, especially as compared with the mother of gods and goddesses, Hera? Do important and powerful women need a Wonder Woman outfit to succeed and be noticed? Are the qualities of a goddess or supernatural power more powerful than those of motherhood (the ability to give life)? Can a migrant mother be a heroine for raising her children against all odds? We take a look at the mothers depicted in war and poverty by various artists: the migrant mother, the protective German mother, or the British women in World War II who took on a variety of roles.

Of Leaders and Warriors

We present one medieval female figure, Hua Mulan from China, and encourage you to compare her with a heroine from a very different place—Joan of Arc from France. Both are what you might call warrior women, taking the part of men to go into battle on behalf of country and family. Each has a story and exudes a sense of heroism outside a traditional female role in almost any society. Students should read these accounts, and compare and contrast them with each other and with the goddesses and queens in this chapter. It is interesting that neither figure is of royal blood or of very high status, Joan in particular being described as a peasant. Hua Mulan and Joan both go on to become revered figures in their own cultures, and you should ask students why they think this might be so. Were they fascinated by the stories, or did they find them unexciting?

Of Rebels, Causes, and Careers

Must a woman stay within assigned and usual roles, or break out of them? Does the nursing done by Florence Nightingale or the success of Oprah Winfrey represent a breakthrough for women or an adjustment to "allowed" types of jobs? Would Rigoberta Menchú, Mother Jones, Olympe de Gouges, or Rosa Luxembourg (look them up) be typical workers, rebels, or revolutionary leaders (or all of the above)? What really makes the difference in how we feel about the importance of a particular woman in history? Do we really admire strong women or do we find them worrisome? Why?

In the third set of examples we further complicate the mystery of the place of women in world history by examining women who represented, led, and spoke for causes that often brought about attacks or death for their views. Some were authors of revolutionary documents, others were outstanding women in their fields—nursing, entertainment, community work, and so forth. These career women represent a more socially acceptable form of achievement, opening questions about their leadership (by example or by speaking out). They are part of the mystery of defining women's roles in history and deciding which ones make it into the ranks of the famous or not-so-famous.

Using the Examples

Use each biography, presented here or researched on your own, to dig into questions of women's roles as leaders, workers, entertainers, and rebels. Are those who work for change taking risks? Ask students how many of their examples were in danger, and from what causes. It is not necessary to glorify each woman, but rather to use her life as an example of gender issues and change. Pursue the question of historical context and which women lived in times of change or status quo. Try to encourage students to develop generalizations, synthesizing what allows women to go outside their traditional roles as mothers and wives, family members, and workers or servants. Remind students to turn to some of the central ideas offered by our experts on history and feminism—Manning, Miles, and Lerner—during the chapter review at the conclusion. Most importantly, we want to invite you and your students to think about women and history more deeply.

We invite evaluation and judgment calls. Who would you describe as revolutionary? Who would be outspoken for women, or for men? What causes did each support and did each risk her life for people and nation, cause and commoners. What were their origins: of low, medium, or high status? Would you describe Rosa, Evita, or Rigoberta as workers, rebels, leaders, entertainers, or role models? In fact, so far, have any of the women whose cases we present been model mothers, wives, or family members?

We invite comparisons and contrasts. How does Olympe de Gouges compare with Joan and Hua Mulan? Who did more for women? All of the women presented may be re-evaluated as potential goddesses and heroines, or as mothers, or potential mothers. Does motherhood mix with revolution; does heroism mix with career? Are the ideas of Rigoberta Menchú a lot like those of Luxembourg, of de Gouge, of Eva Peron? Does Eva

Peron espouse feminist causes? Does each woman complement the others in some way? Is Marie Curie (look her up) a feminist, or just a wonderful scientist? Ask students to read her biography to consider why she is so well known—for her accomplishment in science as a woman, or for her accomplishments in science on behalf of women, or perhaps both. Then compare Marie with Oprah the entertainer, as well as with the examples set by Rigoberta Menchú and Rosa Luxembourg or Eva Peron. Is Oprah outspoken on important social issues? What are Oprah's accomplishments alone, or for women in general, or for African American women? Can an entertainer be a revolutionary and achieve wealth and status? Which of the women do you think should be given more time in your world history books? Which have done the most to change not only their own status, but also the status and definition of women as a whole?

We invite consideration of context. Extend the inquiry by examining what are perhaps the two most famous documents establishing the cause of women's rights, the "Declaration of Women's Rights" of 1792 and the "Seneca Falls Declaration of Sentiments" of 1848. Ask students to put these into historical context and decide whether the times were active and changing or traditional and settled. What kinds of social and political conditions allow women to rise in status or go outside traditional roles and seek positions of work, entertainment, or leadership? What kind of woman would try to achieve what many at the time saw as unlikely or impossible? Would you encourage girls and women to seek their highest levels of accomplishment or stick to traditional roles as mother and wife and sister? Why? Would sticking with traditional roles, like mother, mean that you could not excel or be heroic? Why or why not?

Goddesses and Mothers

We begin with three inter-related examples of goddesses and near-goddesses, all mythological: Athena, goddess of wisdom; Hera, wife of Zeus and mother; and Wonder Woman, an American heroine in cartoon comic form. It turns out that Wonder Woman is a relative of the goddesses and a goddess herself, hence her magic powers. Why use myths to teach history? Because they are part of history and represent human values—you might say the embodiment of values or value projections of female roles.

Why do human beings identify with the goddess idea, or the idea of "mother"? Should "mother" be a heroine, or a goddess, or neither to be part of world history? Athena remains unmarried and unencumbered by kids while Hera is, you could argue, the perfect model of dominated wife: bossy, argumentative, and rebellious combined with submissive, caring, and supportive. Familiar? As you teach these two, think of asking your students for comparisons and contrasts, and then have fun with Wonder Woman as a descendant and modern goddess. Tell your students that the past lives on even in myth, and ask them to take a survey of how many heroes or heroines (in cartoons, games, or fiction) they adore and for what reasons. See if you can generate a discussion of why so many like larger-than-life beings with extraordinary powers.

Ask students to think about women as goddesses, as symbols of beauty and power, and discuss the possible reasons why we need to believe in goddesses—whether these are the real thing, or other callings that rise to a kind of worshipful status: entertainers, stars, power figures, sports heroines. Do we do the same for men, more or less? You might also want to assign research on other cartoon or mythic heroines that are popular right now with your students.

Once you have established female goddess and mythic personalities in history, you can move on to real historical examples, such as the queen of Egypt, Hatshepsut, who ruled a very long time ago and has an interesting story to tell, one that was purposely blotted out by her successor, Thutmose. She may be employed as an example of a royal high-ranking woman who takes the opportunity during a succession problem to ascend to the throne. But, in the process, she has to proceed slowly and carefully by performing male roles and wearing the beard of the pharaoh. Ask students what they think of her as a leader and a woman: would she have succeeded without being a king's daughter, or a royal mother? Why or why not?

Mystery Packet: Mythological Women and Living Myths

Athena

Athena (Figure 9.2) is known as the daughter of Zeus, and she was supposed to have been born as a fully formed adult woman from the head of Zeus. The details of this birth vary.

Figure 9.2 The Goddess Athena. Photo: Yair Haklai/Creative Commons (original in color).

The Greek poet Hesiod says that Athena's mother is actually Metis, the wisest of the gods. When Metis was pregnant, Zeus swallowed her up and afterwards gave birth to Athena himself. Some sources say that Athena sprang from the head of Zeus dressed in full armor.

Athena's parentage explains how she was viewed by the ancient Greeks. Her father Zeus was the most powerful among the gods, and her mother Metis was the wisest. Athena harmoniously combined both power and wisdom: she was a defender of things created out of human cleverness and wisdom—not only agriculture and mechanical, scientific, and artistic inventions, but the state itself, its walls, fortresses, and fortifications.

Hera

Hera (Figure 9.3) had a high place among the gods of ancient Greece. According to one account, she was the eldest daughter of the gods Cronos and Rhea, and sister to Zeus. Homer tells that she was raised by other gods and later became a wife of Zeus.

Zeus relied on Hera's wisdom and confided his secrets in her. However, because Hera was not as powerful as Zeus, she had to obey him. Hera was therefore

Figure 9.3 The Goddess Hera (Recent Marble Copy of an Ancient Greek Sculpture). Photo: Marie-Lan Nguyen/Wikimedia Commons (image in public domain).

considered not a powerful and supreme goddess herself, but the wife of one with such power. (Later, this developed into the idea that she was queen of heaven.)

Homer describes her as cold, jealous, stubborn, and querulous, and prone to frequent disputes with her husband. At one point, she colluded with other gods to imprison Zeus, but he found out and exacted revenge by hanging her from the clouds. Hera, knowing she could not overpower Zeus, resorted to other means to achieve her goals: she became manipulative and cunning, secretive and seductive. Hera had a number of children, some with Zeus, the gods Ares, Hebe, and Hephaestus among them.

Among the gods of the ancient Greeks, only Hera was married, and she was therefore a goddess of marriage and childbirth. She was also thought of as a goddess of the sky and stars and depicted as a beautiful woman with a crown and a lotus-tipped staff.

Wonder Woman

Wonder Woman is an invented character who first appeared in a comic book series and later as a live character on television and film. Her dress is unusual for a cartoon superhero, and she has several powers—she can deflect bullets with her wristbands, run very fast, and make people spill the beans with her "lasso of truth." Wonder Woman is described as having goddess-like powers. Perhaps she is a goddess?

William Marsten, the creator of Wonder Woman, also invented the polygraph test. (His quote is featured at the beginning of this chapter.) What qualities did her creator think Wonder Woman should have? Why did he want to create a character with "the strength of superman" and who is also a beautiful woman? Why do you think Wonder Woman was popular?

Questions for Students:

- Who is Wonder Woman? What does she symbolize?

- What other characters is she like?

- Is she more like Athena or Hera? Why?

- Does she have the powers of a goddess or a human or both?

- Do you like or dislike this character? If you were to create a new female character now for a comic, what would she be like?

- Why do you think Wonder Woman was created during WWII? Is she like Rosie the Riveter? Or is she more like a Greek goddess of long ago?

- Do we still need goddesses, cartoon heroines, movie stars (real or imagined)? Why or why not? Do we still need a wonder woman, and just *who* needs her?

Mother Hero

We have looked at the goddess, the mother, and the warrior as they appear in the guises of Athena, Hera, and Wonder Woman. What about women who are neither warriors nor goddesses, but who play the more traditional role of mother? What about more collective, anonymous portraits of women in the role of mother or hero? Or both?

A deep mystery question is whether mother need be a heroine, or a goddess, or neither, to be part of world history. Here is a brief description of the "Mother Hero" in the Soviet Union. It raises the question of heroism for all of our examples. Are all the goddesses, Wonder Woman, and the unknown mothers heroes? Do any fit the hero mother model that was part of Soviet ideology?

Mother Hero was an honorary title in the Soviet Union awarded beginning on 8 July 1944 and lasting into the 1950s to all mothers bearing and raising 10 or more children. This title was accompanied by a handsomely designed medal representing the "Mother Hero Order," as well as an official government certificate conferred by the Presidium of the Supreme Soviet of the USSR to those women (or men) eligible for the award.

The award, authorized by the government, was given on the first birthday of the last child, provided that nine other children (natural or adopted) remained alive in the household. However, children who had died during World War II under heroic, military or other catastrophic or patriotic circumstances, including those who worked on farms or in factories for the war effort, were also counted toward the award of Mother Hero.

Mother Heroes were entitled to wear a medal, which was a gold star with silver straight rays between the arms; it was suspended on a metal, red-enameled "ribbon" bearing the words "Hero Mother" in Russian. Hero mothers were also entitled to a number of privileges in terms of a better retirement pension than normal, the payment of public utility charges for the household, and an extra supply of food and other goods. One man who raised 12 adopted boys was also awarded this certificate of honor for family and motherhood.

Around 430,000 women and one man were awarded this title during its existence from 1944 until the collapse of the Soviet Union in 1991. Many of the former Soviet Socialist Republics like Kazakhstan, the Ukraine, and Tajikistan have given Hero Mother awards at various times, and recently there has been a movement to restore the award in modified form in the current Russian Federation.

(Adapted from Wikipedia, based on the Russian publication, *Ogonyok*, No. 48, November 25, 1996)

Historical Pictures of Women as Mothers and War Heroines

Questions

- Look at Figures 9.4 and 9.5. How are all of the women depicted here: do they have anything in common? Are they shown emotionally, as different from men? Or could men be shown in the same way in the same poses? Why or why not? Could these be "Hero Mothers" if they had lived in the Soviet Union?

- Are the women shown in Figure 9.5 ordinary or elite? How can you tell?

- What do you think the artist is saying about mothers, about women, about roles? Are the women depicted leaders, workers, entertainers, heroic? Why or why not? Who are they protecting? Why?

- What is the overall mood and message about women's roles and jobs?

Figure 9.4 WWII Australian Poster Recruiting Women to Action. Source: Maurice Bramley, 1943 (image in public domain).

Figure 9.5 "The Mothers" by German artist Kathe Kollwitz (1921) (image in public domain).

Warrior Women

When Judith of biblical times (story in the Apocrypha, texts that were rejected from inclusion in the Jewish or Christian bibles when those documents were canonized) went to slay the Syrian General Holofernes, was that a level of heroism beyond what any queen would perform, and who are the most impressive heroines: Judith, Queen Zenobia, or, say, Joan of Arc, or Hua Mulan, Elizabeth I, Catherine the Great, Mom? Is violence allowed to women as well as to men?

To Do: Joan of Arc

Prepare for your students a packet of sources on the story of Joan of Arc, as a companion to the selections on Hua Mulan included here. Joan's story is quite long and complex with many aspects that can be discussed—her dress, manly demeanor, warlike qualities, leadership, and so on—until the rather depressing ending in which she is captured, tortured, and deceived before being condemned to death by burning at the stake as a heretic.

The Story of Hua Mulan

The story of Hua Mulan is well known and has provided much inspiration for poetry, essays, operas, and paintings, as well as the Disney movie. Look at the image in Figure 9.6 and compare it with images of Wonder Woman, Athena, and Hera. Are there any resemblances? What does this image highlight—is she a goddess, a warrior, or perhaps a mother? Does she look as though she went into history as a man, not a woman? Why is she remembered?

Figure 9.6 A Portrait of the Woman Warrior Hua Mulan (Oil Painting on Silk) (image in public domain).

The Ballad of Hua Mulan

Tsk, tsk, and tsk tsk,
Mulan weaves at her window.
We cannot hear the shuttles sound,
We only hear the girl's sighs.
"Now tell me girl, who's in your heart,
And tell me girl, who's on your mind?"
"There's no one in my heart at all
And no one on my mind.
Last night I saw conscription lists,
The Khan is calling troops everywhere.

The army's rolls were in twelve scrolls,
And every scroll held Father's name.
My father has no older son,
Mulan has no big brother.
I wish to go buy horse and gear
And march to the wars for father."
In the east mart she bought a fine steed,
In the west mart she bought blanket and saddle.
In the south mart bought bit and bridle.
In the north mart she bought a long whip,
At dawn she took her parents' leave.
By the Yellow River she camped at dusk.
She did not hear her parents' calls,
She heard only the sad whinnying
From the Turkish horsemen on Mount Yan.
She went thousands of miles to battle,
She flew across fortified passes.
The north wind carried the sounds of the march,
And cold light shone on her armor.
After many a battle the general died,
After ten years the stout troops went home.
She came back and saw the Emperor.
The Emperor sat in his hall of light,
Her deeds raised her rank by twelve degrees,
He gave her a hundred thousand and more.
The Khan then asked her what she wished.
"I've no use to be grand secretary.
Just loan me a camel with far-running feet,
To carry me on its back to home."
When her parents heard that their daughter had come,
They came out of the town, leaning one on another.
When her sister heard the big sister had come,
At the window she made herself up with rouge.
When the young brother heard that the big sister had come,
He sharpened his knife and got pigs and sheep.
Then Mulan opened the door to her room in the east,
She sat on the bed in her room in the west.
She took off her buffcoat and armor,
And put on the skirt she used to wear.
At the window she combed her wispy locks,
In the mirror she put on rouge.

Then she went to the gate to see her companions,
And all her companions were struck with surprise.
"We marched together for twelve long years,
And you never knew that Mulan was a girl.
The male hare's legs have a nervous spring,
The eye of the girl hare wanders.
But when two hares run side by side,
Who can tell if they're boy or girl?"

—Anonymous, 5 A.D.
(Frankel, 1976, pp. 68–72)

Hua Mulan: Biography in Brief

A historical figure famous for disguising herself as a man is Hua Mulan. Her name has long been synonymous with the word "heroine," yet opinions differ as to whether this is her real name. According to Annals of the Ming, her surname is Zhu, while the Annals of the Qing say it is Wei. Xu Wei offers yet another alternative when, in his play, "Mulan Joins the Army for Her Father", he gives her the surname Hua. Others using *The Ballad of Mulan* as their guide have attributed her surname to be Mu.

There is also some confusion concerning her place of origin and the era in which she lived. She is said by some to have come from the Wan County in Hebei, others believed she came from the Shangqiu province in Henan and a third opinion is that she was a native of the Liang prefecture in Gansu. One thing seems certain though. Hua Mulan was from the region known as the Central Plains.

Cheng Dachang of the Song Dynasty recorded that Hua Mulan lived during the Sui and the Tang Dynasties (581–907 C.E.). Song Xiangfeng of the Qing Dynasty asserted that she was of Sui origins (581–618 C.E.) while Yao Ying, also of the Qing Dynasty, believed she was from the time of the Six Dynasties. No record of her achievements appears in official history books prior to the Song times. Stories circulated in China's Central Plains indicate that she must have lived before the Tang Dynasty.

Both history books and legends do at least agree on one thing—her accomplishments. It is said that Hua Mulan's father received an order to serve in the army. He had fought before but, by this time, was old and infirm. Hua Mulan knew it was out of the question for her father to go and her only brother was much too young. She decided to disguise herself as a man and take her father's place.

The troops fought in many bloody campaigns for several years before they obtained permission to return home. Hua Mulan was summoned to the court by the emperor, who wished to appoint her to high office as a reward for her outstanding service. Hua Mulan declined his offer and accepted a fine horse instead.

Only later, when her former comrades in arms went to visit her, did they learn that she was a woman.

(From the online compilation "100 Celebrated Chinese Women," available at http://www.span.com.au/100women/55.html)

Questions

- Why did Hua Mulan go to war? Did she fight as a man or a woman? Why?

- What might it mean that she declined the Emperor's offer for high office and instead settled for a fine horse—is this the act of a warrior? A woman? What do you think?

- If people found out only later that Hua was female, and not during battle, why remember her at all?

- What role does Hua exemplify: a leader, a warrior woman, and a rebel? Explain.

- Is Hua Mulan's story different from Western examples of warrior women, such as Joan of Arc or the character of Judith in the "Book of Judith" from the Apocrypha?

Rebels and Causes

As warrior women, Joan of Arc, Hua Mulan, and others went on to gain victories for their people, but (at least according to the histories we have) did little or nothing to advance the causes of women in their cultures. However, their lives can be contrasted with many of the case studies that follow, starting with the most unusual figure of Olympe de Gouges, an ordinary woman who became a revolutionary during the French Revolution, and authored a famous document reproduced here, "The Declaration of the Rights of Women and the Female Citizen," designed to supplement and extend the "Rights of Man and the Citizen" recently passed by the National Assembly of France. Olympe was executed during the reign of terror for speaking out, but we have good records of her life and we can also examine the document she wrote. Ask students to examine Olympe's life, and her message as expressed in the "Declaration of the Rights of Women."

Do they see her message as uplifting, moral, and right, or as radical, wild, and rebellious, or as all of the above? What do they think of her views of marriage and family? Why might someone like de Gouges appear during the French Revolution?

Olympe de Gouges (1748–1793)

Declaration of the Rights of Woman and the Female Citizen
Mothers, daughters, sisters and representatives of the nation demand to be constituted into a national assembly. Believing that ignorance, omission, or scorn for the rights of woman are the only causes of public misfortunes and of the corruption of governments, [the women] have resolved to set forth in a solemn declaration the natural, inalienable, and sacred rights of woman in order that this declaration, constantly exposed before all the members of the society, will ceaselessly remind them of their rights and duties; in order that the authoritative acts of women and the authoritative acts of men may be at any moment compared with and respectful of the purpose of all political institutions; and in order that citizens' demands, henceforth based on simple and incontestable principles, will always support the constitution, good morals, and the happiness of all.

Consequently, the sex that is as superior in beauty as it is in courage during the suffering of maternity recognizes and declares in the presence and under the auspices of the Supreme Being, the following Rights of Woman and of Female Citizens.

Article 1
Woman is born free and lives equal to man in her rights. Social distinctions can be based only on the common utility.

Article 2
The purpose of any political association is the conservation of the natural and imprescriptible rights of woman and man; these rights are liberty, property, security, and especially resistance to oppression.

. . .

Article 4
Liberty and justice consist of restoring all that belongs to others; thus, the only limits on the exercise of the natural rights of woman are perpetual male tyranny; these limits are to be reformed by the laws of nature and reason.

. . .

Article 6
The laws must be the expression of the general will; . . . male and female citizens, being equal in the eyes of the law, must be equally admitted to all honors, positions, and public employment according to their capacity and without other distinctions besides those of their virtues and talents.

(Olympe de Gouge, available online at Sunshine for Women, http://www.pinn.net/~sunshine/book-sum/gouges.html)

Olympe de Gouges: A Brief Biography

Marie-Olympe de Gouges was born in 1748, in Montauban in southern France. Sources indicate that she was raised in a family of modest means, the daughter of a butcher, Pierre Gouze, and a housemaid, Olympe Moisset. De Gouges married a wealthy older French officer, Louis Aubrey, when she was seventeen years old, and they had a son two years later. Her husband died after three years, leaving de Gouges with a child to support. She refused to accept her position as a widowed mother or the legal designation of "widow" under French law, and vowed never to marry again. Leaving her son behind in the village, de Gouges went to Paris to take up a career as a writer, and chose as her pen name Olympe de Gouges, a fusion of her father's and her mother's names. She built her career by establishing connections with other famous writers and philosophers and worked her way into high social circles. A largely self-educated woman, de Gouges wrote plays, novels, and social pamphlets, mostly about marriage and social relations. Her career as a playwright had some success, but she turned increasingly to politics. Her work was mainly about human rights, especially those dealing with the place of women in society. France in the 1780s was in turmoil, and Paris was the center of political and intellectual action.

While many of her fellow citizens were deeply revolutionary, de Gouges took a more modest position for reform, and her works tended to reject extremists from both sides, the royalists and the rebels. As talk of revolution began to build, de Gouges still considered herself a royalist. Writing a pamphlet in 1788, "Les Droits de la Femme," the rights of women, she expressed strong support for equality for women while still arguing that the monarchy should be saved for reasons of social stability. However, she became disillusioned after the king of France, Louis XIV, tried to escape the country in a carriage heading to the border, following the storming of the Bastille by a street army of men and women.

De Gouges became more revolutionary in tone, publicly declaring her beliefs in the complete equality of all people, men and women, and joined a feminist organization, the Society of Republican and Revolutionary Women, that encouraged her to create a document that would serve as a (probably the first) declaration of women's rights, one that would be a response to the officially adopted document of the revolution, "The Declaration of the Rights of Man and the Citizen," written and published in 1789.

In October of 1789, now widely known to radical groups, she proposed a radical reform platform to the National Assembly, the governing body of the nation's new leaders. Presenting her ideas to Assembly leaders, she argued for complete legal equality for women, better education for girls, and improved openings to a greater range of occupations for women, as well as a state theater that would show only plays written by females.

In 1791, Olympe de Gouges' work, "The Declaration of the Rights of Woman and the Female Citizen," was published and widely circulated beginning in September of that year. She stated that, "women were equal to men in every respect," and because women participated in the French Revolution, they too should automatically receive the rights extended to their male counterparts.

Because of de Gouges' outspokenness and public activism, she aroused suspicions, particularly after the Jacobin Party took power. This group became increasingly intolerant of dissension and began to reject even mild criticism. De Gouges harshly criticized Robespierre, the Jacobin leader and most powerful man at the time. De Gouges, now thirty-eight years old, was charged with sedition on July 25, 1793, and imprisoned with all her writings reviewed by a public prosecutor. The new government, the National Convention, ordered an interrogation that began on August 6, 1793, and found that she had produced writings that were an attack on the sovereignty of the people, arguing that she had set citizens against each other in civil conflict as well as other charges. The public prosecutor drew up formal charges and ordered Olympe de Gouges held for trial. She was found guilty (no surprise during the Reign of Terror), condemned to death by guillotine, and executed on November 3, 1793. (Adapted from Levy, Applewhite, and Johnson, 1979, pp. 64–65, 87–96, 254–9, and Wilson, 1991, pp. 478–9.)

Questions

- What are some of the ideas about women set forth in de Gouges' preamble and first law?

- How strong are Olympe's ideas for her time, and why do you think they were expressed during the Revolution?

- How did de Gouges start out in life: was she of humble or wealthy origins, and does that matter? Why did she go to Paris to live and what happened to her there? Was she a success in her career, in her cause? How did her life end and do you see her as heroic or foolish in speaking out on behalf of women?

Florence Nightingale: A Brief Biography

Nightingale's foray into nursing came in the form of a "divine calling" in her teenage years. As a woman who came from a highly esteemed and well-off British family, this was a surprise career choice to many, including Nightingale's parents. Traditionally, someone of her status would be groomed to be a wife and mother, and definitely would not take a job as a nurse, which was seen as a beggar's profession. Nonetheless, Nightingale's father granted her permission in 1851 to study nursing abroad in Germany. Two years later, a war broke out between Russia and Germany, and Nightingale was sent to the army hospital in Scutari to care for them. *When she arrived, she found the conditions of the hospital to be the main cause for so many soldiers dying, and soon became an advocate for cleaning up hospitals* [emphasis in original]. It was during this time that Nightingale's mathematical and statistical talents shined as she showed the world new ways on analyzing medical data. Her work here would continue after her return to Britain in 1857. Now a national hero, Nightingale would be invited to meet with Queen Victoria to discuss her ideas in what would end up forming the Army Medical College. The rest of Nightingale's days would involve writing books and manuals for the public and curriculum for medical schools that would shape our modern nursing profession.

(Eric Hebert, "Famous Nurses In History," available at http://www. rncentral.com/nursing-library/famous-nurses)

Questions

- Why is Florence Nightingale considered a special "ordinary" woman? Was she truly ordinary or did she come from a high-status family?

- Is nursing a suitable and understandable job for a woman? Why or why not?

- Did Florence push the envelope in defining her status, job, and gender?

Rigoberta Menchú: A Brief Biography

Rigoberta Menchú (Figure 9.7) was born to a poor K'iche' Maya (one of many Maya ethnic groups) family in Guatemala in 1959. She started out helping her family run their farm, especially when they were away picking coffee in the highlands.

As a girl and young woman, Menchú became involved in community assistance sponsored by the Catholic Church and became an important figure in women's rights in her country. Guatemala has a history of conflict between social classes, particularly those descended from the Spanish and those of native Indian origin, as was Menchú.

Even as a teen, Menchú was criticized and opposed by political leaders. They accused her and her family of joining the local guerilla movement that was fighting against the government. Her father was tortured in prison, although later released. He joined a peasant organization afterward and worked to improve the lot of the Indian peoples, and so did Rigoberta. In 1979, her brother was killed by the Guatemalan army. In the following year, her father was killed by security forces in the capital. He and other peasant leaders lived in the Spanish embassy for protection. Menchú's mother died after having been arrested, tortured, and raped.

Menchú became a leader in the peasants' organization, and taught herself Spanish as well as other Mayan languages. She led a strike for better working conditions and was active in demonstrations in the capital. She joined the Popular Front, an opposition party, and educated peasants on how to the resist armed forces. Then she helped to found a larger political party and, with the help of a French writer, told her life story. Her book, *I, Rigoberta Menchú* (1984), has been published worldwide.

Traveling abroad to raise money for her movement, Menchú has returned many times to protest on behalf of Indian peasants, even though she receives regular death threats.

Figure 9.7 Rigoberta Menchú, Nobel Peace Prize Winner, Attending the International Forum of Peace in Italy. Source: From original color photo by Freddy Ballo/Creative Commons.

She is a popular figure known to many as a spokeswoman for Indian rights and for conciliation. Her work has earned her many awards, most importantly the Noble Peace Prize in 1992. Menchú is still working for her causes in Guatemala and throughout the Western hemisphere.

Questions

- How did Menchú become a leader? Where was she born and how did she start out in life: as an ordinary person, a peasant, or a great leader?

- Why do you think she decided to become so outspoken? Were her actions dangerous in the time and place—Guatemala—that she lived?

- Why, in particular, did Menchú decide to speak for Indian peoples in her country and then go abroad to further her education?

- Do you see hers as an unusual life story or one that any woman could achieve in her social setting? Explain.

You Decide: A Few Big Questions to Think About

- Would Athena or Wonder Woman understand the problems and issues of each woman—mother, worker, or warrior—described here? What do you think they would say?
- What do you think a revolutionary or feminist would say about each picture or description? How did the artists depict the goddesses compared with the way the other women are depicted?

Applying Theories and Explanations to (the Lack of) Women in World History

Women seem to be only casual visitors to world history texts. Although there are enormous numbers of men represented in world history, from ancient times to the present, there are relatively few women prominently displayed in any given epoch, and, worse yet, of those offered to teachers and students of history, most are "top" women—queens, presidents (not very many), and wives of leaders (many more, but still not very many). Because much of what is typically learned as world or U.S. history in secondary and elementary classrooms deals with political leaders and wars, there is a problem, as relatively few political heads of state have been women over the course of history and women have been almost entirely excluded from participation in warfare (name one female warrior/ general who will be recognized by your class!).

Now and again, women appear who are active leaders of less important peoples and places, particularly the downtrodden and oppressed. This often includes women who are advocating or fighting for causes they see as worthy: suffragettes, revolutionaries, rebels, community organizers, reformers, and holy figures. Here we may get a much higher representation of women leaders. Casting a wide net across time and space will yield a fairly surprising number of social reformers, writers, commentators, and community activist types who are not seeking political office and usually do not get the kind of publicity given to their more renowned political cousins. Often, exemplary individual women are smothered textually by the movement they lead which, perhaps rightfully, gets the lionesses' share of sentences in a book. So, even in the social realm women are somewhat at a disadvantage for a variety of reasons, even though they have served as primary leaders of major movements (e.g., the American Progressives). How many of our own home-grown female reformers and suffragists can you name and how many can you actually visualize? Who wrote the famous documents that advanced women in history, such as the "Seneca Falls Declaration of Sentiments" or the "Declaration of the Rights of Women and the Female Citizen"?

Mystery Packet: Women on Coins

Whose images make it onto the money we use? Cultures select people who are admired or who have some special significance to depict on their currency. Compare the depictions of Zenobia and Susan B. Anthony, two women who have made it onto coins (Figures 9.8 and 9.9).

Figure 9.8 Zenobia, Queen of Palmyra, on a Third-Century c.e. Coin. Source: From a public domain image. Modifications © 2006 Jone Johnson Lewis.

Figure 9.9 Susan B. Anthony 1999 Silver Dollar. Source: U.S. Mint.

Zenobia

The Syrian queen Zenobia lived in the third century c.e. She was the second wife of King Septimius Odaenathus and therefore queen of the Palmyrene Empire, which she ruled on behalf of her infant son when her husband died. In 269 c.e., she conquered Egypt and expelled the Roman governor Tenagino Probus, then beheaded him when he attempted to invade his former territory. She proclaimed herself queen of Egypt and ruled until 274 C.E., when she was defeated and taken hostage by the Roman emperor Aurelian. In Aurelian's military parade, Zenobia appeared in golden chains and she so impressed him that he freed her and gave her an elegant villa in Tivoli, Italy. There, she became a prominent philosopher, socialite, and Roman matron. (Adapted from the Wikipedia entry on Zenobia, available at http://en.wikipedia.org/wiki/Zenobia.)

Susan Brownell Anthony

Susan Brownell Anthony (1820–1906) was an American civil rights leader who played a pivotal role in the nineteenth-century anti-slavery and women's rights movements. She is most famous for her fight to win women's suffrage (voting rights). She helped to write the famous "Seneca Falls Declaration of Sentiments" of 1848, and traveled the United States and Europe extensively, giving seventy-five to a hundred speeches per year on women's rights for forty-five years. Throughout this time, she faced arrests, ridicule, and threats. Susan B. Anthony died before seeing the nineteenth amendment passed in 1920, and women's suffrage made the law of the land. (Adapted from the Wikipedia entry on Susan B. Anthony, available at http://en.wikipedia.org/wiki/Susan_B._Anthony.)

Questions for Students

- So, why does Zenobia rate a picture on a coin? Who was she and what did she accomplish?

- How does her image compare with that of a goddess?

- How does her image compare with that of Susan B. Anthony?

- Was Susan B. Anthony a goddess, a queen, or just a commoner? What did Anthony accomplish to rate a coin? Were her accomplishments impressive? Why or why not?

- What does it say on each coin and are the two women depicted pretty much alike or differently? Why?

Student Activity: Women on Coins in World History

- For thousands of years, rulers and the famous have been placed in profile (usually) on coins of their countries. You could argue that getting your image or name or both on a nationally distributed coin means that you rate in some way or another, and that people already know who you are or get to know you when they buy or sell goods.

- Selecting at least two time periods, ancient or modern, find two or three women (or more) who rated enough to be portrayed on a coin. What did each of these women represent: an accomplishment, a title, an office, a mythological figure? Keep a folder of your research and summarize your findings in a well-written essay of about two pages.

- A list of women on coins, titled "Distinguished Women of History: 200 Coin Portraits," can be downloaded from the Internet (see Web Resources below). This list invites us to test our theories about the role of women in world history by examining what type of woman is on each coin.

- Are there a great variety of women, including artists, writers, sports figures, social reformers, or revolutionaries? Do politicos, queens and heads of state make up the majority? Are there women you recognize?

- Do the coins from ancient and medieval times show the same kinds of women as modern examples?

- Can we see any patterns in the roles and status of the women who are placed on coins? Are they generally high in status or low?

- Do "Hero Moms" or "Soccer Moms" make it onto coins? Are there any cultures or nations that have a lot of women on coins? Why might that be?

- If you had to design a coin of your own and place a female figure on it who you regard as a wonderful person, or a great leader, who might that be?

- Research a woman to place on a coin of your design, and then draw a picture of the coin as you would like it to look. Share this with classmates, friends, and family and teacher. Also be ready to explain your choice and to discuss how your choice has improved the role of women in world history, if at all.

Women on Coins: Web Resources

- *Distinguished Women of History: 200 Coin Portraits* (Word document). Available at http://webzoom.freewebs.com/shequality/Women%20on%20 Coins%20%20200%20Portraits.doc.

- *Women on Banknotes*. Available at http://shequality.spaces.live.com, and click on *Women on Banknotes* link.

Theories Explaining (the Lack of) Women in World History

We have looked directly at a small sample of historical sources involving women. In historical research by professional historians, there is increasing recognition of the role of women in world history and we have drawn upon this in preparing these examples. Yet the paucity of women in world history textbooks still confronts us. Why is this the case? We present three views for your consideration.

First, Patrick Manning, an outstanding male historian, recently summarized the state of affairs for women in history. His summary is followed by the views of a noted feminist historian, Rosalind Miles, and by the words of an important female historian of women's history and the Holocaust, Gerda Lerner.

Discuss each excerpt and then go back through single or multiple examples of women in history, or add a few of your own, and decide if these theories help to explain, understand, or provide insights into the quantity and quality of women in the history of the world.

Theory I: A Noted World Historian Offers an Explanation

> For all the new works that one can cite, it remains striking that studies of women and gender roles in world history have developed so slowly and that their development has been restricted to a small number of themes.
>
> Why has gender been such a difficult issue to develop in world history?
>
> What are the lines that have been taken and could be taken?
>
> The well established presumption that women's lives are acted out in the private sphere of the family rather than the public spheres of politics and economy has suggested that women's history is family history, and family plays no great part in world history . . . I argue that women's work can be divided into reproductive, domestic, and social labor. Reproductive life is the bearing of children and bringing them through infancy, mostly completed between the ages of twenty and thirty-five. Domestic labor is that of maintaining one's own household, or the household of one's parents, or the household of one's children or other families; it often takes place for all of one's years. Social labor is the production of economic goods: it may include agricultural work, marketing, artisanal work; it might be paid or unpaid . . .
>
> The lives of most women involve all three types of work, but not usually at one time. For women as individuals and for the societies relying on women's work, the timing of moving from one type of work to another and the social value accorded each type of work provides statements of the destiny of individual women and the structure of society overall. Attention to the patterns of these types of work and to changes in them may offer a way to include the lives of women in history, to link the them to gender roles generally, and to show the place of family history in society more broadly.
>
> (Manning, 2003, pp. 210–11)

You Decide

- Do you generally agree or disagree with Manning's analysis of the problem, that is, women's roles in the family have held them back from a prominent treatment in historical texts, or might you consider this a male bias? Why?
- If you wrote a supplement or challenge to his statement, what would you say, or are you pretty much satisfied with the conclusion offered?

Theory II: A Feminist Historian's View

Professor Manning's research conclusions can be contrasted with those of the feminist historian Rosalind Miles, who argues that the absence of women in history has occurred for several reasons. Here is a quote from her work for you to analyze:

> A women's history, then, must hope to explain as well as narrate, seeking the answer to two key questions: How did men succeed in enforcing the subordination of women? And why did women let them get away with it? At the origin of the species, it is suggested, Mother Nature saddled women with an unequal share of the primary work of reproduction. They, therefore, had to consent to domination in order to obtain protection for themselves and their children. The historical record shows, however, that women in "primitive" societies have a better chance of equality than those of more "advanced" cultures. In these, male domination has been elaborated into every aspect of life, indeed strenuously re-invented in every epoch with a battery of religious, biological, "scientific," psychological, and economic reasons succeeding one another in the endless work of justifying women's inferiority to men. Traditionalist arguments of masculine supremacy have been remarkably resilient over time—all democratic experiments, all revolutions, all demands for equality have so far stopped short of sexual equality—and women, seen as biologically determined, continue to be denied the human right of full self-determination.
>
> (Miles, 1989, p. xiii)

You Decide

- How would Miles answer Manning's views about family being the cause?
- Do you agree with Miles' placement of responsibility in equalizing the role of women in history? Are male authors to blame or are women to blame as well?

Theory III: A Noted Feminist and Holocaust Historian Offers Her Own View of Women in History

Yet women's culture has remained largely unrecorded and unrecognized. It must be stressed that women have been left out of history not because of the evil intent of male historians, but because we have considered history only in male-centered terms. We have missed women and their activities, because we have asked questions of history that are inappropriate to women. To rectify this we must, for a time, focus on a woman-centered inquiry, considering the possibility of the existence of a female culture within the general culture shared by men and women. As we ask new questions and consult formerly neglected sources, we uncover the record of women's unrecognized activities. For example, when we ask the traditional question, "What have women contributed to reform activities, such as the abolition movement?" we assume that male activities are the norm and that women are, at best, marginal to the male-defined movement. In answer to such a question we learn that abolitionist women demanded the right to lecture in public and to hold office in antislavery societies and thereby, in 1840, provoked a crisis that split and weakened the antislavery movement. What is ignored in this interpretation is the fact that the increased participation of women and their greater activism actually strengthened antislavery ranks. Had we asked the question, "What was women's role in, perception of, and experience in the antislavery movement?" the answers would lend themselves to a somewhat different interpretation. If one looks at the impact of the antislavery movement solely in terms of voting behaviors and politics (male activities), the contribution of women may seem unimportant. But reform movements in antebellum America can also be seen as efforts to adjust personal values and public morality to the demands of a rapidly industrializing society. Moral reform, sexual purity, temperance and abolition became the symbolic issues through which women expressed themselves in the public sphere. Antislavery women's activities—organization building, the spreading of literature, petitioning, participation in slave rescues—helped to create changes in the climate of opinion in the North and West that were essential to the growth of the political antislavery movement. Men and women, even when active in the same social movements, worked in different ways and defined issues differently. As historians are uncovering the record of women's activities and correcting the bias in the interpretation of the past, which has assumed that man is the measure of all that is significant, we are laying the foundation for a new synthesis.

(Gerda Lerner, "The Necessity of History," 1982 Presidential Address to the Organization of American Historians, reprinted in *Why History Matters*, 1997, pp. 119–20)

Women have always been half the human race, but have often been treated as second-class citizens. Exemplary women, however, have abounded in almost every time and place, and have inspired others across the ages, breaking the boundaries of culture and politics to effectively influence the formation of new ideas and self-images. These women are Jewish, Greek, Chinese, African, South American, and others, and are exemplars for both the real and the ideal. Some women, and men, have espoused ideas of equality and justice for women that have influenced individuals and groups in many places, jumping over many geographies and societies to encourage more attention to and support for women as leaders and liberators.

Which women do you admire most? Which do the students admire most? Collect reasons for each choice and summarize these for the class as a whole. Do any patterns appear? Are there unusual and commonly expressed reasons? How do students explain the lack of women in world history, and which women whom they have studied and/or researched would they give special attention to in a world history textbook? Ask them to write an argument in favor of two women of their choice who they think should be give serious attention in any commonly used textbook. Start a club, write a letter to a publisher, pass a law for equal time in texts and websites for women in world history compared with men. Let's go fifty-fifty, okay?

References and Further Reading

Adovasio, J. M., Soffer, O., and Page, J. (2007) *The Invisible Sex: Uncovering the True Roles of Women in Prehistory*, New York: HarperCollins.

Aristotle. (1983) "On the generation of animals," in M. B. Mahowald (ed.), *Philosophy of Woman*, Indianapolis: Hackett, pp. 266–74.

Barber, E. W. (1994) *Women's Work: The First 20,000 Years*, New York: W. W. Norton.

Bock, G. and James, S. (1992) *Beyond Equality and Difference: Citizenship, Feminist Politics, and Female Subjectivity*, London: Routledge.

Clark, R., Allard, J., and Mahoney, T. (2004) "How much of the sky? Women in American high school history textbooks from the 1960s, 1980s, 1990s," *Social Education* 68: 57–62.

Clark, R., Ayton, K., Frechette, N., and Keller, P. J. (January/February 2005) "Women in American world history high school textbooks from the 1960s, 1980s, and 1990s," *Social Education* 69: 41–5.

Clay, C., Chandrika, P., and Senecal, C. (1949, reprint 1989, 2009) *Envisioning Women in World History*, vols. I and II, New York: McGraw-Hill.

De Beauvoir, S. (1949) *The Second Sex*, New York: Vintage Press.

De Gouges, O. (1791) *Declaration de Droits de la Femme et de la Citoyenne*. Paris: Self-published by the author.

Eisenstein, H. (1983) *Contemporary Feminist Thought*, Boston: G. K. Hall.

Frankel, H. H. (trans.) (1976) "The ballad of Hua Mulan," in *The Flowering Plum and the Palace Lady: Interpretations of Chinese Poetry*, New Haven, CT: Yale University Press.

Freidan, B. (1963) *The Feminine Mystique*, New York: W. W. Norton.

Gornick, V. and Moran, B. (1971) *Woman in Sexist Society: Studies in Power and Powerlessness*, New York: Basic Books.

Gross, S. H. (1987) "Women's history for global learning," *Social Education* 31: 194–8.

Lerner, G. (1979) *The Majority Finds its Past: Placing Women in History*, New York: Oxford University Press.

Lerner, G. (1982) "The necessity of history," Presidential Address to the Organization of American Historians, reprinted in Lerner, G. (1997) *Why History Matters: Life and Thought*, New York: Oxford University Press.

Lerner, G. (1987) *The Creation of Patriarchy*, New York: Oxford University Press.

Lerner, G. (1997) *Why History Matters: Life and Thought*, New York: Oxford University Press.

Levy, D. G., Applewhite, H. B., and Johson, M. D. (trans. and eds.) (1979) *Women in Revolutionary Paris, 1789–1705: Selected Documents*, Urbana: University of Illinois Press.

Lloyd, R. (n.d.) "Distinguished women of history: 200 coin portraits." Online. Available as a Word document at http://webzoom.freewebs.com/shequality/Women%20on%20Coins%20%20200%20Portraits.doc (accessed March 14, 2010).

Mann, S. (1990) *Women's and Gender History in Global Perspective: East Asia*, Washington, D.C.: American Historical Association.

Manning, P. (2003) *Navigating World History*, London and New York: Palgrave Macmillan.

Menchú Tum, R. (1984) *I, Rigoberta Menchú. An Indian Woman in Guatemala*. Edited and introduced by Elisabeth Burgos-Debray. New York and London: Verso.

Menchú Tum, R. (1998) *Crossing Borders: An Autobiography*, New York: Verso (first published in Italian, October 1997, and in Spanish, April 1998).

Miles, R. (1989) *The Women's History of the World*, New York: Harper & Row.

Morgan, R. (ed.) (1970) *Sisterhood is Powerful*, New York: Vintage Books.

Pernoud, R. (1994) *Joan of Arc: By Herself and Her Witnesses*, Lanham, MD: Scarborough House (first French edn 1962).

Reiter, R. R. (ed.) (1975) *Toward an Anthropology of Women*, New York: Monthly Review Press.

Sadker, M. and Sadker, D. (1994) *Failing at Fairness*, New York: Scribner's.

Stone, L. (1996) "Feminist political theory: Contributions to a conception of citizenship," *Theory and Research in Social Education* 24 (1): 36–53.

Strobel, M. and Bingham, M. (2006) *The Theory and Practice of Women's History and Gender History in Global Perspective*. Washington, D.C.: American Historical Association.

Tetrault, M. K. T. (March 1987) "Rethinking women, gender, and the social studies." *Social Education,* 170–8.

Ulrich, L. T (2007) *Well-behaved Women Seldom Make History*, New York: Vintage Books of Random House.

Vivante, B. (ed.) (1999) *Women's Role in Ancient Civilizations*, Westport, CN: Greenwood Press.

Wilson, K. A. (1991) "Olympe de Gouges," in *An Encyclopedia of Continental Women Writers*, vol. I, New York: Garland Publishing, pp. 478–9.

Websites

Women in World History. A project of the Center for History and New Media at George Mason University, providing primary sources, curriculum modules, teaching case studies, and discussion forums for educators wanting to include women in their history teaching. Available at http://chnm.gmu.edu/wwh.

Women in World History Curriculum. Large, well-organized interactive site about women's experiences in world history with lessons and plans for teachers. Available at http://www.womeninworldhistory.com.

About.com: Women's History. A blog and resource on women in history, by professor of women's religious history Jone Johnson Lewis. Available at http://womenshistory.about.com.

Worldwide Guide to Women in Leadership. Available at http://www.guide2womenleaders.com.

Sunshine for Women. A major site for women's history and documentation. Available at http://www.pinn.net.

Shequality-Parity Democrats. An organization promoting political parity among women and men by educating about women leaders. Available at http://www.freewebs.com/shequality.

The Oxford Encyclopedia of Women's History. A fully searchable collection from Oxford's works in print (requires hosting). Available at http://www.oxford-womenworldhistory.com.

ten
Finding Mysteries Everywhere
Sources, Resources, and Outright Fabrications

Mysteries are everywhere! Just look for them!

(Jack Zevin and David Gerwin)

Teaching history as mystery is an idea that seeks to return the study of history to its roots in observation, analysis, and inference. Put another way, we are trying to recapture a sense of history as a kind of "undiscovered" country in which students and teachers can play detective—finding and interpreting primary evidence. Some of the evidence is missing, some is faulty, some biased, and some frequently misleading. This is to our benefit as teachers. Why?

Well, the whole idea is to do your own digging and draw your own conclusions; better yet, to learn *how* to do your own digging. You may seek help from others: teachers, parents, resources, professional historians and social scientists, scientists, and artists. But the joy of solving mysteries, or finding out that they cannot be solved or can be only partially solved, is that you get to play Nancy Drew or Sherlock Holmes. Everything is *not* handed to you. Rather, you get to enjoy the struggle for knowledge in much the way historians do when they confront new and perplexing data, or find they must rethink existing interpretations and judgments. Contrary to what you might think, history is not "dead" at all, but living within us, and our culture, and evolving with us as we travel through time and space.

For example, people we once thought quite unimportant or non-existent turn up, and are re-evaluated, and gain a new sense of status and importance; while others who we once doted on turn out to be quite flawed and go down in our estimation.

Indeed, one of the truly scary things about history is how changeable it is depending upon whose eyes we are looking through, and the temper of the times. Historical revision and transmogrification mean that prevailing norms wrap around our minds and may very well blind us to current or past realities, while other events may open our eyes to new possibilities.

In addition, you get to sharpen your collective wits, honing intelligence and investigative skills against what may be very broken, confusing, and conflicting data, or worse yet, data shaped and edited through the lenses of biased sources who have agendas, conscious or unconscious, to push onto their audiences. So, hey, look out, be sharp, and don't take the first pretty solution you come across as the right answer. Go back and question answers, question historians and social scientists, question news sources, and question yourself. It is a bit exhausting but very exciting to make your own discoveries, even if they seem ordinary at the end, but you may also discover interesting facts, and lies, and prevarications, and machinations, and (every now and then) great truths and judgments.

You may find that sources have been lost, hidden, and purposely misrepresented to attain ends and goals that you may not fully understand until later. All to the good!

You may find sources that are genuinely and passionately emotional about historical and mythological people, places, and events. All to the good!

You may find sources that offer theories about historical causation—theories that are illuminating and exciting, but perhaps not fully supported by evidence, maybe not even directly connected to evidence. Well, all to the good?

You may find sources that are way too familiar and have been interpreted many times, laden with references and interpretations and judgments: these are prime material to decimate and fragment, creating missing pieces of your own for student interpretation.

All such problematic sources (or those familiar ones rendered problematic by a process of deconstruction) are exactly what we need to teach world history as mystery, because they invite and sustain problem finding and problem solving by students. Problems drive inquiry and discussion, and promote conversation and critical thinking, factors that make for high levels of motivation and participation.

History and social science employ methods that we have used in this book: investigative approaches such as close observation, comparison of sources, corroboration of witnesses, and connecting conclusions to evidence. These are all sound historical techniques for reasoning and testing interpretations, and should be part and parcel of your daily teaching repertory.

History and the social sciences may also be used by those who want to shape our minds so that we *miss* certain ideas and events, making us blind to some things but very aware of others. For example, one could argue that the place of women in history has been "hidden" or repressed, perhaps so that we will be relieved of thinking about the problem of balancing the place of women in human affairs. History may also be used to encourage us to worship certain ideas, events, and people; to like *our* leaders but dislike others.

However, aspirations to find truth in history are quite elusive as we are all prone to certain beliefs, prejudices, and philosophic assumptions that may shape our conclusions—basing them as much on sentiment and compassion, or loyalty and faith, as on facts and reason. Thus, we have a great many problems interpreting and understanding the past, but rather than worry about or deplore the human condition in studying history, we as teachers should welcome these problems as potential motivators for student inquiry into world history.

Missing evidence may make a problem more enticing, providing us with the opportunity to fill in the blanks by research, or by extrapolation, extending what we know to make reasonable assumptions about what the lost portions might be like. Realizing that multiple causes and effects are common in any historical event offers the chance to promote a more complex vision of historical thinking, one in which we can collect, analyze, rate, and debate which causes or consequences are connected and which are most important. Identifying causes, and pinpointing effects, is a form of mystery that *could* be quite enjoyable if we didn't feel we must drive ourselves, and our students, to "*a*" definite conclusion about "*the*" causes of WWI, for example.

Conflicting sources, unreliable witnesses, multiple overlapping witnesses, and clashing views of experts, although potential headaches in a history classroom in which answers are everything, are allies in a classroom in which the questions are more important than the answers. Conflict between sources, criticism among witnesses, and secondary sources with dramatically different interpretations create a sense of vitality (that history *matters*!) but give us decisions to make about truth, reliability, and interpretation.

Finally, emotional reporting and moral issues in history, particularly those that draw us into an argument we care about, are wonderful in motivating learning and stimulating creative teaching. After all, if we don't care about history, past or present, why even bother to have a debate over good and evil, over whether the past is prologue, about the precise interpretation of a new find, or over an old set of evidence and its newfound meaning? Placing a value on historical evidence and giving meaning and admiration to a decision is involving us, and our students, in the process of history as it is and was lived by those we are studying. We, too, are part of the process, and it matters just who we will ascribe the role of hero to, who we vilify as evil, and what we see as good, defensible choices for leadership, or faith, or economic decision making. Heroism itself is a value issue in history, and may lead us to wonderful ideals or lead us astray into the hands of demagogues and charlatans.

Thus, thinking about world history as mystery is welcoming the subject in its "raw" form, comprising one or more of the following problems:

- sometimes plentiful, sometimes missing or misshaped or one-sided evidence;
- multiple causes and effects for events, which need to be ranked or rated;
- a wide range of witness reliability validity, and agreement or disagreement;

- overlapping, conflicting, and converging interpretations by experts; and
- descriptions, views, and judgments of people, places, and events, permeated by values, biases, prejudices, and ideologies.

Therefore, the excitement of teaching and learning history as mystery is confronting face to face the evidence and the interpretations. This is the trip we need to take to create our own personal sense of history as meaningful and delicious, arguable and entertaining, and always open to renewal and revision.

You Decide

Take a look at Figure 10.1. Where in history is the fine fellow and his horse from? When did he live and where did he ride? What culture did he belong to, as far as you can tell? Can you interpret the clues and come up with an answer? Even if you know the horseman is Pazyrik, does that do much for your understanding and interpretation?

Figure 10.1 A Rug Woven with the Image of a Pazyrik Rider (State Hermitage Museum in St Petersburg) (image in public domain).

A Note of Caution about the Wonders and Pitfalls of the World Wide Web

Caution! Download ahead: many websites, lots and lots of data, words I don't understand, dates that are confusing, and biases that may be undetected in the rush to finish my paper!

The websites available now, as of this writing, are simply grand. It seems as though everything we could ever have wanted and then some can be obtained by going online and "Googling." This wonderful state of affairs has resulted in excellent research on occasion, but also in plagiarized and copied papers—with large sections taken right out of historical sources but empty of meaning to students. You can check quite easily whether students understand their downloads by asking them to pick out a passage and explain it in their own words. If they can, fine—and if they cannot, then they are simply parroting what they collected uncomprehendingly.

Carrying out historical research online, in our view, is wonderful for teachers *if* the sites are previewed, regulated, selected, and planned so that the plethora of sources students encounter fit together and are approachable. In our opinion, it is important that you use the marvelous resources on the web, and we will suggest some to you, and as you may note in this book we ourselves have taken considerable advantage of what is available.

However, there are issues. For example:

- Sites may contain vast amounts of data, and require guidance to use intelligently, picking and choosing sources that fit a question or topic.
- Sites may be confusing to navigate, offering what amount to sales pitches along with important data. These should be previewed, and you should prepare a short guide to help students navigate specific sections and subjects rather than wander through (unless that's what you want).
- Sites sometimes cite (pun intended) sources for images, music, documents, bios, and so forth. But sometimes they don't, or they cite them in a way that is incomplete or unclear to students. As historian-detectives, we prefer to know our sources clearly: author, date, place, publisher, artist or photographer, as this information may be important.
- Sites may provide links to related sources and databases that are quite valuable, but require a great deal of time to travel through, particularly if an assignment or reading is due. Selection based on teacher criteria will reduce confusion and save time.
- Sites may be suspect as having a bias, good or bad, or a hidden agenda to promote, and these need to be identified and then, if time permits, checked against other sources, or (in historical terms) *corroborated*.
- Sites may be overly helpful, friendly, and interpretive for students, leaving almost nothing to do except copy or acquire, without asking for much critical review or

personal understanding. These sites should not be on your preferred list if you want the students to do the problem solving, unless they are advanced thinkers who know how to critically analyze the way a site is put together by the professionals—not an easy task.

So, with these words of warning, we encourage you to make use of the web to create your own mysteries in history, carefully identifying the sources and materials you want students to consider before they draw conclusions of their own, and as a prelude to more wide-ranging investigations into extensive databases on a given historical or social science topic.

Why History Should Be Problematic

You may have heard professors talk about "problematizing" an issue for students—this is not a bad thing! Problems are central to studying history as mystery:

First, a problem built into the mystery has the potential to foster at least several alternate solutions. A problem opens up possibilities and probabilities. There should not be "one right answer," as that would not fit our definition of a mystery in history. You already know the answer, so that would simply be a fishing expedition to find out what the teacher wants as a conclusion.

Second, a problem should be approachable from several angles, both theoretical and practical. Problems might invite skill development, for example in the use of testing analogies, such as is one revolution really like the other, or is it quite different.

Problems may also draw from two or more competing or overlapping theories about why actions take place in history, for example for largely economic, social, or political reasons.

Third, a mystery problem should offer richness and variety if possible, utilizing several kinds of media, images, sounds, texts, each incorporating layers of messages and meanings within the whole. Multiple meanings and messages provide a richness that allows teachers and students to extend and deepen their inquiry into many areas from the relatively simple interpretation of data to discussions of cause and meaning and then on to conversations and debates about human values and beliefs, including our own about the factors that influence human behavior in a particular time and place and across all human history.

Thus, we are advocating a bold approach to defining and using mysteries in history, whether or not these are concocted to entertain and elucidate, or reflect truly unresolved and perhaps eternal debates about mysteries in history, cause, ideology, structure, connections, and ethical and moral values.

To review, we advocated looking at mysteries using a simple sliding scale or "rubric" in terms of dealing with a minor, medium, or major mystery. You are invited to assist in modifying these definitions based on your problem-finding and problem-solving experience with this book and the whole idea of mystery in world history.

You Decide: Approaching Art from Different Angles

Look at the Cycladic figures in Figure 10.2 and try to answer the following questions:

- From a personal angle: do you understand these figures?
- From a historical angle: when, where, and why?
- From an esthetic angle: are these figures lovely?
- From a sociological angle: is this a family?
- From an economic angle: did the artist make a living?

Figure 10.2 A Set of Cycladic Figures from the Bronze Age. Photo: Smial/Creative Commons (original in color).

Minor Mysteries

We have defined a minor mystery largely in terms of data: whether parts are missing, or if there are enough data, or whether the data are the right kind from good sources, etc. The data puzzle is our model, with a focus on the quality and quantity of information available to us.

The complexity of the mystery then would be determined by how many pieces are missing or suspect. Questions could be developed around the meaning and messages built into evidence. Thus, you could develop an easy or difficult classroom mystery by controlling the amount of information and by stressing the degree of suspicions about reliability.

In our book, Stonehenge offers an example of a true mystery because there are many elements missing or challenged, particularly as we have no written records by its builders telling us their goals. Using raw materials juxtaposed with scholarly interpretations—although focused largely on artifacts and documents, reports and scientific analysis—makes for a very satisfying minor mystery.

Medium Mysteries

We have defined a medium mystery as one that has data issues, but that also raises the level of problem solving by focusing on *interpretation* and *causation*. Interpreting data and giving it meaning, or debating its meaning, is enriched by questions about how and why an event occurred, and what were the consequences for the actors in history. The case of the Incas and Spaniards is, in our view, a good example of a medium mystery in the sense that we are questioning just *why* the Inca Empire collapsed—particularly from the historical evidence and point of view of our major source, Guaman Poma de Ayala, which also raises interesting questions of viewpoint and bias as well. Why was he acting as a witness, presenting his woodcuts to the king and queen of Spain, and are his loyalties mainly with the Inca people or the Spanish newcomers? Thus, a medium mystery looks deeply at the data, but also demands work toward a comprehensive examination and interpretation, one often subject to multiple viewpoints.

Major Mysteries

In reviewing the idea of a major mystery, we return to our argument that deep and abiding mysteries raise questions about beliefs, values, and morals that are imbedded in our notions of historical change and the impact of both personal and collective decisions.

Within major mysteries there are data problems, interpretational issues, points of view to consider, and that all-important element of depth: moral codes and values to examine and to act upon. For example, the place and role of women in world history almost immediately raises questions about gender, to which there are answers from many wildly different ideological and theoretical frameworks. Feminists of many persuasions cast very contrasting views of history to those commonly found in secondary and elementary school textbooks, and to some historians still believing in male superiority. Marxist historians' views of women's roles might or might not square with those of noted feminist historians, but contrast with mainstream thinking. And thus we have a great big theoretical fight about what to do with women in history, how to teach about gender and sex, marriages, and alternate families.

The chapter on heroines in world history raises questions about just how, who, when, and where we define some people as heroic and others as not, or as villains—a big and potentially emotional topic, depending on the culture and time we belong to or the cases we wish to analyze.

Gender and heroism run throughout human affairs as far back as we know, and often greatly influence the choice of leaders, resulting in what are sometimes very happy and well-off eras and sometimes depressing and contentious periods. We think that the reason for all these problems and issues is that major mysteries probe eternal and universal human values.

Asking Mystery Questions: Big Questions and Small Questions

- *Meeting the raw, primary source data*: Examining evidence on a face-to-face, word-by-word, basis without preconceptions is always a good start to a mystery lesson.
- *Bringing together theory with evidence*: Reviewing familiar lessons and the data they are based on in the light of new evidence, new theories, and/or alternate perspectives is also a good start to a mystery inquiry.
- *Connecting local and national with global*: Finding links between the object of your study and related, connected, and/or shared people, ideas, and artifacts.
- *Thinking about values and debating issues*: Examining moral and ethical questions that have an emotional impact, and that lead to recognition of issues and controversies.

Constructing or inventing questions is a critically important teaching skill, and just what type and level of queries are posed, their order and overall effects, are key to a successful mystery lesson. This is vital to the process of inquiry because sustaining a mystery investigation depends on the quality of the problem and the questions driving it.

We are very sensitive to *questions*, favoring questions of judgment, synthesis, and analysis over recall, comprehension, and application, but we strongly believe that you need to cycle through the whole of Bloom's taxonomy of questions for a wholly successful mystery. However, the key questions, the ones that set your goals, need to be "big" because the entire unit is built around them.

Big questions tend to ask for value judgments: "How do you rate a heroine or hero: who qualifies?" Or they are "wrap-up" synthesis questions: "What social conditions allow women more freedom?" Or analytical questions: "Why did Rome last so long?" None of these is easy, but they do form overall objectives to work toward and provide for many smaller questions along the way, as well as give you a guideline for your choice of content.

Smaller, but important and beautiful, questions focus on the building blocks of the bigger questions: recall, comprehension, and application. One can always go back to these in the midst of dealing with the big questions, which may set students back for a while (after all, they are quite difficult).

Of special importance to us are questions of definition, as these build clarity and can mutate into questions about standards. Something as innocent as "Who is a hero or heroine, and who is not?" can be rephrased to promote competing definitions, applications of examples, and eventually standards for evaluation. Application too is important because this serves to test students' big ideas, interpretations, value judgments, and reasons against additional examples, comparisons, and contrasting sources, for example "Was the KKK like or unlike the new example of the Serbian Black Hand?"

Thus, inventing questions for mystery lessons, units, and courses isn't that difficult if you have a fix on what you are really after, your objectives. Questions, objectives, and problems, in creating mysteries for the classroom, are all of a piece, and it helps to do some serious historical and/or social science and/or literary reading and study to accomplish this task.

We love to mull over problems that have not been addressed much or at all, or turn to historical examples that have been taught and re-taught to the point of triteness. We particularly dislike what we call "National Enquirer" kinds of mystery questions, for example "Is Anastasia still alive?" Or, "Were the pyramids designed and built by space aliens?" Or, "Where is Atlantis buried?" These sensationalist questions draw attention but don't go very far, because (if you take a close look) the questions themselves are low level, and because the data do not usually support them very much.

You Decide

How do you separate fact from fiction in world history?

Questions that Look at the Past in a New Way

As a start, we prefer to read a text and look for all-too-pat answers, or look at a body of data—documents, songs, stories, images, and so forth—that have been taken for granted. Consider the raw material yourself rather than a text's, or even a professional interpretation, and see what you come up with. For example, Guaman Poma's amazing woodcuts sat on a shelf for centuries, and then were used as textbook illustrations to show Inca life without much reflection, and then re-examined to find out that they may be social criticism of the Spanish conquerors—or maybe not. They require a good deal of observation and detail work and offer a real life mystery that promotes as many questions as answers, including those of professionals.

The Serbian Black Hand, whose oath appears in the Secret Societies chapter, usually gets one or two lines because of its part in assassinating Archduke Ferdinand of Austria and setting off WWI. But upon closer inspection of the oath and the background, it turns out that the Austrians gave good reason to the local Serbs to form an underground organization, to promote their own nationalism in a Europe swept by national feeling that was often denied by dominating powers.

Looking at familiar or unfamiliar Roman documents in the light of theories about the sustaining qualities of empires may throw common preconceptions about Rome and Romans out the window and permit new ideas to form and be tested. Taking another look at Stonehenge and the Bronze Age cultures around it, along with new archeological research, may lead to hypotheses about its purpose that go counter to the "clock or worship" ideas prevalent in most history texts. There are always new and old theories to be tested against the evidence.

Topics and people are often taught as unrelated to each other in many history courses and textbooks. Therefore, drawing and testing connections is another way of promoting mystery. Looking for links may confound your ideas about human history and lead to new ideas about warfare, trade, medicine, conquest, and world culture. Pizza, for example, is a combination of New and Old World foods, both probably ancient in origin: bread, cheese, and tomatoes. How they come together and the amusing claims made about the invention of pizza provide a great case study in cultural diffusion and, if pursued, the Columbian Exchange as a bigger topic.

Questions that Ask Us to Feel, Value, and Judge

Some historians get quite nervous about comparing times and places, people and literature, or ideas and philosophies peculiar to a specific context, particularly when seeking universals and common patterns, because they see events as unique and separate. We disagree, at least for pedagogical purposes, because it is just these *BIG* universal questions that motivate interest and promote inquiry, e.g., Why build giant circles of stone? How do you organize a rebellion and find followers? Who is a heroine or hero?, Why do empires last or fall? Why are the women in world history in such low proportion to the men? How do we make meaning from historical events, from the lives of people, and who are we willing to follow?

The emotional appeal is buried but still there, trying to fight its way out of figures like Joan of Arc, like Eva Peron, like Mother Jones, like Napoleon, all of whom had points of view, sacred beliefs, and personal values, each imbued with an electric charge of morality, each leading to taking stands on the issues of the time and place in which they found themselves. Art and literature have no compunctions about expressing emotion, and are often interesting indicators to historical changes such as revolutions, coups, and uprisings.

The realm of values and beliefs, in both a personal and social sense, also provides clues to how the past lives within us now. We are heirs to the past even though some of us may be a-historical, not knowing or caring whence we or our ideas came from. But in a crisis, attention suddenly is riveted on "How did this happen?" Indeed, when confronted by changes that make our lives more difficult, we usually begin questioning the past. Our current financial crisis, perhaps a world depression, is being questioned, examined, reflected upon, and fought over, as we write these words. Many analogies, both accurate and spurious, are being made to the Great Depression, toward which we suddenly exhibit curiosity and perhaps an emotional reaction.

History is full of moral decisions, but we usually don't like to talk about these in class for fear we will get in trouble, as there are no settled answers to value questions. We are stuck with many competing philosophies and views, past and present, and certainly more in the future, and it gives us a headache to deal with the whole thing. Much easier are answers to questions such as "What is Genghis Khan's middle name?" or "Did Joan of Arc wear makeup?" than trying to come to grips with eternal, and perhaps universal, questions of aggression, hero-worship, subversion, terrorism, and imperial ambition.

Many of the topics in this book raise difficult questions about our values and beliefs, now and applied to the past. Gender issues and arguments over the identification of heroic qualities call upon us to render judgments, even where we want to remain neutral and just absorb the "facts." Secret societies that begin by trying to liberate people from oppression but move into terrorism raise deep issues about causes and consequences of pressures exerted by internal or external forces on restless populations.

You Decide

Take a look at Figure 10.3.

- What is the artist's goal?
- Why the dancing skeletons? What emotions are they projecting?
- How does this image make you feel: sad or happy, both or neither? Why?

Figure 10.3 "Gran Fandango" Woodcut Engraving by José Guadalupe Posada (Mexico, 1852–1913) (image in public domain).

Finding Mystery in Everyday History

A wide range of materials—literary and musical, artistic and documentary, cinema and sculpture, coins and artifacts—can provide us with clues to the past and to our own time, forming the basis for teaching sources as mysteries to discuss, interpret, applaud or criticize. You don't really need too much to work with at one time; in fact, pick two or three images or juicy dramatic documents, or perhaps a short movie clip of no more than fifteen minutes, as the basis for your mystery. Above all, make sure you have a real mystery to work with that springs out of your evidence.

You too, and your students, are invited to take stands on the moral issues of our time and place, and even to venture forth into the past, evaluating and re-evaluating the people we know and the people we don't know as guides to perhaps making our own choices in world history, however small, as in voting, or however big, like joining a movement or global organization.

You Decide: Keeping Secrets?

Take a look at Figure 10.4.

- Who are these people?
- What is the central figure doing?
- Is this a meeting of a secret society or someone keeping secrets?
- Is this a religious or political ritual?
- Where are we? When are we?

Figure 10.4 An Old Theory about the Building of Stonehenge (image in public domain).

Content and Corroboration: Sources, Checking Authenticity, and "Cleaned Up" Entries

Allow us a few words on sources, primary, secondary, and tertiary texts, and their presentation in the classroom. As good historians and social scientists, we value our data, our professional interpreters, and the summaries presented in overarching textbooks seeking to encompass the totality.

However, we must teach and learn to exercise caution. Each source needs identification as to its origins: *who* wrote it, *when*, *where*, and *why*, and sometimes *how*. Remember, eyewitnesses and reporters of history, including historians, may be compromised by an agenda, a sales pitch, an ideology, and/or an emotional attachment that needs to be brought to light as we proceed with our investigation. That doesn't make the sources unusable or ugly; it actually makes them more fun to use, as long as we are aware of these issues.

We still need to practice the rules we began with: checking sources, looking for corroborating witnesses, making sure evidence and reasons are given for conclusions, admitting assumptions and identifying overall or underlying philosophies that shape interpretations.

Summary and Conclusions

Mystery in history develops out of the admission that we don't know it all, that even the familiar and settled can be unsettled and re-examined with profit. The mundane and familiar can be subjected to new theories and new evidence leading to (horrors!) revisionist thinking about the past and the present.

At one time, in the not too distant past, world history almost did not exist as a high school and college course. It was taught—but as international relations, or as Western history with a few admissions that other places outside Europe existed (but were kind of dangerous), or as a litany of strange names and empires and exotic people who had nothing to do with us here in our snug environment at the top of the food chain. Well, the time and place for that sort of world history is long past, and probably has been long past for a while. In the twenty-first century we have connections with a vengeance as everything is shifted around, bought and sold, polluted and used up, exchanged and adopted, linked and made newly utilized—to create an interactive world symbolized by the Internet itself and the massive diffusion of computer culture.

We have more knowledge available than ever before, yet few seem to care and we are still repeating the mistakes of the past. Viewing the world as a single interactive whole, a concatenation of cultures long in contact, an economy that is totally connected, is now well accepted.

Yet, despite the availability of knowledge and the ease of travel, we don't really know much about each other in a deep historical kind of way—only about ourselves. That, too, is a mystery that needs exploration, and so in this book we have offered a series of case studies that range across time and space, people and places, to invite you to "solve" as a prelude to designing your own mysteries for the students in your classrooms. We hope that you (and they) will enjoy, be stimulated by, and reap the benefits of all this scholarly and not-so-scholarly detective work.

References and Further Reading

Barton, K. (1997) "I just kinda know: Elementary students' ideas about historical evidence," *Theory and Research in Social Education* 25 (4): 407–30.

Barton, K. and Levstik, L. (1996) "Back when God was around and everything: Elementary children's understanding of historical time," *American Educational Research Journal* 33 (2): 419–54.

Bausum, A. (2004) *With Courage and Cloth: Winning the Fight for a Woman's Right to Vote*, Washington, D.C.: National Geographic Society.

Brophy, J., VanSledright, B., and Bredin, N. (1992) "Fifth graders' ideas about history expressed before and after their introduction to the subject," *Theory and Research in Social Education* 20 (4): 440–89.

Downey, M. (1994) "After the dinosaurs: Elementary children's chronological thinking," paper presented at the annual meeting of the American Educational Research Association, New Orleans, LA.

Gerwin, D. and Zevin, J. (2003) *Teaching US History as Mystery*, Portsmouth, NJ: Heinemann.

Levstik, L. and Pappas, C. (1987) "Exploring the development of historical understanding," *Journal of Research and Development in Education* 21 (1): 1–15.

Levstik, L. and Barton, K. (1996) "They still use some of their past: Historical salience in elementary children's chronological thinking," *Journal of Curriculum Studies* 28 (5): 531–76.

Levstik, L. and Barton, K. (2001) *Doing History: Investigating with Children in Elementary and Middle Schools*, 2nd edn, Mahwah: NJ: Erlbaum.

National Geographic (2007) *Mysteries of History*, Washington, D.C.: National Geographic.

VanSledright, B. (2002) *In Search of America's Past: Learning to Read History in the Elementary School*, New York: Teachers College.

VanSledright, B. and Frankes, L. (2000) "Concept-and strategic-knowledge development in historical study: A comparative exploration in two fourth-grade classrooms," *Cognition and Instruction* 18 (2): 239–83.

Zarnowski, M. (2006) *Making Sense of History: Using High-Quality Literature and Hands-On Experiences to Build Content Knowledge*, New York: Scholastic.

Index